A New Social Contract in a
Latin American Education Context

Palgrave Macmillan's
Postcolonial Studies in Education

Studies using the perspectives of postcolonial theory have become established and increasingly widespread in the last few decades. This series embraces and broadly employs the postcolonial approach. As a site of struggle, education has constituted a key vehicle for the "colonization of the mind." The "post" in postcolonialism is both temporal, in the sense of emphasizing the processes of decolonization, and analytical, in the sense of probing and contesting the aftermath of colonialism, and the imperialism that succeeded it, using materialist and discourse analysis. Postcolonial theory is particularly apt for exploring the implications of educational colonialism, decolonization, experimentation, revisioning, contradiction, and ambiguity, not only for the former colonies, but also for the former colonial powers. This series views education as an important vehicle for both the inculcation and the unlearning of colonial ideologies. It complements the diversity that exists in postcolonial studies of political economy, literature, sociology, and the interdisciplinary domain of cultural studies. Education is here being viewed in its broadest contexts and is not confined to institutionalized learning. The aim of this series is to identify and help establish new areas of educational inquiry in postcolonial studies.

Series Editors:

PETER MAYO is Professor and Head of the Department of Education Studies at the University of Malta, where he teaches in the areas of sociology of education and adult continuing education, as well as in comparative and international education and sociology more generally.

ANNE HICKLING-HUDSON is Associate Professor of Education at Australia's Queensland University of Technology (QUT), where she specializes in cross-cultural and international education.

ANTONIA DARDER is a Distinguished Professor of Educational Policy Studies and Latino/a Studies at the University of Illinois at Urbana-Champaign.

Editorial Advisory Board

Carmel Borg (University of Malta)
John Baldacchino (Teachers College, Columbia University)
Jennifer Chan (University of British Columbia)
Christine Fox (University of Wollongong, Australia)
Zelia Gregoriou (University of Cyprus)
Leon Tikly (University of Bristol, UK)
Birgit Brock-Utne (Emeritus, University of Oslo, Norway)

Titles:

Education and Gendered Citizenship in Pakistan
M. Ayaz Naseem

Critical Race, Feminism, and Education: A Social Justice Model
Menah Pratt-Clarke

A New Social Contract in a Latin American Education Context
Danilo R. Streck

A New Social Contract in a Latin American Education Context

Danilo R. Streck

Foreword by Vítor Westhelle

A NEW SOCIAL CONTRACT IN A LATIN AMERICAN EDUCATION CONTEXT
Copyright © Danilo R. Streck, 2010.

First published in 2010 by
PALGRAVE MACMILLAN®
in the United States—a division of St. Martin's Press LLC,
175 Fifth Avenue, New York, NY 10010.

Where this book is distributed in the UK, Europe and the rest of the world,
this is by Palgrave Macmillan, a division of Macmillan Publishers Limited,
registered in England, company number 785998, of Houndmills,
Basingstoke, Hampshire RG21 6XS.

Palgrave Macmillan is the global academic imprint of the above companies
and has companies and representatives throughout the world.

Palgrave® and Macmillan® are registered trademarks in the United States,
the United Kingdom, Europe and other countries.

ISBN: 978–0–230–10538–6

Library of Congress Cataloging-in-Publication Data

Streck, Danilo Romeu.
    A new social contract in a Latin American education context / Danilo
R. Streck ; foreword by Vítor Westhelle.
        p. cm.—(Postcolonial studies in education)
    ISBN 978–0–230–10538–6 (alk. paper)
    1. Education—Social aspects—Latin America. 2. Democracy and
education—Latin America. 3. Social contract. I. Title.

LA541.S77 2010
306.43′2098—dc22   2010017025

A catalogue record of the book is available from the British Library.

Design by Newgen Imaging Systems (P) Ltd., Chennai, India.

First edition: December 2010

10 9 8 7 6 5 4 3 2 1

Printed in the United States of America.

Contents

Foreword

Vítor Westhelle

In the early 1990s, on the walls of the University of Bogotá, Colombia, a graffiti set the terms of the dilemma this book is addressing. The graffiti said: "When we had almost all the answers, the questions were changed." This was a commentary on the veering in geopolitics at the time, symbolized by the fall of the Berlin Wall in 1989. Questions were indeed changed, as if the rules of a game were altered in the midst of its being played. In Latin America, political consciousness and the social models offered as alternatives were by and large guided by the political polarization between the two world powers. These poles did not offer primary strategic allegiances, but a vague—yet definitely recognizable—demarcation of ideological arenas for the exercise of citizenship. Many of the countries of Latin America, among them some of the economically and politically most influential, were just coming out of brutal dictatorships carried under the complacent watch of Washington, and often directly aided by it.

In the same emblematic year of 1989, the city of Porto Alegre, the capital of the most southern state in Brazil, and the most important metropolis in the south of the country, launched a program called the participatory budgeting. Its core principles and modus operandi as a matrix for rewriting a social contract offered a curricular design for the exercise of citizenship. The participatory budgeting became such a landmark that it was not only successfully sustained over the years but also adopted and adapted to different social locations worldwide.

A New Social Contract in a Latin American Education Context, by Danilo Streck, offers an empirical study of the participatory budgeting as a map that explains the new terrains in which civil society renegotiates its contracts and fosters its citizenship. Yet this work not only offers a map that detects and describes a topography, but also creatively provides an itinerary for exploring paths yet to be crossed and trajectories to be pursued. It offers a compelling architectural model for how these two pedagogic-political roles work in the sketching of successive drafts of social contracts, their explanatory function, and their exploratory task. Even though the reader will find the details of the field research done on the participatory budgeting only toward the end of this study, a well-planned travel brochure with the map and the itinerary informs and guides this work. And consistent with his pedagogical commitment, the author in conclusion suggests very concrete proposals for the new social contract already in the making.

The treatise starts with an insightful discussion about globalization. The word is derived from the Latin *globus,* meaning a round mass or a sphere. It entered the English vocabulary in the sixteenth century to designate the terrestrial planetary sphere. But "globalization" is a rather recent word to describe a chain of events wherein actions that take place in a given location are immediately also of planetary consequence, creating a common exchange market where desires, punishments, and satisfactions are bartered. The Indian writer Arundhati Roy properly defined globalization as a mode of standardization where everyone desires the same thing but only few are able to have it.

Globalization is not a new-fangled phenomenon. Its awareness can be traced back to the late fifteenth and early sixteenth centuries, when "globe" became an operational concept. Columbus had it wrong when he thought to have reached the coast of India by sailing west, but he set the trend for the unmindful nature of globalization when he established at least the possibility of traveling around the globe and arriving *without* returning to the same place of origin. The actual circumvention of the globe was accomplished by Ferdinand Magellan, twenty-eight years after Columbus reached the Americas. Since then, an incredible intensification of global traveling has reduced the size of the planet, as it were. Not only has physical mobility dramatically increased, reaching supersonic velocities, but virtual traveling and transportation have made it possible to circle the globe at the speed of light. In all of this drastic increment in velocity and mobility, however, one thing remains the same: the forward motion that brings one to the point of departure without necessarily having to return! This phenomenon means one simple thing: it is a process of moving forward without a return, without having to be accountable back. While Columbus still kept the practice of writing *back* to Spain about his discoveries, his reports answered for the conquest and landfalls but not for the others he had actually met. Tzvetan Todorov once said it well: "Columbus discovered America but not the Americans." If Columbus wrote back to Spain, even if only about his spoils, Magellan did not even write back to account for his deeds and, as far as we know, did not even keep a journal. He was only moving forward.

Against this backdrop, this book deserves special attention because it is about responsibility. It questions a process of forward movement, of a "progress" without accountability, or, in other words, without responsibility. The words "responsibility" and "response" literally mean to pledge (*spondeo*) back (*re*). The Latin *spondeo* is the root of the English word "spouse." To respond, therefore, is something akin to the exchange of vows in a marriage ceremony in which each partner pledges to the other the commitments being made; responsibility is to answer back, be accountable to those pledges. Globalization, we are hereby instructed, averts responsibility in the same way as Magellan averted landfall by circumnavigating the continents. After all, his greatest accomplishment is emblematic; he bypassed what is now Latin America by being the first known navigator to cross Cape Horn without making landfall. Globalization is when rules of accountability or responsibility no longer apply. The globalizing phenomenon means moving on oblivious to what is left behind.

The onset of the globalization era in the sixteenth century simultaneously marked the beginning of a crass era. On the one hand, virtual traveling had reached its zenith and insurmountable problems were solved, while on the other, people and places were muted and rendered invisible. Where in the world is Porto Alegre, Port Adelaide, Port-au-Prince, or Portugal? At the click of a key we are instantly transported to our favorite vacation spot or served our choice of menu while missing or misplacing the city, the country, or even the continent where millions of people live. Thomas Friedman tells the story of why he entitled his bestselling book *The World is Flat*. He was playing golf somewhere in India, and all the external references—billboards, commercials, posters, brand names, and so on—were about the same as when he would be playing golf in New York or anywhere else. When he came home he confided to his wife: "Honey, I think the world is flat." A "flat globe" is an oxymoron that has come to symbolize what globalization means. Streck's analysis of the three axes of globalization (politico-economic, cultural, and technological) and the pedagogical strategies that address them reflect the same conundrum, while at the same time offering an Ariadne's thread out of what he calls the "educational labyrinth."

However, as this book relentlessly reminds us, what is more insidious and pervasive is the fact that the other to whom supposedly one owes a response becomes faceless; he or she is excluded from the conversation, is no longer taken into account. The other becomes what Kafka called a nonperson, an expression Peruvian theologian Gustavo Gutiérrez applied to describe the excluded ones in third world societies, people who live in what he called the "underside of history." These people are "invisible," in the sense Ralph Ellison alludes to in *The Invisible Man*, or as Manuel Scorza, in *Garabombo, the Invisible*, described them. It is a social, political, and economic invisibility that allows for nonresponsibility, and even its justification.

If nonresponsibility is a feature of globalization, invisibility is the other. However, invisibility, as it is used in the works of literature mentioned, functions as a metaphor. It is not that these people are translucent or that they can be seen through, but that their individual existence is so dispensable that one does not need to see them. Their invisibility is such that one need not be responsible toward them, to address them. Invisibility, thus, has a Janus face. The invisible also becomes picturesque. Pictures in magazines, newspapers, TV shows, and other media make people ultravisible, and that only magnifies the irresponsibility. One does not write back to the aboriginal people one finds beautifully portrayed, say, in the *National Geographic*. You see the picture, but you don't see the person. You remember the picture, not the person; one knows the framed photo, but not the complex and multidimensional reality that exceeds any frame. Presented in this book are others whose presence is engraved in these pages, from a slum woman in Porto Alegre to a barber in Los Angeles.

The author adroitly takes the reader from a general discussion about globalization and pedagogical strategies encrypted in the resilience of popular education (particularly as it was in gestation during the years of military dictatorship) to the shaping of a new social contract and the pedagogical process through which it is obtained. The middle section of the book offers the theoretical core to sustain the argument in a very original pairing of the great eighteenth-century French political philosopher Jean Jacques Rousseau with the celebrated twentieth-century Brazilian educator Paulo Freire. If the former provided the author with the pedagogical implications of a political social contract, the latter offered him vistas of the political consequences of education when exercised for the common good of things public. Autonomy is a key word that yokes the two thinkers in a common project. For the Anglophone world it is a salutary discussion to learn how the autonomy exercised by the two authors that inform the theoretical frame of the book differs from the dominant definition of freedom in the tradition of John Locke (something that might be missed by the English edition of Freire's last book, *Pedagogia da Autonomia*, translated as *Pedagogy of Freedom*). This becomes rather clear in the chapter on *conscientização*, a notion that is still in want of a proper English rendition, precisely because it does not conform to the negative definition of freedom dominant in the Anglo-Saxon world—and by implication what "conscience" usually means in these Nordic latitudes as opposed to its use and implementation in Latin America.

One of the strengths of this book is that it is rich in the theological and religious dimensions of the pedagogical process. Paulo Freire, though not a theologian by training, was a seminal figure in the formation of liberation theology in the late 1960s. Tenderness, care, joy, solidarity, and responsibility are some key concepts that the reader will encounter in the following pages; these notions born from Freire's pedagogy are couched in the pedagogical work of the authors included in this volume, who happen to be stalwarts in the theological landscape of Latin America. For Streck, pedagogy is about resilience, resistance, responsibility, survival, and liberated citizenship in the kingdom of this world, because this is what first matters in this divine playground of ours.

The struggle for visibility is the struggle to elicit a response, a call to be addressed, which is an act of gentleness and tenderness. But to be addressed is to have one's address. This is the pedagogical challenge this book presents: to have one's "address" defined in the quest of affirming an identity that can be claimed and acclaimed. Yet this identity is always fluid and hybrid, which defines the signature concept of Freire's pedagogy: a participatory or "nonbanking" form of education. An identity is not attributed or even possessed, but always enmeshed in the dynamic dance of entering systems of knowledge and power, while constantly leaving them in search of other paths. Antonio Machado, a Spanish poet of a century ago, expressed what could be the epigraph for this book: "Walker, there is no path, you do the path by walking." This is the merit of this work and its author, who knows that even the participatory budgeting may (or has) become a system of knowledge and power that needs to be revisited in search of new liberating ideas and practices. This book is a splendidly drafted map of the pedagogical challenges and the itinerary for a path ahead not yet traversed.

Series Editors' Preface

Peter Mayo, Antonia Darder, and
Anne Hickling-Hudson

This book by Danilo Streck is a welcome contribution to the current debates surrounding education for citizenship, particularly where civil liberties are trampled upon and public spaces are rapidly shrinking, given the growing context of privatization and commodification. In this scenario, there is constant talk about the shredding of the social contract in many parts of the world. The history of Latin America, which provides the postcolonial context for the ideas in this book, is alas tainted with various episodes marking the most brutal dismantling of this contract through military interventions and their suppression of human rights. In the case of Chile in 1973, the intervention against a democratically elected coalition government was intended to allow the ideology of the marketplace to hold sway, as a "trial run" for what was to become a global ideology. And yet, as the author so clearly affirms in this book, Latin America, despite being marginal in the global economic system, has time and time again proved a fertile ground for the incubation and proliferation of ideas that served as antidotes to the prevailing ideologies manifested at all levels of social life, including education, the main site of social practice focused in this work.

Danilo Streck draws heavily on the ideas of the eighteenth-century French philosopher Jean Jacques Rousseau and fellow Brazilian educator Paulo Freire. A foretaste of the bringing together of these two figures was provided in a chapter in a recent anthology of writings inspired by Freire.[1] For the most part, Streck draws from Rousseau's education classic *Émile,* focusing the discussion on a broad notion of education (beyond schooling), which therefore takes on board the area of nonformal education, precisely the area in which Latin America has arguably made its greatest contribution to educational thought and postcolonial educational thought. The juxtaposition of Rousseau's and Freire's ideas in this context is interesting from a postcolonial perspective, in view of the manner in which a concept connected with the European Enlightenment and tied to the birth of modernity is here given a strong postcolonial and subaltern meaning within the Latin American context. It would not be amiss to say that Freire helped inspire one of the most important Latin American projects concerning a participatory deliberative democracy, namely, the Participatory Budget as developed in Danilo Streck's home city of Porto Alegre in Rio Grande do Sul. It was, subsequently, reinvented in other cities, including European ones, albeit with contrasting outcomes. This project is given prominence in Danilo's Streck's book, providing the basis for what a social contract would mean today and what it would mean when viewed from the vantage point of a people who, although variegated in terms of identities and subjectivities, have traditionally been regarded as "subaltern" and "oppressed." As Streck points out, it is a view of participatory democracy coming from the margins and from the global South. It is a view that, true to its postcolonial nature, is characterized by a hybrid of Western concepts (deliberative democracy with its echoes of Dewey and Habermas, social contract with its echoes of Rousseau and the Enlightenment) and others that have their basis among historically colonized peoples (e.g., Latin American popular education, which itself is not immune to hybridization). These are concepts that challenged the status quo at the time and which, in Rousseau's case, led to reprisals.

In keeping with Dewey, the Participatory Budget represents an educational space.[2] It has often been felt that, when participating in a process of deliberation about social issues, which can be broadened to incorporate biodiversity issues, one could well be engaging in a process of learning. This contains echoes of Dewey's well-known dictum that one learns about democracy not by simply hearing about it, but by doing it. It is also typical of learning that occurs within social movements. Latin America has had its fair share of postcolonial social movements, including the Frente Zapatista in Chiapas, with its various approaches to education in the region, also involving postcolonial reinventions of ideas associated with Illich;[3] the popular education movements; the Christian base community movement; the Liberation Theology movement; and the landless peasant movement (MST).

These and others are the sorts of movements that can help revitalize the drive for the recuperation or retention of public spaces and the construction of a public sphere relevant to our times. They can also strive, perhaps abetted in certain Latin American contexts by recently elected left-wing leaders, for the creation of a new social contract predicated on the Freirean concept of authentic dialogue and the legitimization of cooperative ways of working and learning, which have characterized the Latin American scene but have remained within a marginal position. It involves a contract that allows spaces for a "thick democracy" characterized by a process of "conscientização," a term that Freire borrowed from Dom Helder Camara, viewed, as in chapter 6, in its political, ethical, aesthetic, and epistemological dimensions. This social contract is based on an alternative view of power that constitutes a healthy utopia, the kind of utopia that guided the thinking of several Latin American intellectuals such as Freire himself, Frei Betto, and Rigoberta Menchú.

It is the sort of utopia that helps one maintain coherence in one's critical engagement with social and political life, preventing one from lapsing into the contemporary malaise of cynicism. And yet, Streck argues, the education and action involved in this regard is one that should extend beyond the legality of a social contract to embrace such values as being sensitive to solidarity (*sensibilidade solidaria*), caring (*cuidado* in Leonardo Boff's terms with its echoes of Lorenzo Milani's "I Care"), and showing the kind of tenderness (*ternura*) that Jose Marti advocated and that was echoed in a slightly different context by Ernesto "Che" Guevara ("one must be tough without losing one's tenderness.").

This book provides a steadfast case for a critical democratic citizenship that has its basis in Latin American thinking and action and is drawn from a variety of sources, including both European and indigenous ones, reinventing them in accordance with the specificities of this postcolonial context. This unmistakably Latin American postcolonial view provides a much-needed antidote to the static view of citizenship projected globally through states, markets, and communication technologies (the topic of the first chapter), which reduces people to what Herbert Marcuse would have called one-dimensional persons, or rather, we would argue, two-dimensional persons: producers and consumers. The postcolonial ideas that Danilo Streck draws on speak uncompromisingly to an alternative concept of citizenship, one forged within a new postcolonial social contract, characterized by social actors,[4] and critically engaged in the life of the polis.

Notes

1. D. Streck, "The Utopian Legacy: Rousseau and Freire," in *Social Justice Education for Teachers: Paulo Freire and the Possible Dream*, ed. C.A. Torres and P. Noguera (Rotterdam and Taipei: Sense Publishers, 2008).

2. D. Schugurensky, "Transformative Learning and Transformative Politics: The Pedagogical Dimension of Participatory Democracy and Social Action," in *Expanding the Boundaries of Transformative Learning: Essays on Theory and Praxis*, ed. E. O'Sullivan, A. Morrell, and M.A. O' Connor (New York and Basingstoke: Palgrave Macmillan, 2002).

3. M.S. Prakash and G. Esteva, Escaping Education: Living as Learning within Grassroots Cultures (New York: Peter Lang, 1998).

4. I. Martin, (2001). "Reconstructing the Agora: Towards an Alternative Politics of Lifelong Learning," *Concept* 11, no. 1 (2001): 4–8.

Previous Publications

Dicionário Paulo Freire. Belo Horizonte: Autêntica, 2008; 2010. (Edited with J. Zitkoski and E. Redin)

José Martí e a Educação. Belo Horizonte: Autêntica, 2008.

Educação em Nossa América. Ijuí: Ed. Unijuí, 2007. (Editor)

Religião, Cultura e Educação. São Leopoldo/RS: Editora Unisinos, 2006. (Edited with C. Scarlatelli and J. I. Follmann)

Pesquisa Participante: a partilha do saber. Aparecida/SP: Idéias & Letras, 2008. (Edited with Carlos Rodrigues Brandão)

Erziehung für einen neuen Gesellschaftsvertrag. Siegen: Athena, 2006.

Educación para un nuevo contrato social. Buenos Aires: Stella/ CELADEC/La Crujía, 2005.

Pedagogía de otra manera de convivir: Diálogo con la Teología. Bogotá: Dimensión Educativa, 2004.

Rousseau e a Educação. Belo Horizonte: Editora Autêntica, 2004, 2008.

Pedagogia no encontro de tempos: ensaios inspirados em Paulo Freire. Petrópolis: Vozes, 2001.

Paulo Freire: ética, utopia e educação. Petrópolis: Vozes, 1999, 2008. (Editor)

Educação e igrejas no Brasil: um ensaio ecumênico. São Leopoldo: Editora Sinodal, 1995. (Editor)

A educação básica e o básico na educação. Porto Alegre: Sulina, 1996. (Editor)

Correntes pedagógicas: aproximações com a teologia. Petrópolis: Vozes, 1994, 2003.

Credits

Translation: Marie Krahn and Hedy L. Hofmann
Cover Photo: Painting by Flávio Scholles (www.fscholles.com.br)
Research Grant: CNPq—Conselho Nacional de Desenvolvimento Científico e Tecnológico (BRASIL)

Introduction

This book is about social justice and the role of education within the social processes of change. Researchers from different fields tell us that certainties, if there are any, are provisional, and very few would risk a forecast about how the world will be in a decade or in the years to come. Educators, on the other hand, even when sharing this assumption, wage their time and life in favor of a world project they anticipate in every history or physics lesson. Beyond the naiveness of wanting to arrest the future in a permanent present or the belief in a kind of magic of transformation, there is the possibility of caring for and cultivating a future that, although still unknown, is pregnant with the dreams and projects for a world of justice and peace. Or, using Margaret Mead's beautiful metaphor, the challenge is to cultivate this unknown future as the mother cares for the unborn child in her womb.[1] This is, finally, the assumption that sustains this book.

New Social Contract in a Latin American Education Context is an attempt to understand the educational praxis within the current discussions summarized in the World Social Forum's slogan *another world is possible.* Since the first Forum in 2001, in Porto Alegre (Brazil), thousands of people met in the search for making this world a better home for all. Of course, the Forum is only an iceberg of a movement embedded in the complex social fabric as a sign of resistance and transformation. While referring to the Forum, I point to the contextual character of these writings, beginning with the conception, passing through the choice of the field for developing the research, to the ideas and authors engaged in the discussion. In a broad sense, the book is committed to what has been labeled *perspective of the South*, understanding the South not as a geographical reference but as a vindication of the existence of ways of knowing and of living that struggle for their survival and for a legitimate place in a world where the respect for difference is balanced with the right for equality. The metaphor of the *new social contract*, much in use especially in the first editions of the Forum, stands for the desire to envision *another world*, which paradoxically cannot but spring out of the entrails of the existing one. A shift in recent discussions within the Forum (Porto Alegre, 2010) toward a *crisis of civilization* is an indication that ecology and the future of the planet have gained prominence in the agenda, but they certainly cannot be considered apart from social, economic, and political arrangements.

The recent financial crises have only made it more explicit that a globalized world requires the recreation of the ways we relate to each other as persons and as nations. The metaphor of the social contract represents both the possibility to understand how the modern social organization has been constructed and its limits in a time when we experience paradigmatic transitions in many fields. Could the same contract under which the colonial orders were erected serve as a tool for decolonizing relations, knowledge, and power? Consequently, what kind education could effectively contribute for structuring a new social contract?

While inspired in the broader discussions about the world order, the book is grounded on empirical research on participatory budgeting. This experience of linking representative and direct democracy started in Porto Alegre (1989), and since then has been adopted by communities around the globe, in various forms, and under different names. Participatory budgeting is certainly only one of the many local experiments within the growing consciousness about the need to find other ways of living together. In Latin America today one could not forget to mention the innumerous organizations of popular cooperatives that may represent a relatively small proportion of the GNP, but stand for an alternative way of organizing production, distribution, and consumption of goods. There is precious learning going on in these social experiments, and it is the role of pedagogy to understand and enhance their emancipative potential.

The opening chapter is an attempt to draw a scenario for education today. It is an exercise of making sense of what is happening around us, and of the multitude of explanations, many times conflicting among themselves. The intention is to identify some axes around which to center the discussions and the search for alternatives. It is founded on the belief that in education we are daily responding to a set of challenges, and that the reading of the world—as Paulo Freire has taught us—precedes the reading of the word. The instruments may be more or less sophisticated, but there is no way of abdicating this task if we are committed to participating in *pronouncing our world.* The arguments in this chapter are constructed around three basic ideas. The first one refers to the emblematic and polemical concept of globalization. Notwithstanding its ideological charge, globalization is here taken as a phenomenon that encompasses the following three thematic nuclei: The state, the market, and citizenship; culture: identity and hybridism; knowledge and technologies of information and communication. At the end of this section there is a brief reference to some absences in the discussion about globalization, namely, the issues of religion, race, and gender. It is argued that the discourses that avoid seeing the differences or that do not project them against the background of equality do not allow us to evaluate how much societies are actually divided. The second section deals with September 11 as (also) a theme for education. The event is interpreted as an iceberg of the manifold manifestations of a world still impregnated with a culture of violence.

In the second chapter popular education is taken as a pedagogical movement that together with liberation theology, the theatre of the oppressed, the Ecclesiastic Base Communities, and other grassroots manifestations reveal the creative potential of people in their struggle for justice and liberation. I argue that Latin America occupies a paradoxical place in the global context: on one side, within the world market, the subcontinent has a relatively small impact, figuring at best among the *emerging* markets; on the other, Latin America, maybe because of this marginal position, functions as a kind of social laboratory. An example, as developed in chapter seven of this book, is the process of participatory budgeting, which grew out of the demands of popular movements in the region.

The third chapter deals with the discussions around what is here named as *new social contract,* to differentiate it from the modern social contract, the great narrative that guided Western societies in the last centuries. After the erosion of some classical answers, and in the aftermath of the neoliberal avalanche, some convergences tend to appear on the horizon. The other social contract, so far, is much more about this effort of rearticulating forces around common agendas than as a finished proposal. In this chapter I discuss the origin of the idea of the social contract, identifying it as the founding political and social metaphor of modernity. In short, the social contract implies a new self-understanding of the individual and his/her organization under an authority. Among the themes related to the social contract there is a brief discussion about the invention of a state of nature as an anchorage for the use of reason as source for explaining life in society. There follows an analysis of major topics that reveal the limits of the modern social contract: the *natural contract* (Michel Serres) denounces the detachment of men and women from nature, as if they existed solely in history; the *sexual contract* (Carole Pateman) denounces the contract as absurdly onesided, leaving out of it half of the population; the *racial contract* (Charles Mills) shows how the original contractors were not only male, but also white. Afterward there is an attempt to understand some of the meanings of the "new social contract," namely on three dimensions: an enlarged social contract, a planetary social contract, and a new political social contract.

Rousseau and Freire, in chapters four and five, are at the heart of the book. Rousseau is an obligatory reference in the discussion of the social contract as well as in modern pedagogy. Is the Emile, Rousseau's educatee, the same on both sides of the Atlantic? It is argued that the story of Emile's hero, Robinson Crusoe, serves as a paradigm to understand the colonizing relationship that took place under the modern social contract. There was no problem in enslaving the strange Friday to assure Robinson's survival on the island, and create the conditions for a happy return to his home, richer and self-fulfilled.

Chapter four, under the title "Emile and the limits of citizenship," is basically dedicated to Rousseau. What makes this author of such interest today is that he criticizes Enlightment from within the lights themselves. Of special interest is his influence on the nineteenth-century emancipatory movements in Latin America. Liberators such as Simón Rodríguez, Simón Bolívar's teacher, had read Rousseau or at least been influenced by his ideas. The basic critique of Rousseau follows Galvano Della Volpe's argument regarding the abstracness of Rousseau's subject. Apart from the real world, Emile stands for the general subject, more often associated with the hegemonic visions of society and of men and women.

Paulo Freire, on the other hand, is a landmark of contemporary pedagogy. His *Pedagogy of Oppressed* is indeed the pedagogy of the enslaved Friday, who can be found at any place where colonization produces its victims. In chapter five, "Autonomy Revisited: From Rousseau to Freire," special attention is given to autonomy, a key concept for both Rousseau and Freire. As far as Paulo Freire's pedagogy can serve as reference for education toward another social contract, his idea of autonomy provides important insights for reinventing autonomy. Once, situating the subject within the movement of history, with its many tensions and contradictions, and having no intention to preserve men and women from the "bad influences" of a corrupted society. Second, by working on the presupposition that men and women become human through dialogue, in an intersubjective relation.

In order to apprehend Freire as a reference for recreating relations and organizations, there is a return to his concept of *conscientização*.[2] The discussion in chapter six attempts to show that *conscientização* should not be seen as a fixed concept, but as a construct originated and recreated within the praxis of people who struggle against oppression and for liberation. Social movements, more precisely, popular social movements can be seen as inspiring forces for reinventing pedagogy. Four dimensions to *conscientização*, namely the political, the ethical, the epistemological, and the esthetic, are also discussed. No claims could be made about the exclusive or all encompassing character of these dimensions.

Participatory budgeting, the subject of chapter seven, has revealed itself an innovative social and political experiment. There is an attempt to look at the process from the perspective of education, based on the presupposition that while discussing the budget, citizens engage in teaching and learning. It is assumed that inasmuch as we are able to identify the pedagogical mediations that promote citizenship in the movements of reinventing the social relations and institutions we will be able to contribute more effectively for their efficacy, but also for the education of citizenship in institutionalized pedagogical practices. In this chapter, there is a brief introduction to the praxis of participatory budgeting, and an analysis of some of the major contributions of the process for citizenship learning. These contributions are organized around three topics, based on empirical research: (1) the enlargement and construction of knowledge: about the budget itself, usually a process restricted to a very small and "specialized" group of people; about the local and regional reality, providing access to information and exchange about difficulties and projects; (2) participation and power: presenting a brief description of what citizens understand under participation and their relation to the instituted power; (3) the negotiation of consensus, describing the process of reaching decisions, based on some examples from popular assemblies. At the end of the chapter there is a note on children's involvement in participatory budgeting as protagonists.

The *Propositions*, in chapter eight, are an agenda for meeting others and continue the dialogue. Finishing the book with the experience of participatory budgeting would lend a too much technical character to the book, almost as a recipe. The agenda is made up of eight propositions covering a wide scope that intend to articulate some of the discussions from previous chapters, and at the same time add new ingredients to a discussion that necessarily has to remain open. The inspiring metaphor for proposing the agenda is Freire's book *À sombra desta mangueira [Pedagogy of the Heart]*. The shadow of the mango tree is a place—physical and metaphorical—where he liked to go in order to be by himself, and in so doing, to be with others. Today his image and his work can be compared with this mango tree where people join to recover their strengths, to sharpen their imagination, and for preparing the next step of their action.

To end this introduction, a brief note about my Mexican barber in Los Angeles. I am used to listening to my barber in Brazil talk about horse races, and since I don't know much about the subject, the conversations are usually quite monosyllabic. But this one wanted to know what exactly I was doing at UCLA (University of California, Los Angeles),[3] and when I told him that I was researching social contract he wanted to know more, and asked very frankly: "Could you just tell me in plain English what it is about?" I thought to myself: This man is right; if I'm unable to make myself understood by this barber, my work may be of little value. And so we engaged in a dialogue about millions of Latin Americans fleeing to the United States, where many live illegally. We talked about how people organize themselves for producing food and automobiles, how they participate in deciding where public resources are spent, and how they are involved in discussing the type of school they want for their children. I don't know whether this conversation made much sense for the barber, but I had been reminded of a basic lesson in social research. Although this book is not written for barbers, it only makes sense if at some time it finds an echo in the lives of barbers, janitors, farmers, industry workers, the unemployed, among citizens who feel that this world can be a better place for all.

"My books reflect the pain of the world." With these words José Saramago once spoke about his novels and about his commitment as a writer-citizen. I hope this same pain is heard behind the words and between the lines of this book. Paradoxically, as we know, it is from this pain that so much active and contagious hope emerges. However, we should not move on to this hope too fast, without allowing ourselves to feel and express indignation, in as much as we still have this capacity. In biblical images, for the great part of the Latin American population, as for much of what is known as the Third World, the great march of the Exodus has been substituted by the silent waiting imposed by the new Babylonian servitude. But at the end of the deluge there will be a rainbow as a sign of a new covenant—the promise of a reinvented living together.

1

Daily Life, Globalization, and Education: Educational Practice and the Reading of the World

We live in a paradoxical time. A time of vertiginous mutations produced by globalization, the society of consumption and the society of information. But also a time of stagnation, frozen in the impossibility of thinking social, radical transformation.

—*Boaventura de Sousa Santos*

The September 11 attacks were a monstrous calling card from a world gone horribly wrong.

—*Arundhati Roy*

Scene 1: In a seminar as part of the International Doctoral Program at the Siegen University in Germany, a group of German and Brazilian students had as a debate theme—globalization. Concerned that the linguistic factor might impede communication I proposed that, to initiate the reflection, each one of the participants write down some ideas about the theme based on their experiences. Upon opening the debate, various German students presented their annotations, stressing in their presentations positive aspects such as access to goods produced in other parts of the world, communication with people from other cultures and nations, and the possibility of travel. Given the silence of the Brazilian group, I asked for the reason. I thought that maybe they had not understood the exercise itself. They said this was not the case and as they began to speak I realized that the reason for their silence was the difference in points of view. For them globalization was associated with job instability and the maintenance of unequal relations between class and countries.

Scene 2: On the campus grounds of the University of California in Los Angeles (UCLA), among the tables, a cigarette butt lay burning. A young woman who was reading while drinking her coffee complained about the smoke. She said it would be good if it could be put out and maybe even removed from there. The young man, who was conversing with a female friend, at the table at the side, did not hide his irritation at the request and grudgingly crushed what was left of the cigarette with the point of his shoe. He commented something to his friend, took his motorcycle helmet, and went away, but not without first casting an angry glance and showing the finger in a sign of contempt. The woman who was reading, if she saw anything, made as if it had nothing to do with her. Some time later, she looked at that cigarette butt as something that was definitely out of place. Important to say that she was an Anglo-American, blond student. He was an Arab type accompanied by maybe a Korean or Chinese girlfriend. Completing almost a triangle, in the other corner there was a couple of Latino students. The incident, as mentioned earlier, took place at UCLA, where, as in the majority of the large universities of the First World, there is a large contingent of foreign students.

These relatively common scenes contain important ingredients for comprehending what is going on in the world. Much of what is discussed about globalization and about the current conflicts is revealed in that classroom and around that cigarette butt. Facts such as these, from daily life, permit the comprehension that globalization is not something that happens out there, with others or with the economy. It has to do with each person's daily life and conditions educational practices. I intend to use the relation between these facts and the theoretical discussions as an exercise in learning how to read the world, somewhat in the way that Paulo Freire taught: the world being opened up into themes and these becoming denser based on the experienced reality.

Using the language of photography, this introductory essay seeks to capture some of the moments that represent important movements of the scenario in which education is developed today. I begin with a reflection about some of the overlapping themes in the discussion about globalization, covering the dimensions of politics, culture, and knowledge. I then move on to the issue of gender, which is not easily understood within one or all of the prior discussions although it is present in them. The same goes for racial, class, and religious issues, although these will just be mentioned in passing. Finally, I establish the relation between the cigarette butt and September 11, an emblematic date about which much has been said and written, and which, as all seems to indicate, will pass on to history books with very different meanings.

Three Faces of Globalization

In the two scenes described earlier, each person or group had their projects, but suddenly they found themselves side by side or in front of another. I believe that the presence of these people in these places can be understood as an expression of a process of, among others, cultural, political, economic, and academic relations that has received the name "globalization" and that, in spite of being on the political and academic agenda for more than a decade, continues to generate polemics. Some point to the perverse side of the process and tend to assume a contrary position; others mainly see the advantages and desire a deepening of the process; a growing group is in favor of a different globalization or world process, guided by the needs of the majority of the planet's population, which is at the margins of the current process. Education, as we know, is always present in the disputes, simply because it always has to do with world projects and conceptions of the human being.

Many articles and books about globalization begin with a warning that one is dealing with a complex, controversial, and slippery subject. Octavio Ianni will say that it is a phenomenon similar to those brought about by the epistemological ruptures represented by the discovery by Copernicus that the earth is not the center of the universe, by Darwin's claim that humans are not simply the children of God, or by Freud's finding that humans are a labyrinth of unconscious thoughts and feelings.

> The discovery that the earth turned into a world, that the globe is not just an astronomical figure, but the territory on which all are related and bound together, differentiated and antagonistic—this discovery surprises, enchants, and brings fear. It represents a drastic rupture in the ways of being, feeling, acting, thinking, and imagining. A heuristic event of broad proportions, shaking not only convictions, but also the visions of the world.[1]

For example, from a Marxian point of view, globalization may be seen as just another name for a new face of imperialism.[2] According to McLaren and Farahmandpur, the concept of globalization may indeed camouflage the expanding role of capitalism in the last decades, the outcome being "a community of mutual interests—a countervailing and mutually reinforcing coalition that legitimizes itself through an appeal to geopolitical correctness."[3] *Globalization*, therefore, just as probably any other term that could substitute it, carries with it an enormous ideological baggage that can either facilitate one's identification with one side or the other or lead to the simplification of the facts and a distorted comprehension. Confronted with this, a new definition or an option of one of the definitions does not help us much. In all of them, there is something lacking or something left over, as is prone to happen with themes in which there is much at stake. At this moment, it seems to be more productive to identify some thematic axes that present themselves as challenges for the elaboration of a position in relation to the theme.

The literature indicates that there are three broad axes that cross through the discussion, with differentiated emphases, depending on the context and on the interlocutors. They are complex thematic blocks involving always more than one element: the state and its relation with the market and with citizenship; culture and its link with the discussion of modernity and postmodernity; knowledge related with the new communication and information technologies. In this chapter we seek to elucidate some of the arguments around these issues to make up the background of the discussions on the new social contract. More precisely, we will present some of the issues that will accompany us in the discussion throughout the chapters of this book.

State, Market, and Citizenship

Globalization has to do with the comprehension of the role and size of the state, that is, with a geographic and political reference that deeply conditions our way of living and our subjectivities through public policies. Burbules and Torres call attention to the fact that the postmodern theories, with all their merit, have underestimated the strategic role of the state in the formulation and execution of the public policies when they attribute a supposed autonomy to the postmodern culture.[4] These theories, thus, reinforce the neoliberal argument of the reduction of the state due to the increase of the space for self-regulation of the relations through the market. The strong financial crises that shook the world these last years, demanding the intervention of the state to save the economy from imminent collapse, seems to prove the thesis that its role must neither be underestimated nor overlooked.

This state, certainly, is suffering deep transformations, which, in their turn, are manifested in the exercise of citizenship. Capella suggests that for the first time after its emergence in modernity, the public power tied to the nation-state can no longer be defined in terms of simple sovereignty and legitimacy.[5] For him, the force field of current polity is constituted by the inter-relation of a "vague suprastate private ruler," formed by large corporations and financial capital and by "an open state" or "associations of states" such as the European Union. They are two sectors that, although not autonomous, find their legitimatization in different spheres—in the private and public spheres, respectively.

The legitimatization of the first happens through the discourse of efficaciousness, while the second seeks its legitimacy through the discourse and the defense of rights. Capella records that with globalization, the field of influence and decision of the citizen diminishes since the suprastatal agency escapes its control by being in the private field and through the discourse of efficaciousness. A consequence of this fundamental change in the political system is the increasing weakening of the culture of citizenship.[6] For example, when an industry is transferred from one region to another or from one country to another, the citizen has little or nothing to say about it, since it is done in the name of efficaciousness, a self-legitimizing argument. The years or decades of union struggles for labor rights count for very little when a decision of the private sphere totally escapes their action and takes away the job itself.

The role of the state in education is equally an object of concern and controversy and gains new contours. For example, Blackmore argues that there was a transference of control to the state of education issues due to its loss of control in the economy.[7] In many countries the decentralization policies, in reality, had as a result a greater centralization in what the author calls "centralized decentralization." The author's comments regarding educational policies in countries such as England and Australia apply to others as well: "Devolution in many Anglophone education systems has produced even stronger centralized controls through curriculum guidelines, financial management, accountability mechanisms, and weaker decentralization tendencies."[8] The standardized national exams are becoming the strongest control mechanism of the center. One knows that much of this is beyond the actual decision of the states themselves.

Looking at the issue from the perspective of insertion of educational policies at the macro level, Susan Robertson and others show the problems arising from the "structural porousness of the national frontiers," in a process wherein the horizon of the economies is ever more being constituted in regional and global terms instead of national ones. With education being included as a service within the agreements of the WTO (World Trade Organization) through the GATS (General Agreement on Trade and Services), the traditional role of the national states in organizing an educational system according to their own development polity can become definitively compromised. Education will tend to be regulated like other services open to the law of supply and demand on the international level.[9]

One of the effects of this process is what can be called pedagogical consensus, on the lines of the consensus of economic policies. In 1989 the English economist John Williamson of the Institute for International Economics, Washington DC, used the concept *Washington consensus* to summarize some points that seemed consensual to promote the development of Latin America. Within these can be highlighted the discipline of fiscal politics, the redirectioning of public spending to basic services, such as basic education, basic health care, and investments in infrastructure, broadening the tax base, and adopting moderate taxation, competitive commercial exchange taxes, liberalization of commerce from import restrictions, and legal security for property rights. If, in the economic area, as everything seems to indicate, this consensus is being overcome, in education it still exerts strong effects. It must also be said that a consensus always has its margins, its out sides and its contradictions that reveal its weaknesses and fallacies of which the following can be highlighted:

The fallacy of the policies and techniques: The educational world has been caught up in a true fever of reforms and the discussions are largely dominated by the issue of policies. There are policies for literacy training, inclusion, basic education, higher education, research, and so on. There are and there should be policies for all sectors of life in society and no one doubts their importance as regulating and inductive elements. The problem is with the belief that it is sufficient to have an adequate policy for there to be a different education. We have already learned that even in those places where we have among the best policies on the planet—such as the ECA (Estatuto da Criança e do Adolescente [the Statute of the Child and Adolescent])—Brazil is counted among those who have the worst performance in the area.

The fallacy of quantity: Education on all levels is taken over by a syndrome of haste, of acceleration. To do more in less time, which, in education, is translated into obtaining more information through optimizing the time of the teachers and using new technologies. Professional education is reduced to basic training; children and young people are submitted to marathons of classes and courses because of future needs. Today Rousseau's recommendation sounds like an almost incomprehensible provocation: "Do I dare expound here the greatest, most important, most useful rule for all of education? It is not about gaining time but losing it."[10] It is quite true that the forty hours of the literacy training program begun in Angicos,[11] the pioneer experience of Paulo Freire in Northeastern Brazil, have become legends in the history of our education. But let us not forget that this reading of words was just one moment in the reading of the world that was already in process and would continue after this. Besides this, it was an emergency program aimed at integrating into the reading world the enormous contingent of illiterate people.

The fallacy of competencies: In our society the responsibility for the destiny of each one is increasingly the individual's own responsibility. Success and failure depend on the competencies that each individual supposedly can acquire at any moment in his/her life. The first observation is that this responsibilization is disconnected from the conditions to effect insertion in society. We see how compensatory strategies such as the family grant or payment of a grant for students who pass can minimize the problem, but are far from providing a more definitive solution. The second is that competency cannot be seen as a merely personal attribute. There are individual interests, there is a greater or lesser effort on the part of one or the other, but there also are structural and conjunctural factors that promote or facilitate successes or failures and that are protected by the current consensus around the functioning and organization of society.

The fallacy of inclusion: Inclusion has become the word of order, a part of the new pedagogical consensus. There are policies for the inclusion of blacks, the poor, deaf, women, young people, among others. There is an undeniable pragmatism derived from the conflicting interest games to which the governments will always attend selectively and partially. However, already in *Pedagogy of the Oppressed* Freire denounced that marginalization would not be resolved with the simple "integration" of marginalized persons, since this marginalization was inherent to the system.

> The truth, however, is that the oppressed are not "marginalized," are not men living "outside" society. They have always been "inside"—inside

the structure that made them "beings for others." The solution is not to "integrate" them into the structure of oppression, but to transform that structure so that they can become "beings for themselves." Such transformation, of course, would undermine the oppressors' purposes; hence their utilization of a banking concept of education to avoid the threat of *conscientização*.[12]

Today the discourse of social exclusion tends to suggest that in this world, at the same time unified and divided by the market, the only alternative possible is that of inclusion in the existing reality. It is presupposed that the existing reality is the best possible for all. Within this perspective, the only reasonable policy is to work for the inclusion of those who "still" are excluded; is to take the advantages of the technical-scientific progress to those who still do not have access to them, through the expansion of the markets, through always new products, and to always new consumers.

The fallacy of participation: Just like inclusion, participation has become a sort of panacea to resolve the problems of society and is part of the political agendas of the right and the left parties, as well as of the programs of national and international development agencies, with very distinct if not antagonistic political intentionalities. Even in research and in teaching, participation and dialogue have gained a consensual place. For what reasons? One of the motives is a merely technical-instrumental one. There are indicators that participation increases the efficiency in carrying out the tasks, be it in industry or in the implementation of public policies. The call to participation has the added advantage of displacing the responsibility for failures onto whoever had the opportunity to participate and possibly did not correspond to the calling or made ill use of the opportunity that was given. There are also political motives, in the sense that today democracy is seen, almost consensually, as the most appropriate government system, although in a paradoxical way, this recognition is accompanied by a disbelief in the political institutions and a decrease in the effective exercise of citizenship. Even so there seems to be a tacit consensus that no power system or government can maintain itself for very long without some type of popular participation.

Within the framework sketched here in which new "places" of decision-making for educational policies are configured, Burbules and Torres[13] argue convincingly that, despite everything, the state survives as a decisive institution for mediation seeking to balance four imperatives: transnational capital, the power of global agencies such as the World Bank and the United Nations, the internal demands of the population, and its own interest in survival. It is an optimistic position, considering the real conditions of survival of many national states as agents of their social and educational policies, but who knows, maybe because of this, it is important to signal that to this decision-making territory, at this moment in history, are linked the hopes of many people who are left behind by the process or thrown to the margins of development. Placed before research in education is the challenge of comprehending the complex and changing relations within the state and between the states, these no longer understood as self-determining spaces but as part of a complex force field.[14]

Returning to scene number two, around that cigarette butt crucial issues for citizenship in the globalization era are manifested. For the young American woman, possibly from California, where the reaction to smoking is very strong, her space was being invaded by the smoke of a cigarette that had been thrown in an improper space. She had the right to not be bothered. For the young Arab man, throwing a cigarette butt on the ground did not perhaps have the same esthetic, moral, or health restrictions. He had the right to use this space. What is citizenship in the situation described? Who defines it? It is defined on the basis of what principles and with what criteria? Would the current moment be demanding a new type of citizenship that, although passing through the power of the individual states, surpasses the traditional geographical, cultural, and political limits?

Culture: Identity and Hybridisms

What is obvious by the appearances is that the actors of scene two belong to distinct cultures. It is even possible that, as in California it is politically incorrect to smoke in public places, in the country where the young man came from the problem would be the girl sitting in that public place. This obviousness, however, is crossed by many problems. Beginning with the question of whether each of them are, in fact, mutually considering each other as cultural beings, that is, having a personal and collective history that makes them be and act in that way. What makes this happen? Could the young woman's *reason* have to do with an economic power that creates and undoes needs? These are some of the issues that are also present in the pedagogical scenario and are widely debated by the theoretical currents of multiculturalism, which, according to Torres, "whatever the form or color, (...) it is related with the politics of difference and with the emergence of the social struggles against racist, sexist and classist societies."[15]

An issue that has assured presence in the discussions and is of special interest for our *case* is the homogenization or fragmentation of identities. On the one hand, there is the concern with the successive "ethnocides" that, in the end, would reduce the world to a cultural homogeneity according to the dominant culture's patterns. On the other, there is the concern of an excessive fragmentation that can undermine the foundations for integrated actions.

In this scenario of cultural reconfigurations the idea of hybridization gains relevance, overcoming the strict dichotomization of maintaining or losing the identity, and eventually maintaining the two poles within a wider and permanently tensioned comprehension. For Canclini there are fallen fences at all (cultural) boundaries, and therefore, there is no culture that maintains itself *pure*.[16] This hybridization can be verified today in phenomena such as the *deterritorialization*, through which the facts no longer remain bound to certain geographical contexts, and the *declassification,* a process that abolishes standards that determined, for example, popular and classical or regional music and rock.

This discussion has profound implications for educational practice. For example, does the idea of "cultural invasion" denounced by Paulo Freire in the 1960s still apply? Could there be an undue victimization of the supposedly invaded cultures? Luke and Luke, writing from the Thai perspective, affirm that the very idea of "subordinate" or "inferior" is a Western construction that does not apply to their reality. They refuse, with this, to assume as true a "victim's narrative." In their words: "This, then, is not a victim narrative, not a story of economic brute force exerted by Wall Street, Ford, or News Corporation. (...) No Western product, cultural symbolism, or social practice maps into *blank slate* indigenous or national cultures. Rather such forces dovetail in unpredictable and unsystematic ways into local histories and relations."[17] A similar argument is presented by Rizvi when he studies the westernizing effect of the education that Malaysian students undergo studying in Australia.[18] His findings support the conclusion that the fear of pervasive westernization is unfounded, and that what results from this exchange is a new global generation that, however, is neither necessarily nor strictly Western.

What these studies reveal is that the relation between culture and power is not a uniform process. Each culture creates its forms of communal interaction with the world, making adaptations and creating survival and resistance mechanisms. That is why the idea of cultural negotiation is especially relevant for education. Education, as Paulo

Freire defined it, is "cultural action for freedom" through dialogue, which, in turn, is always traversed by power relations. Because of all this, the educational process goes beyond a simple exchange involving complex negotiations of knowledge, values, and world perspectives.[19]

Knowledge and Information and Communication Technologies

A third thematic block in the discussion on globalization is the issue of knowledge, mainly in its relation to the new information and communication technologies. For the group around the cigarette butt the presence in that place probably did not exclude permanent and instant communication with research sources, with colleagues, friends, and families of very distant regions. Globalization has to do with the abolition of some space and time boundaries. Be they crimes against innocent populations in the war against the terrorists of Afghanistan or dictatorial ravishments in any country, even though silenced by the larger press, a significant portion of the population has access to other sources and develops alternative ways of thinking.[20]

A key issue in the context of the rapid changes in the development of information technologies has to do with the possibility of developing a true community through the virtual network. Or, on the contrary, would it be dividing citizens placing each one in front of the monitor at their home or office, to better transform them, in the end, into individual consumers, not lastly of the technologies themselves and their facilities?

Nicholas Burbules' argument allows an advance in the reflection in an objective way, without divinizing or satanizing the new technologies. After proposing that the idea of a community is sustained on two principles—(a) that of cooperation and shared responsibility and (b) the presupposition that close ties between people are important for carrying out their objective—he argues that all relations in a community are mediated, even those face to face. Rituals, gestures, and words, as we know, can have very different meanings depending on the context. He calls attention to the myth that closer relations are always the most honest, open, and intimate. That is why, before anything else, it is necessary to see what the specificity of each type of mediation is and not make a value judgment a priori. "I think," he writes,

> That these are not degrees of mediation, or contrasts between mediated and unmediated (face-to-face) interaction, but rather alternative forms of mediation, each of which works in its own distinctive ways

to disclose and conceal—which is what media do, and what they are often explicitly designed to do. Any medium acts as a type of frame, highlighting certain elements of interaction and making them more visible while at the same time serving to block out elements that fall outside the frame.[21]

For Burbules, Internet is becoming not a community—it is too diffused for that—but a meta-community in two ways: it gathers within itself various communities and it propitiates conditions for the creation of communities in a type of relation that re-signifies the ideas of materiality, identity, temporality, and proximity, among others.

At the same time in which it broadens the possibilities of constructing new relations of communal interaction and of learning, it also accentuates the perception of knowledge as merchandise. The attention of international agencies directed to education has to do with the fact that in this area there is one of the greater concentrations of resources: the sector put in motion, in 1997, 1.29 trillion dollars, that is, more or less, 25 percent of the total circulation of merchandise.[22] In some countries, for example, higher education is seen effectively as an exportation product and markets are sought out for "exchange" like selling Coca Cola. We know that not all are benefitted in the same way by this business; suffice it to take a look at the disparity of expenditures toward education between rich and poor countries and, within these countries, between the different social classes. The great majority of the students from the lower social background will most certainly be outside of this global meta-community that generates information with the same speed as it discards it.

Some Absences

There were two women and a man at the center of the scene. One of the women complained. The man showed the finger. I thought: What if the man had asked to snuff out the cigarette butt? And if he had asked would he have received the same answer? And if the woman had thrown out that cigarette butt? Or, even, would that have been possible? And if there had been a young man with the young woman who complained?

They are merely hypothetical questions that however show the complexity of the gender relations intertwined with the issue of race, class, religion, and, in turn, are re-signified in the context that we call globalization. Blackmore observes that in the globalization discussions the gender issue generally is absent as is also the case in the discussion on educational reform.[23] In the new, conservative "fundamentalism," she notes, there is a regression, in terms of prejudice, as to race and gender. "Women feel both the pain and the pleasure associated with seductive notions of choice, but they largely bear the responsibility as the competitive state withdraws from its social welfare obligations while reprivatizing women's productive labor."

This argument is reinforced by an analysis of the situation of the women in Latin America. Studies show how due to economic adjustments, homes have been forced to make internal adjustments that, in the end, result in a greater work load for the woman. This is manifest in various ways, one of them being a change in buying habits. With smaller budgets, things that were once bought in supermarkets need to be made at home (food, care with clothing, etc.), work that, even if other members of the family participate, is understood as being women's work. The crises has also diminished the possibility of leaving the house for leisure or gathering with relatives and groups, once again forcing mainly the woman to remain "tied" to the house and its care. Besides this, to survive, many women join solidarity projects from community ovens, exchange clubs to cooperatives. While this brings unquestionable gains in terms of political consciousness, this work generally is added on to what the woman was already doing. Summarizing, economic efficiency and lower cost of production represent transferring the cost of the market to the homes, where, in turn, the women take on the greater load.[24]

The same type of questions regarding gender can be made regarding social class, race, and religion. Although the concept of social class may have gone out of style, in reality we know and feel that there is a concentration of capital and power never before seen leaving the greater part of the population at the margin of the system, as much as producers as well as consumers. The idea of race, on the other hand, is often subsumed within the broader (and blander) notion of ethnicity, coming to be, in some circles, a politically incorrect concept, unfortunately leading to an occultation of discrimination.[25] The color of the skin continues to cause the emergence of reactions and prejudices that are deeply rooted in the history of the nations. "It is painful to know that the color of the skin of the children who wander the streets, of the majority who are in the prisons and of those who live in the slums is black," said Benedita da Silva, referring to Brazil.[26] And finally, religion also imposes itself as an important variable in comprehending the social processes. We could ask if the phenomenon known as the *emergence of religion* or the *return to the sacred* means an almost magic return of the divinities and of religiosity or if the academic world, within a positivist posture, was not able to see it. Thus, it is more elegant to speak of the return of religion than to recognize the theoretical and instrumental deficiency.

The discourses that avoid seeing the differences or that do not place them in tension having equality as the background, be it for political delicacy or for ideological astuteness, do not permit the evaluation of how much the majority of the societies are divided. For example, Douglas Kellner shows how the presidential election of 2000 in the United States revealed a nation divided by race, gender, class, religion, region, and political ideology. Similar data can be found in other countries and serve to reaffirm the importance of multiple perspectives in order to comprehend reality, in a relation of dialogue, complementation, and mutual criticism.[27]

September 11 and After: New Challenges for Education

"The September 11 attacks were a monstrous calling card from a world gone horribly wrong."[28] This phrase by Arundhati Roy places September 11 at the point of an iceberg that has been in formation for a long time and that, once revealed, can no longer be ignored. Douglas Kellner formulated the issue with these terms:

> The terror attacks of 9/11 put in question much conventional wisdom and forced U.S. citizens and others to reflect upon the continued viability of key values, practices, and institutions of a democratic society. In particular, the events of September 11 force the rethinking of globalization, new technology, democracy, and national and global security. 9/11 and its aftermath demonstrate the significance of globalization and the ways that global, national, and local scenes and events intersect in the contemporary world. The terror spectacle also pointed to the fundamental contradictions and ambiguities of globalization, undermining one-sided pro or anti-globalization positions.[29]

The date will possibly enter history with crossed signals: for some, it is a threat to the world of progress and of freedom and for this reason it brought on a "just" revenge; for others, it will be, up to now, the most eloquent sign of the frailty of a type of world, and for this reason itself, should liberate creative forces to rethink and construct a different one. A sign that we live in a make believe world, as were the giant towers that crashed before the stupefied eyes of the whole world, live and in color, in a spectacle worthy of Hollywood.

What is intriguing is that, if this is a sign of a world gone wrong, this world was created with the help of self-sacrificing educators in all parts of the planet. Those who planned the attack and piloted the airplanes that destroyed the World Trade Center and hit the Pentagon as well as those who, some time later, began to plan and execute a war of retribution and promise to take it to all places of the world wherever there is "evil," and the thousands of journalists who have the role of passing on the information of the generals and us, who watch everything, complacent or revolted, we all have been educated, some of us within the modern standards, very well educated, with the right to university and access to all sorts of information. It has become common to use the phrase that education alone will not be able to generate a different world, but a different world will not be possible without education. It seems that the effect of this phrase has often been not only to exempt us from guilt and liberate us from the complex of Atlas, the mythological figure who carries the world on his back, but also to turn us away from the fundamental issues, always pressed as we are by the need to present results according to the competencies of the day.

In a very brief way, I outline some arguments to show that September 11 is also a problem of and for education. Asked about the role of education, Chomsky, an uncontested leader in the movement for a globalization founded on justice, argued that far from creating independent thinkers, schools have always played a special role in reinforcing the system of control and coercion. There is a kind of vicious circle: once one is educated and socialized within a given power structure, this same structure takes care to provide the corresponding compensation.[30]

Is that the destiny of education? I believe it depends a lot on the readings we are able to do of the world, of the scenarios that we are able to construct and the dreams we permit ourselves to dream and to nourish. And foremost, of the future that we start to build now with our actions. In the scene of the cigarette butt there was smoke rising between people of different cultures and origins. Eduardo Galeano made a very pertinent comment that September 11 provoked a curtain of smoke that continues enveloping persons on all continents.[31] Maybe one could broaden Galeano's image by saying that this curtain of smoke already existed and September 11 made it denser and life much more vulnerable.

Smoke makes people confused, inept for rationalizing due to the lack of oxygen. Ben Bella has a phrase that warned: "This system, that has already made mad cows, is making mad people too."[32] A symptom of this are the word plays that seem to have lost any relation to reality.[33] Many of those who today are terrorists some time ago were acclaimed as "freedom fighters." President Bush's promise that the United States were entering into a "long, long war" leads one to understand that in the near future the distinction between time of war and time of peace will no longer exist.[34] And, as the popular saying goes, war is war. That is, war is (or was) a state of exception where freedom is sacrificed and resources redirected to defense because of a cause that one won or lost. Then one would expect return to another time, of cultivating the land, taking care of life. The brother of one of the victims of the World Trade Center, David Potorti, writes: "There is a moral corruption that comes from living in a militarized society. When military debates continually defy debate, hold center stage at the expense of monumental human need at home and consume resources essential for the well-being of people, our culture is diminished, and we are diminished along with it."[35] I would add that these human needs are much more monumental outside the United States, where many nations have become accustomed to the minimum of humanity due to this same politics of war.

It is inevitable that there is an association between the accumulation of bellicose power in the Persian Gulf Region with the petroleum industry, which in its turn has ties with the war industry, which in its turn has ties with the information and entertainment industry (mass media), which in its turn... "America (sic!) has always viewed petroleum as a security issue and protects it in all ways that it considers necessary. Few of us doubt that its military presence in the Gulf has little to do with its concerns with human rights and almost exclusively to do with its strategic interest in petroleum."[36] In other words, a circle is formed that feeds itself and that, depending on the perspective, is a virtuous one (see the good portents for the American economy with the injection of resources into the army and into security and the guarantee of the flow of petroleum for a few more decades) or a vicious one (see the lack of perspectives for a great part of the peripheral world).

The press has an important role in maintaining this curtain of smoke. Douglas Kellner, in the book *Grand Theft 2000: Media Spectacle and a Stolen Election*, shows the role of the television media in the fabrication of a candidate. For example, George W. Bush was propagated as the heir of a political dynasty committed to a "compassionate conservatism," which had nothing to do with his practice as governor with a record number of execution of prisoners and with a significant cut in social programs. Today, this same media eat up the news of the war from the hands of the officers. It is enough to watch one session of briefing to understand the game in scene. In one of these sessions, after one of the North American soldiers had fallen from the helicopter, the questions were if he had been hit before or after falling from the helicopter, if he suffered much before dying. It was also asked if the last "smart bombs" were efficient enough to destroy the caves of Afghanistan, all of which are supposedly infested with dangerous terrorists ready to launch a new attack on some power symbol in the United States or manufacturing dangerous chemical weapons in sophisticated laboratories. This is sold as truth and, what is worse, it is bought as truth.

September 11 has yet another reading. It is unlikely that we will ever know if this date was chosen because in 1973, on September 11, the socialist government of Salvador Allende in Chile fell. Roger Burbach writes: "On the morning of September 11, I watched aircraft flying overhead. Minutes later I heard explosive sounds and saw fireballs of smoke fill the sky. As a result of theses attacks thousands died, including two good friends of mine."[37] The author was not describing the happenings in New York, but what he experienced in Chile when a military coup with strong North American support overthrew the people elected government and installed one of the bloodiest dictatorships of Latin America. It is, at least, an irony.

This reading of a double September 11 raises up the many faces of terrorism. Noam Chomsky, among many others, has denounced the current American intervention in Afghanistan as state terrorism, as were dozens of other actions carried out without respect to the still fragile international conventions. Arundhati Roy listed the countries that the United States has attacked and bombarded since World War II. The number and geographical range is impressive: China (1945–1946, 1950–1953), Korea (1950–1953), Guatemala (1954, 1967–1969), Indonesia (1958), Cuba (1959–1960), Belgian Congo (1964), Peru (1965), Laos (1964–1973), Vietnam (1961–1973), Cambodia (1969–1970), Granada (1983), Libya (1986), El Salvador (1980s), Nicaragua (1980s), Panama (1989), Iraq (1991–2001), Bosnia (1995), Sudan (1995), Yugoslavia (1999).[38] Currently it is Afghanistan's turn and there are already new targets announced. This is not counting the participation in state coups that have also cost thousands of lives, as was the case in Latin America.

September 11 then, at the same time as the smoke gets denser and good is confused with evil, liberty with control and war with peace, also causes a greater quest for the figures behind the smoke and above all, for air to survive. Education can have an important role, be it to widen and spread the cloud of smoke or to create spaces of oxygenation. It is not about returning to the dichotomous pattern of clear-dark, with the intention of seeing things clearly and distinctly, as Descartes wanted, but of exercising the intelligence or the intelligences and senses to perceive that there exists the possibility of living outside the smoke, that we are not Kafkalike enmeshed in a present without a way out.

The changes that have been talked about for decades and the emblematic events such as the fall of the Berlin wall in 1989, and the attack on the World Trade Center and on the Pentagon on September 11 of 2001 demand, minimally, that deep attention be given to the discourses of change of epoch or paradigmatic transition. In education this need is manifested, above all, in the sensation that it is not being able to handle the responsibility that the world demands. Would this be the end of an education? Through where would a different education pass? This question will serve as the base for the investigations that follow, not without first reflecting on the place of Latin America and on what here is qualified as its pedagogical labyrinth.

2

The Latin American Pedagogical Labyrinth: A Popular Education Perspective

In our Latin America, there is much more meaning than one thinks, and our peoples which are considered lesser—and they are lesser in territory and inhabitants much more than in purpose and judgment—are saving themselves with the secure rudder of the bad blood of yesterday's colony and the dependence and servitude to which a false and criminal concept of Americanism was beginning to lead them, through an equivocal love of foreign and superficial forms of republic.

—José Martí

The Paradoxical Place Called Latin America

It is appropriate that we reflect more specifically on the place and role of Latin America within the scenario presented in the previous chapter. As indicated in the subtitle, this reflection will take place within the perspective of popular education, a pedagogical movement constructed in Latin America during the second half of the past century and that has within its characteristics: (a) the fact that it is rooted in the concrete struggles of the people; (b) the clear assumption that it is a transforming political activity in favor of justice and equality; (c) the aim of being developed through a methodology based on dialogue and *conscientização*.

Within this reading perspective, Latin America and the Caribbean occupy a paradoxical position. On the one hand, having as one of the indicators the scarcity of media exposure on international means of communication, we are dealing with a relatively irrelevant subcontinent within the world scenario. With some exceptions and in spite of recent news that puts Brazil as an emerging power (we need to remember that some decades back there was the so-called *Brazilian miracle*), the subcontinent does not stand out as an essential source of products; as a consumer market it also does not greatly attract the appetite of investors, since its population does not numerically represent as attractive a market as, for example, China or India. Besides, only a reduced part of the population effectively participates in the market beyond that which is considered essential. From the military point of view, even the civil war in Colombia does not seem to fit into the parameters of the war against terrorism since the conflicts remain more or less within the territorial limits. Thence occurs the displacement of resources to other more strategic places, from the point of view of maintaining the economic hegemony. The World Bank as well as the International Monetary Fund perceived, in the war against Iraq, an opportunity to revert their own legitimacy and identity crises by placing themselves on the side of the fight against terrorism, where they carry out the "soft" side by giving support in strategically dangerous situations that can be sources of generating terrorists, while the Pentagon takes on the "hard" side of combating the terrorists directly.[1]

This is one side of the story. Paradoxically, however, Latin America is also one of the places that is looked to in terms of alternatives for this world that showed its monstrous side on September 11. The World Social Forum, which in 2010, on its tenth birthday, returned to Porto Alegre, is an expression of a broad movement of resistance and quest for alternatives, which has in one of the cities of Latin America its point of reference. Porto Alegre, earlier nonexistent on the political map, has become a symbol for the quest for alternatives, expressed in the slogan of the Forum: *Another world is possible*. The fact to be highlighted is that this type of experience becomes possible and viable in a place that is at the margins. But it is in the frame that the termites install themselves and from there begin to gnaw at the picture. Just so, it is at the margins that alternatives emerge.

The World Social Forum represents a convergence of the movements that, from Seattle to Copenhagen, reveal the limits of the current model of development and social organization, as well as the quest for alternatives. It is the pacifist movements, the movements for human rights, the anticorporate globalization movements, the ecological movements, and in Latin America the movements of the Indigenous peoples and the Afro-Brazilians that find a platform in the World Social Forum for gathering and for dialogue. Among the lessons that are being learned in the discussions and that are put forth as references for the construction of another possible world are the following: (1) that the globalization dominated by the interests of the market is unsustainable; (2) that what is in progress is an alternative globalization; (3) that the dialogue between the proposals of globalization is difficult, but is necessary and urgent, aiming at the construction of a new social contract and at confronting what is turning out to be a crises in the civilizational model; 4) that the responsibility of the resistance movements at the level of organization, objectives, and projects grows.[2]

In the last years the political map of Latin America reveals a strong inclination to the left with the election of governments identified, to different degrees, with policies that introduce alternatives to or attenuations of the dominant neoliberalism of prior decades. This has some important implications for the social movements and for education. On the one side, it would be contradictory to not recognize that the presence of these governments is due to the intense mobilization of society, with conflicts that cost the lives of many co-citizens. The election of Lula in Brasil, of Evo Morales in Bolivia, of Fernando Lugo in Paraguay, of José Mujica in Uruguay, and of Rafael Correa in Ecuador, in spite of the differences, was celebrated as a victory of the forces that have been constructing their participation in power throughout decades.

On the other side, hanging in the air is the feeling that the changes are far from what was expected. From the tension between the conquest of the social movements and the force of the elites to hold on to their power, there arise what Zibechi calls "new governabilities," in other words, new forms of governing states and peoples as spaces without fixed boundaries and as a collective construction in movement.[3] We would no longer be in the context of welfare states, nor in neoliberal states in the strict sense, but in states that seek to maintain the survival of the existing policies with new forms of legitimization and new strategies of governing the movements from below. Examples of this are the compensatory policies, the many types of grants that interfere in a direct way in the life of the people, and, although not substantially altering the picture of inequalities, they present the opportunity for a certain degree of social mobility.

Within this discussion it is important to highlight the role of the nongovernmental organizations, or NGOs, which have proliferated in the last two decades. Although there are controversies about the function that they carry out in the current political conjuncture, there seems to be a certain consensus that they have passed from a contesting role to a collaborating one, motivating participation on the local level, but not interfering in macroeconomic politics. This adaptation to the system is tied mostly to the emergence of second degree NGOs, that is, those designated to channel help for development. Zibechi presents an example from Chimborazo, a region of Ecuador of a predominantly indigenous population: with 28,000 inhabitants the region had 158 first degree NGOs and 12 second degree ones.[4]

In the context of this new governability many social movements have been transformed into NGOs or have become associated to those that supported them. The characteristics of protests and demands have been put aside and they have gone to a language of projects and programs. According to the analysis of Maria da Glória Gohn, a new grammar has been created subject to deadlines and project results, even if these attend to only a small portion of the population. "The militant turned into the organizing activist of clients who use the social services."[5] Her analysis coincides with that of Zibechi, when the latter analyzes the new type of leader that arises from the NGOs, being that the capacity of the leaders is not evaluated by the political, formative, and organizational quality of the movement, but on the ability to capture resources. As one leader of an NGO argued, it is about an issue of scale. In other words, the world is more or less in order, one only needs to broaden the existing projects.[6]

It must be said that this is not about denying the seriousness of the work of the NGOs or their right to capture resources for their projects through partnerships. The work carried out by these institutions is as worthy as that carried out by schools and universities and in some regions it represents possibilities for jobs for professionals of various areas, from agronomists to pedagogues. However, the analyses call attention to the fact that they also help "educate" the movements in the sense of adapting them to the hegemonic rationality, integrating them in subordinate ways. In this process the popular education methodologies are widely used as instruments to perpetuate domination. It is a case of sorcery that turns against the sorcerer.

The interaction of the political and social movements with different agendas, as well as the cultural diversity, causes the question about the individual and collective identity to become a permanent figure in the life and history of Latin America. Alcira Argumedo affirms that "the problem of the social and cultural identities constitute an essential facet for the matrix of the Latin American popular thought pattern."[7] To accept that the search for identity itself is constitutive of what one is as a people implies another type of attitude in facing our reality. The Venezuelan philosopher Ernesto Mays Vallenilla suggests that the originality of the Latin American thought system will not appear with the use of artifices or even through force—such as forceps in birthing. It would also not make sense to project futures full of novelties but disconnected from reality. Rather we should be as the poets: "instruments of being and porters of its mysteries." The secret of the poet lies in letting him/herself be penetrated by the mysteries of the reality that, in their turn, are found in daily living and are familiar. "Let us let America appear and the experience of being come to light, through the rapt time of the future."[8]

In this sense it is not the case of talking nostalgically of recovering an identity of Latin America or popular education, which in fact never came to exist as a fixed point. The priorities and emphases of this endeavor to make education a part of the movement for change varied according to the needs and challenges presented by a given context. Considering that popular education affirmed the non-dichotomization between theory and practice, one of the tasks for reflection was and continues to be the definition of articulating themes. Among these themes there has already been the resistance to the dictatorship, the participation in the definition of the educational policies that would guarantee the right to school education, the revision of the epistemological foundations, and more recently the confrontation with the issue of cultural diversity.

One of the great generating themes today is the construction of the public as a common good. This is verified in the breakdown of representative democracy and in the quest for complementation through forms of direct participation and through valorization of the community processes. Examples of this today are found all over, through mechanisms such as participatory budgeting and the installation of planning and social control instruments with the participation of citizens. In Brazil, the creation of councils, stemming from the Federal Constitution of 1988, in all spheres of public life, signals another moment in the comprehension of citizenship. The limitations, in practice, for example, with the representatives of the social and popular movements assimilating the logic of the governments, indicate the distance, if not the abyss, that separates the reality from the possibilities.

It is pertinent to return to Hanna Arendt when she identifies two correlate characteristics in the concept of public. First, public is the place of appearance, that is, where everything can be seen by everyone and has the greatest possible divulgence. The *polis*, in this sense, is not a physical place, but the "organization of society that results in joint actions and speaking."[9] It is through the speaking of and the being heard by others that the public sphere is constituted.

Second, the term public remits us back to the world itself being a shared space and constituted by mediations created by men and women. For something public to exist one of the essential conditions is permanence. In other words, there needs to be a certain degree of conviction that this world will not end tomorrow, that it will survive my death as an individual. According to Arendt, the belief in the imminent Parousia of the first Christian communities (the end of the world with the second coming of Christ) would be an example of a belief that did not favor the development of the public sphere.

Popular education sought to be a pedagogical-political practice of formation of the public based on a place that identified itself with those who were left out or were on the bottom of the social scale. In the theory of Freire literacy training was part of the possibility of saying one's word, a word tied to action. The utopia of a transformed society fed these practices. Today, there are, minimally, new factors to be considered. One of them is that the place of *appearances* has become more complex, especially through the role carried out by the new communication and information technologies. The current *agora* is formed by neighborhood associations as well as by virtual communities.

Besides this, the level of disillusion leads to no longer believing in the Parousia but in the lack of perspectives for the future. A poll carried out among young Argentineans (Boletin IESALC) revealed that no less than 37.8 percent of these young people stated moving to another country as a future goal. Interviews about the perspectives for the future of young people in a poor neighborhood of a south Brazilian city revealed that the job of their dreams was no more than becoming a watcher of cars, if not some explicit involvement with drugs.[10] What conditions would exist here to generate a culture of the public? Or, to put it in Habermas' terminology, what conditions would exist to generate an argumentative community with the minimal conditions for social and political efficacy?

Within this context it is understandable that many practices of popular education tend to close in on themselves in an attempt to survive, or they take on a demanding character with regard to the state as the great social actor. Analyzing civil society and the alternatives of action within it, Margarita Bonamusa identifies three tendencies that can help in guiding educational practices. The first emphasizes the strengthening of the organizations, especially grass roots ones, those not necessarily identified with the state. Democracy is carried out and terminates within the organizations. Margarita Bonamusa calls this tendency *sociocentric*. Maybe we would find within this category many of the solidarity based economy businesses.

Another tendency organizes its actions in relation to the state that is seen as the main actor and representative of the public. Bonamusa calls this tendency *statecentric or neo-corporative*. The priority goal of educational action and the social practice would be to generate capacity for specialized interlocution with the government, which has the prerogative of interpreting what is of public interest. The specialization in the social movements to create intervention mechanisms is one of these ramifications. Also inscribed in this tendency is the current debate within popular education about its capacity to influence public policies.

A third tendency relates the strengthening of civil society with the strengthening of the public. The public is not to be confused with the state, but refers to a sphere of negotiation of the collective interest among the various groups and with the governing entities. According to Bonamusa, "the relation between government and organizations of the civil society is placed as an intermediation mediated by the multipolarity of the public space, going beyond the bipolar and direct relation of the second tendency."[11] An essential part of this concept is the deliberation between the different actors of the civil society and the government in open public spaces with the control of the citizens.

These three perspectives do not need to be seen as mutually exclusive or in a linear way. What is put up for debate is the importance of clarifying the focus or directing the action as one begins to understand education as a political-pedagogical intervention. The argument is that the notion of public as a common good could be today an important convergence point in the discussion on issues such as cultures, methodologies, and institutionalities, in sum, about the possibility of a new social contract.

Looking from the Perspective of Hidden Pedagogical Strategies

Having as a presupposition that education can carry out an important role in filling in the deficit of the comprehension of and especially in experiencing the public, I propose a broadening of the vision, which can go in various directions. I limit myself in this chapter to what I call hidden pedagogies, inspired by two thinkers who seek to help in this articulation of the public "from below" or from the "community of the victims." The first is Boaventura de Sousa Santos,[12] who propounds the need for a sociology of the absences in order to give visibility to the non-hegemonic practices, and the second is Enrique Dussel, who, on the occasion of the celebrations of the fourth century of the "discovery of America," published the book *1492: O encobrimento do Outro [The invention of the Americas: eclipse of "the other" and the myth of modernity]*. Today one perceives that a great part of our pedagogical history of Latin America is hidden and that its reconstitution is an exercise in pedagogical archeology that is fundamental for giving roots to current practices so that these might be effective instruments in the construction of a public sphere where there are conditions for each citizen to have his/her say as well as to have a sense of belonging to a world whose permanence is constructed and guaranteed collectively.

A Haitian story talks about how on dark nights the sorcerer, the Lord of the Word, disinters a previously sleeping body that, through sorcery, is converted into a slave, and sells his workforce to the owners of the lands of the region. He becomes a worker without a conscience, willing to obey any order without resisting, without arguing, without questioning, without asking, and without organizing in self-defense. However, the dwellers of the region know the antidote and also know that the version that the slave is a live-dead person taken over by Mu-Ntu (the soul of a dead person) is false. The people then get salt, the antidote, and go into the gardens and plantations to sprinkle salt on the slave until he wakes, returning to being a person, a human.[13]

The days and nights of Haiti are, in different proportions, the days and nights of Latin America and the Caribbean. Put in better terms, they correspond to the way this part of the world was invented by the most brilliant thinkers of the West. Hegel, for example, is categorical when he affirms that the distinction between the Old and New World is not only external. According to him, the Spirit has not manifested itself here yet, and when it does, as in the case of Peru and Mexico, it has the character of "an entirely particular culture which expires at the moment that the Spirit gets near it."[14] It is this one and only true spirit, so many times installed in the cannon balls and the tips of the swords, that can destroy without scruples, together with temples and libraries, the way these peoples had created to make themselves humans on these lands.

The five hundred years since the arrival of Columbus (1492) and Cabral (1500) to what today is America served to put side by side, when not in conflict, the versions that surround these happenings. On the one side were celebrations because of the integration into the world of the European civilization and on the other, denouncements because of the usurpation of the lands and the destruction of cultures. This other side of the story interests us in the hope of recovering some of the lost links that could help in the reconstruction of our pedagogical memory. The presupposition is that together with the silencing of the cultures their pedagogies were silenced as well, but continued surviving in clandestineness.

While living and working with the population of a poor neighborhood, the Venezuelan social scientist Alejandro Moreno Olmedo observed a fact that is assuredly the experience of most educators. In his words:

> I understood then, what was the great abyss that separated my science and my methods from the reality which I intended to use with them. (...) The discussion of paradigms pointed me to a clue, but soon that revealed itself to be insufficient, since the discussion always gyrates within the field of meanings of the world that is external to the people.[15]

His analysis led him to the conclusion that there exists something like a popular *episteme* that is distinct from modern *episteme* as well as from post-modern *episteme* and therefore impossible to be captured by the theoretical instruments provided within these references.

This *episteme* is understood by him as a matrix that "defines the conditions of possibility of what one can think, know and say in a certain historical moment, besides the possible way of a certain 'doing' and the existence itself of some 'doings.'" In this sense he would say that the *episteme* is not thought, but that one thinks within it and from it. His argument is that there exists something like a popular *episteme* with a distinct logic from that which rules hegemonic thought and science.

In this same direction, Alcira Argumedo rejects as absurd the idea that the popular-political traditions of the subaltern classes of Latin America have an eclectic formation: a little of Marxism, a little of Christian social thought, of liberalism and fascism, among others.

> Based on the various factors that are at work in the political realities of Latin America, it is not so easy then, to make a *tabula rasa* with

the popular conceptions, considering that one is in the presence of a mixture without essential contents or boundaries, of non-processed experiences, of blind activisms, of politics without culture.[16]

There would be a matrix of popular thought historically constructed based on which the ideas are adapted, transformed, or rejected.

She identifies four historical periods for the constitution of this matrix. The first is of the pre-Columbian cultures. Among them we find nations that depended on hunting and gathering, but also nations with an elevated level of scientific development. The Mayans had a more sophisticated calendar than the Gregorian calendar and the architecture of the city of Tenochtitlán was equal to the best European cities of that time. Among the Aztecs as well as the Incas there was an educational system that sustained their technological development. In the less developed nations from the technological point of view, the pedagogical strategies were built into their elaborate religious rituals or in the richness of the myths. Or, how to negate the competence of education when a boy is able to proffer 661 names of plants and 336 names of birds?[17]

The second period is that of conquests, a period of devastation of the Indigenous and African cultures, with strong and violent conflicts. The colonial period follows, between the seventeenth and eighteenth centuries, when open resistance had become practically untenable. Finally there is the period of the cultural-political processes stemming from emancipation, with the integration of new social actors and a growing formation of an intellectuality identified with the subaltern layers. This division of periods of the formation of a matrix of the popular source of Latin American thought makes it possible to identify some pedagogical strategies that further on will serve as support for the emancipatory pedagogical proposals. Here they are understood as pedagogies since they form a set of knowledge and practices with their own relative internal coherency.

A Pedagogy of Survival

Pure and simple survival constitutes a distinctive feature of a great portion of the Latin American people. Today it is the problem of chronic unemployment for some, of underemployment for others, and of precarious and subhuman living conditions for approximately fifty million Latin Americans who live with a daily income of up to one (one) North American dollar, according the data from the World Bank. Throughout history survival was part of the experience of the

Indians, the African slaves, the immigrants, and growing portions of the population, marginalized in the name of progress and of civilization or simply of the greed of the dominant classes.

Surviving, in these conditions, is an art and requires pedagogical strategies with a level of sophistication equal to or greater than those found in the didactic manuals of the hegemonic pedagogy. It is a pedagogy about which little is known because it is generated in clandestineness, many times outside of the legal environment or official formality, amidst needs for eating and healing, in sum, living. The situations herein have the intention of pointing out dimensions or identifying elements that in this context are understood as making up a pedagogy of survival.

In the cathedral of Lima, Peru, an indigenous woman prayed, kneeling in front of the coffin with the mortal remains of Pizarro placed at the entrance of the temple. The first reaction vis-à-vis this scene is one of revolt on seeing this woman possibly from some poor neighborhood imbedded in the Andes humbling herself in front of someone who had transformed those descendants of the Incas into strangers and undesirables in their own land. What could one ask for in a prayer to Pizarro if not for clemency to continue alive, which with time gained the form of a plea for health of a child or employment for the husband?

I interpret the scene as an expression of an attitude of survival within a world that had become overwhelmingly cruel in its domination and where the forces of open resistance had been annihilated. The dominated had learned disguise tactics: under the apparent acquiescence (in Pizarro's case even of veneration) they maintained complicity through the original languages, the festivities, and other customs. I cite Argumedo once more: "They are destroyed, annihilated peoples, who defend themselves in ancient codes to maintain their human condition in the face of a devastating power."[18]

Another situation is the expression through trances in mediumistic religions or through glossolalia in Pentecostalism. This phenomenon can be rejected as manifestations of deformed or incapable rationality, but it can also be seen as a subversive and clandestine strategy to create and legitimize truths and knowledge. When it no longer is John on the corner or Mary the faith healer who is speaking but an *orixá* [African divinity] or the divine spirit that is manifesting itself, one is outside the parameters of judgment to which the "normal" rationality is submitted. They are ways of surviving that in academic language came to be known as *epistemecides*.

Not rarely, the learning from survival gives rise to practices that later are assumed by society as a whole or are validated by normative science. The *feijoada* [black bean dish] with pig's feet and skin—the leftovers of the master's house—became a typical national meal, served as *Brazilian food* in fine restaurants in New York and in other global metropolitan centers. The medicinal herbs, many a times associated with practices considered charlatanism, can give clues to pharmaceutical laboratories to *discover* chemical elements for their new medications. Or the church can learn that the touch of a friendly hand can do miracles.

In the field of arts the origin of the *tango*, of *capoeira*, and the *samba* schools are examples of how survival generates its own knowledge and esthetics. From the maneuvers of the body that is preparing to escape the whippings is born a game of great rhythmic wealth. From the music of the Buenos Aires workers in their leisure hours in the bars arise some of the most beautiful expressions of sensuality and movement. From the periodic and controlled invasion of the central streets of the cities by the poor dwellers of the hills, most of them black, are born the samba schools.[19]

A Pedagogy of Resistance

The history of Latin America is also a history of resistance and all that was said earlier could be described as a way of resisting domination. The intention, distinguishing between survival and resistance, is to reinforce the intentionality of the latter. Following this logic, all survival is certainly resistance, but there are resistances that are placed at the level of intentional and purposeful struggles.

Once more we observe that we know very little of the pedagogical processes that took place and continue taking place within these resistance movements. The books on the history of education in Latin America inform us that the first universities were founded in Lima and Mexico in the year 1551, much before the first university on North American soil, which was Harvard, founded in 1636,[20] but they do not tell us how the indigenous peoples organized themselves to resist the force of the weapons and the imposition of the language of the conquistadors. We learned about the coming of the Jesuits and of their efforts to catechize the pagan Indians, but we do not learn about the faith expressions of the local communities and how this faith was an instrument of resistance. Considering that in the mid-nineteenth century the official Brazilian educational system reached around 107,000 students in a population of 8 million inhabitants one can observe that the history of education tends to pass over the knowledge and the nonformal *educational systems* of the vast majority of the population.[21]

The same can be said with regard to the *quilombos* [refuge communities for fugitive slaves] that were formed by fugitive slaves. How could Palmares, the best known among them, have resisted more than half a century (1630–1697) without training, educating men and women who, in that place, fed their hopes for a life of freedom and sought strength and the means to fight for it? What knowledge circulated in this community in the form of myths, of artistic expression, of sayings and relations, of knowledge of geography, of the culture of the dominator, and of their instruments of violence?

The resistance from early on created its intellectual leaders. Amidst so many voices one that became emblematic was that of José Martí, the Cuban writer and poet who died in the struggle for the independence of Cuba. For him, resisting did not mean to give in to blind xenophobism. José Martí was a man of cosmopolitan experience and spirit who lived in Europe, in the United States, and in various places in Latin America, without ever losing his Cuban and Latin American roots. The popular pedagogical matrix is not constructed on the principle of excluding what is different, but on the radicality of affirming from what place one speaks. Thus, the issue is not whether universities should be created in a land where they originally did not exist, but what type of university should be created and what content of teaching and research is relevant in them. Martí said: "The world can be grafted into our republics; but the trunk must be that of our republics."[22]

Also the political dimension of the pedagogical action must be highlighted in these emerging pedagogies. Education could not be reduced to technical training. It should be human formation in the fullest sense, combining scientific knowledge with passion and sensitivity. Martí wants the ambulant educators to take to the fields the scientific knowledge together with the "knowledge of tenderness [*ternura*], of the needs and pleasures of life," all necessary knowledge for a people who would not want to be condemned to die.[23]

A Pedagogy of Relation

Another important element in the pedagogical matrix can be found in the already referred study by Alexandro Moreno Olmedo when he proposes that the popular *episteme*, different from the modern and outside the parameters of the traditional discussion between modernity and postmodernity, is an *episteme* of relation. The man and the woman of the people, according to him, is neither a modern *homo faber* nor the postmodern *homo ludens* but the *homo convivialis*.

He warns that the relation, as an epistemic matrix root, is not a concept and therefore it cannot be explained with words within a discursive logic. Its proper language would be the myth and the symbol. And, as we know, every symbol that is explained is a fractured symbol. At the same time, being as one cannot but talk about this *mystery*, everything said should be understood also as something unsaid. Let him explain it himself:

> The man of the people is not a being in the world, but is a living relation, who exists in this situation. He is not subjectivity, nor rationality, nor individual, but relation. It is in the relation that subjectivity, rationality and singularity will be constructed—and reconstructed, if there is no more remedy for it other than continuing to talk in the only language we have.[24]

Consequently, people cannot be reduced to an aggregate of individuals who contract to live together, as implied in the modern social contract, but is constituted by a complex network of relations that include approximations and distancing, encounters and missed encounters, unions and oppositions. Based on the relation one also cannot idealize the people. Suffice it to look at the statistics to see how a great part of the assassinations and rapes occurring happen within the most intimate relations. In other words, in identifying the relation as the base of the popular knowledge one is not proposing a moral judgment of this relation in confrontation with other epistemic bases.

The challenge is to open up to other rationalities, as Mário Peresson put it:

> The question we ask ourselves with regard to this is if there exists only one universal rationality or if, on the contrary, there is a *plural rationality;* we want to verify if there exist popular logics, that is, their own forms of elaborating the knowledge of reality and of expressing it and how much these rationalities are being taken into consideration in and are having a determining impact on popular education.[25]

He then identifies, alongside the technical-scientific hegemonic rationality in the formal educational processes, logics whose contexts are the popular groups: the symbolic rationality and the sapiential rationality. The first of these, as it remits to the depth of experience, has as its goal to enter into relation with the other, as indicated by the etymology of *symbol* (gather together, join). The second indicates a quest for a "radical wisdom" about the ultimate meaning of life and also does not take place prioritatively in the world of ideas and concepts but in the area of interpersonal relations.

The centrality of dialogue in the pedagogy of Paulo Freire can be understood as the recognition of this episteme of relation. For Freire, as we know, dialogue can never be reduced to a technique or simply one more tool in the box of methodologies of teaching. Dialogicity is nothing less than the essence of education as practice for freedom. Dialogue, as a way of being in the world, is founded on a set of well-defined anthropological presuppositions that are carefully described in *Pedagogia do Oprimido[Pedagogy of the Oppressed]*: a profound love for the world and for men [meaning all humans], humility, faith in people, trust between the subjects, hope and critical thinking. Summarizing, here is his definition: "Dialogue is the encounter between men [*sic*] mediated by the world, in order to name the world, not ending, therefore, in an I-You relationship."[26]

Education and Its Labyrinth

The labyrinth is an emblematic metaphor of Latin American literature. Gabriel García Marquez in *O general e seu labirinto [The General and His Labyrinth]* describes Bolívar, at the end of his life caught between his ills and his dreams and asking how to get out of this labyrinth. The image of the world as a labyrinth, Moacyr Scliar reminds us in *Saturno nos Trópicos: a melancolia européia chega ao Brasil [Saturn in the Tropics: The European Melancholy Arrives in Brazil]*, "is very illustrative of a time in which the ancient socio-economic references disappear, giving place to doubts, dilemmas and uneasiness."[27] Scliar is referring to the Renaissance period when the European melancholy is also transplanted to this continent and here encounters a fertile field in which to bloom. "There was reason for sadness (. . .), a historical, social reason: indigenous genocide, African slavery, pestilence, poverty."[28]

What characterizes the labyrinth is the perplexity when faced with paths that can lead to nowhere if not back to the starting point, in an apparently interminable walking around in circles. For Octavio Ianni the Latin American labyrinth consists in this feeling of living in a borrowed world and time, in an opaque reality in permanent quest of concepts, where the announced exits will rarely transform themselves into real exits.[29]

Education today, maybe more than ever, finds itself confronted with its labyrinth. Less than two decades ago, during the debates of the Constitution in Brazil, Paulo Freire defined popular education as "an effort in the sense of mobilizing and organizing the popular classes aiming at creating a popular power."[30] Naturally, as he himself liked to emphasize, one is dealing with a power in permanent re-creation. Today we are living between the disenchantment with the possibility itself of re-creating power, and on the other side, the untested feasibility (*inédito víável*) that insists on arising in the society in movement through innumerable projects and practices. It is our challenge and task to recognize the signs of these new possibilities as well as to embrace and cultivate them.

3

The New Social Contract: A Brief Map for Educators

Well, if I am not mistaken, if I am not incapable of adding two and two, then, among so many other necessary and indispensable discussions, it is urgent, before it becomes too late, to promote a world wide debate about democracy and the causes of its decadence, about the intervention of citizens in political and social life, about the relations between the States and world financial economic power, about that which affirms and negates democracy, about the right to happiness and to a dignified existence, about the miseries and the hopes of humanity, or speaking with less rhetoric, of the simple human beings which make it up, one by one and all together. There is no worse deceit than when one deceives oneself. And this is the way we are living.

—José Saramago, *"Da justiça à democracia, passando pelos sinos" [From Justice to Democracy, Passing through the Bells"—article written for the closing of the II World Social Forum*

Education and the Social Contract

We have sought to show how education is part of this scenario in which life is developed in a double manner: it is conditioned by the power relations and makes this world work by training people to occupy various places in society, but it also carries a tradition of creating different scenarios. This dimension is often forgotten. Thus, for example, the theory of the *tabula rasa* of Locke or of the natural goodness of man, of Rousseau, is studied as individual attributes of the children, without any relationship with the visions and political projects that were at play at the time and that cause impacts still in our days. With this, education loses its power as political action.

In this chapter the goal is to start weaving the relation around the concept of social contract. In the quest for a key to understanding the multifaceted changes and crises that the current society is experiencing, the concept of social contract seemed adequate as it covers the relations between persons, the configuration of the institutional apparatus, and the forms of exercising power, among other aspects that have to do with human life in society and on the planet. Besides this, the idea of social contract is inseparable from the discussion now taking place about modernity and the *postmodernities*. That is, it remits to the question of the continuities and ruptures that we are experiencing and to the meanings that we attribute to one and the other.

At the same time, a look at the current discussions about contractualism recommends caution, since it is a subject discussed by jurists, philosophers, social scientists, and politicians. This multiple interest signals the relevance of the discussion, making it important to ask how educational theory can participate and eventually contribute in the debate that is being constituted as a specialized field. The problem of this study, however, is not so different from all the others in the area of education, since this one is necessarily constructed in dialogue with other areas of knowledge. Philosophy, anthropology, and psychology, among other areas of knowledge, are essential for handling the task of teaching and learning. The alternative to the silence of someone who assumes he/she should not talk because he/she does not know and the attitude of someone who talks amateurishly about everything without caring that others might know more and better, is to engage in a serious and honest dialogue with other areas of knowledge and other fields of social practice, often at the same time, by demand of the pedagogical practice itself. Education, by its very nature, demands crossing epistemological boundaries, with all the risks that this can entail. Not being at home is in itself a place to be cultivated. I see pedagogy as a platform where the various areas of knowledge meet in that which, in the end, is what matters: the formation of the human being and the destiny that one envisions for the world.

It is against this background that I use the concept of social contract, without the intention of discussing Hobbes or Rousseau as jurists and political scientists do. What is important, above all else, is to understand the interfaces of this discussion with education, maybe constructing a place or movement where one can engage in a new dialogue. Pedagogy is here understood as a partner in this dialogue because education is part of life, and the way we organize ourselves in society, an inherent subject of the social contract, has to do, fundamentally, with the quality of this life.

The subtitle, *A Brief Map for Educators*, summarizes the intention of this chapter: to share some of the paths on which the current quest has led me, having in mind the perspective of educators. For sure, there will be many other paths. I argue that the social contract can be seen as a story created by modernity to explain itself, that this story finds itself in crisis, and that there are many attempts to find common ground on which to walk in the search for new practices and a new language.

The Social Contract: Origins and Themes

Critics of the theory of the social contract seem to coincide on an ironic comment on the origin of this contract: They joke that it is difficult to believe at a given moment the men (*sic*!) would have gathered together to decide how to live together and who would govern them.[1] They are correct as to the nonexistence of such a meeting, and they are also correct when they point out that it is fiction, in other words, that it is a story told to give meaning to life in society.[2] Boaventura de Sousa Santos will say that the social contract is "a founding metaphor for the social and political rationality of western modernity."[3] In that he coincides with Carole Pateman, when she says that we are dealing with "the most famous and influential political story of modern times."[4]

Although it is possible to identify contracts from ancient times or from the Middle Ages, it seems pertinent to view the social contract as a modern happening. It arises out of the need for there to be organization and regulation among individuals, when the predefined relations, in a world structured within a theocentric conception, can no longer be sustained. In this sense the social contract is a product of modernity.[5] Among the classic authors on the constitution of the social contract we will find as obligatory references Hobbes, Locke, and Rousseau, all of them committed, in their own way, to seeking a new way of being and of understanding themselves in a world that was no longer the same, and among them, at least Locke and Rousseau as obligatory references in education as well. With time there developed the idea that there were rights, some of them inalienable and inviolable, so that people would not simply have to submit to authorities, but would be able to choose among alternatives regarding the exercise of authority over the members of a given community. In other words, the social contract implies a new self-comprehension as an individual gifted with free will and freedom, as a collectivity and as an organization under one authority.

Following Gough's analysis, this contract was in gestation for a long time, since the idea of the alliance in biblical times, through the Greek democracy, and, in a very special way, through the debates in the Middle Ages. The Greeks very early discovered that there were differences between some more or less stable principles to explain the natural phenomena and the precariousness of human relations, thus, leading to the need of another type of approximation to the social and political phenomena. The disputes of Plato with the sophists are a good example of this. In the Middle Ages he highlights the two currents that marked Western thought, both of them a mixture of theology and Greek philosophy, with distinct political implications. On the one side is the Aristotelian conception that man is a political being by nature and that the state develops more or less naturally based on the family relations and regulations. On the other is the Augustinian theory of the fall of man, which opens the path for a regulation of the "city of men" by men, separating it from the divine sphere and its (the divine's) direct interference. Feudalism itself had contractual elements, alongside those of loyalty and personal devotion. The vassal swore loyalty to his lord, but was obligated to fulfill this oath as the lord fulfilled his functions of maintenance and protection.

The story that begins to be told has a very complex and often contradictory plot. Even so, one is able to identify some themes or arguments that repeat themselves, making up a plot that continues to be fascinating. It is important to recover, even if only briefly, some of these themes that have a more direct and immediate relation with education.

As the backdrop of the social contract there is the *invention* of a state of nature that could serve as a reference for constructing and legitimizing the idea of the human rationality being the source or matrix of civilization. This backdrop can have very different tones. Thus, Hobbes describes a state of violence, of war of everyone against everyone, that will demand a Leviathan (the state) to legitimately wield control for the survival of all. The condition of human nature "is a perpetual and restless desire for power and more power, which ends only with death."[6] The possibility of escaping this design resides in part in the passions and in part in reason:

> The passions which make men tend to peace are the fear of death,
> the desire for those things which are necessary for a comfortable life,

and the hope to gain them through work. And reason suggests adequate norms of peace around which men can reach an agreement. These norms are those which, on the other hand, are called the laws of nature (...).[7]

On the other side, we have Rousseau with the belief in the natural goodness of the human being. The known opening phrase of *Contrato social [The Social Contract]* announces his vision: "Man is born free and on all sides finds himself within bars."[8] The fact that *Emile* begins with the same idea is not a mere coincidence, but indicates a presupposition on which is founded the social organization as well as the educative practice. "All is good when it comes from the hands of the author of all things, everything degenerates in the hands of men."[9] There is a natural goodness, derived from a good creator, which the person loses as he/she lives in society and creates civilization. The way out is not in the simple return, now impossible, to the state of nature, but in the control of the passions and in the development of reason, as Rousseau will didactically show in his *Emile*.

The search for a state of nature is related to the emergence of a new mythology to anchor the use of reason as a source to explain life in society. We know how this theme crosses through the discussions on education giving rise to very different practices. Today, on the one side, there is a generalized criticism of what could be considered an original essence of human nature as the starting point. On the other side, a new line of biological research tries to show how solidarity and love, as original feelings, are responsible not only for the maintenance of life on the planet, but for the genesis of the human through language.[10] In other words, it is an ongoing discussion, in spite of the different clothing and new arguments.

The modern theories about the state of nature, however, are not as innocent as they may seem at a first glance. Boaventura de Sousa Santos points out that the theories on social contract from the seventeenth and eighteenth century are as important for what they say as for what they silence about. What they say is that there are an expressive number of modern people, of metropolitan individuals, who leave behind the state of nature to enter the social contract. What they do not say is that on the other side of the line there are millions of human beings condemned to live in the state of nature, without a possibility of creating or being part of a civil society.[11]

Another fundamental theme of the social contract is the emergence of the individual, who, with his/her acquired self-consciousness, needs new references for life in society. It is not mere coincidence that Rousseau deals with the education of one man and citizen, Emile, and not of a group or a class. Although public education is not missing from Rousseau's concerns the reference is *Emile*.[12] In the same way, John Locke, in his essay on education, is concerned with the formation of the "gentleman." For the poor there should be work schools where they would learn some manual abilities besides moral norms.

The emergence of the individual is tied to the struggle against the absolutism of the time, founded on the divine right. In this sense, the well-known affirmation of Locke that the mind of the child when it is born is a *tabula rasa* is much more than a caricature for pedagogical empiricism. This affirmation, in its context, was strongly loaded with political meaning. In other words, nobles and princes are born with the same attributes as other human beings, there not being any type of aptitude or knowledge from birth that would guarantee ascendance over the others. Rousseau, in like manner, will say that men are born equal and that, as a consequence, inequality is a product of human society. The implications of this same principle of equality at birth, however, are told in different ways. For Locke, this idea is associated with the defense of private property as an inalienable right of the individual whereas Rousseau sees in it the compromise of the individual's freedom and the origin of all evil. These observations permit us to see how, from the beginning, the same story was told in various versions with very distinct political-pedagogical implications.[13]

It is not necessary to say much about how freedom, autonomy, and authority are part of the modern pedagogy. Distinctions between freedom and licentiousness, autonomy and egocentrism, individual and individualism, authority and authoritarianism are permanent concerns in educational practice and have a guaranteed place in the pedagogical discussions. The contextualization of these discussions in the social contract allows us to see them as part of a broader political dispute. They definitively tie the didactical to the political.

What this exercise reveals beyond the content per se is that the origin and the themes of the social contract should challenge us as educators to the involvement with the root issues in comprehending education as political action. It is about not losing sight of the *permanencies*, by remaining at the superficiality of the fashions. In the expression of Miguel Arroyo: "What about our pedagogical theory being less 'modern.'"[14] Or, in the image of Ítalo Calvino, to keep in mind that the classic discussions constitute the background melody that helps us to make sense of the enormity of the sounds and noises that surround us.[15] We need these sounds and noises expressed in ideas, in books, in articles, in films, in music, in various practices, but we also need this background as a deeper layer or dimension of the same map.[16]

Note on the Hypothesis of the "Iberian Choice"

During the period of the constitution of the Latin American and Caribbean nations we encountered a strong debate about the causes of the differences among the civilization in the Americas of the North and of the South. José Martí, in his long exile in New York (from 1881 to 1895), from where he led the independence movement of Cuba, recognizes the technical progress of the United States and sees in scientific education a model to be followed.[17] At the same time, he denounces from the "guts of the monster," the new empire that was in formation at the time, with the annexation of the territories that today constitute the states of California, Texas, New Mexico, and Arizona. The independence of Cuba and of the whole Caribbean region would be, in his viewpoint, a fundamental issue for the *balance of the world. Our America,* a term he used to identify the peoples of Latin America and of the Caribbean, is neither better nor worse than the other America, but it is different and will only be able to develop as it recognizes its own nature.

In this sense, his rationale differs from that of the Argentine Domingo Faustino Sarmiento, for whom the history of Latin America is situated between civilization and barbarity, and the way out is to imitate civilization and combat barbarity. "If barbarity perpetuates itself, if immorality grows, the blame is on the limitations of the means of action put in practice to combat it, and the moral base that exists in man must be very great to resist this abandonment."[18] The instruction of the people has to do with inculcating the civilized values—to be read as European and United States values—which range from ways of dressing to ways of thinking. For Martí, on the contrary, the struggle is not between civilization and barbarity, but between false erudition and nature. The new reality will not be a copy of the old, European one, because transplants do not work; nor will it be the recovery of a past civilization that no longer exists. *Our America* will be built based on the natural forces that exist in different ways in the various nations.

This debate challenges us to seek within history not a justification for what we are, but a comprehension of the way the nations of this subcontinent were constituted so as to evaluate the alternatives in the present. A study that presents a challenging perspective is the already classic O *Espelho de Próspero: culturas e idéias na Américas* [*Prospero's Mirror: a Study in New World Dialectics*] by Richard M. Morse. In this book Morse goes back to the Middle Ages to identify the birthing place of mentalities that later were the support for the distinct political options. According to him, the *Iberian-America* cannot be seen as a case of failure, but as an expression of a cultural life that has its own history and identity. Aware of the mutually accusing and recriminatory tone that permeates the North-South relationship, the author warns that he intends to "consider the South Americas not as victims, patients or 'problems,' but as a mirror image in which the Anglo-America will be able to recognize its *own* infirmities and 'problems.'"[19] Maybe Prospero, the bloody colonizer of the play *The Tempest* by William Shakespeare, who metamorphosed into the "prosperous" United States, is not the only option possible for what one knows as Western civilization.

Morse's study leads him to Pedro Abelardo (1079–1142), in whom he identifies two basic contributions to the development of Western thought. The first that faith issues can be expressed within the laws of logic and grammar, thereby passing from a demonstrative character to an explicative character; the second that sin would not be a transgression of a law, but a despising of God, from whom the laws are derived, thus revealing the subjective aspect of the action. In Morse's own summary: "Abelardo, therefore, outlines two notions that are fundamental for any consideration of western civilization: that of *science* which applies the first principles of the intellect to the theoretical order, and that of *conscience,* which applies them to the practical order."[20]

These premises would be the starting point for the choices made in the middle of the sixteenth century by the Iberian world and by the English in the middle of the seventeenth century, respectively. What characterizes the Iberian "choice" however is its connection with the later rediscovery of Aristotle and with the theology of Thomas Aquinas, which deals with the subjects of the faith and with those of the natural world as complementary within that which Morse calls the *architectonic principle*. It is an inclusive logic, in which the church is seen as a "mystical body" and the state as a "political and moral body," as an expression of the harmonious structure of society. This is why no movements of individualism or theory of social contract would have emerged in Iberian America, in spite of important contributions in the field of the philosophy of law.

One of the consequences of this option is that the promoted consensus also represented a broad space for divergent manifestations. Morse cites the tense discussions about the human statute of the Indians, in which even the radical position of Las Casas did not propose a rupture with the ecclesiastical institution but moved within its scope. This *understanding* and *unifying* matrix, however, had little to do with the scenario of polarization between the castes and classes, lords and slaves, civilized and barbarians and its crisis was revealed in the period of the independence movements, when neither the integrating Iberian option, nor the atomism of Hobbes or the contractualism of Rousseau were able to impose themselves as hegemonic options:

> The issue that arises with the Iberian-American independence is not the schizophrenia of the intellectuality, torn between the perspectives of the Iberian world and the Anglo-French world. What happens is that neither of the two versions, nor a mixture of both, could offer a "hegemonic" ideology which would find acceptance or even passive acquiescence in societies (a) whose national identities were improvised, (b) whose internal articulation was invertebrate, (c) where no sovereign power was legitimized and (d) whose relations with the external world involved an uncertain mixture of external concession and internal liberalization.[21]

Morse's study is relevant in order to comprehend how in Latin America and in the Caribbean we have a confluence of disparate traditions that have to do with the paradoxical character of Latin America as pointed out in the previous chapter. The diversity of experiences in the social, political, and economic field seems to confirm the hypothesis pointed out by Morse that the "Iberian-American is better equipped and situated than the Anglo-American to maintain alternative constructions of the social reality."[22] The labyrinth character of Latin American thought, expressed in the work of a Borges, or the fascination for the baroque manifested in the Brazilian carnival should not be seen, because of this, as an excrescence to be eradicated or a stage to be overcome, but as a part of a way of life historically constructed within a determined version of modernity. In education we have a good example of the comprehensive and cosmopolitan thought of Paulo Freire. Those who accuse him being eclectic and not rigorous enough forget that he moves within a field of very secure ethical-political-pedagogical options that constitute the foundation to be able to affirm a different rigorousness and directivity of the educational process.

It must also be highlighted that Morse's analysis seeks the origins of modernity and the models that ended up competing for hegemony. However there is also an America that is outside the parameters of modernity, which Rodolfo Kush calls the *América Profunda [Deep America]*.[23] It is the America that blooms in the indigenous movements of the Bolivian plateaus, between the Andes mountains in Ecuador or in Chiapas in Mexico, bringing to the spotlight other forms of communal interaction and of dealing with power. It is the hidden America that has little to do with the Anglo-French or Iberian modernity. On the contrary it has survived and resisted at the margins of both. In general, Kush reminds us, we do not very well know what to do with this America because the *smell* of its people and of its streets offends our sense of purity and our esthetic sensibility. More than this "the truth is that we are afraid, we fear all of this which bothers us and is on the outside, this fear makes us feel defenseless and imprisoned."[24]

The Crisis of the Modern Social Contract: The End of a Story?

The earlier reflection about the cultural matrix, however, should not serve as justification for the internal inequalities and for the "colonial wound" provoked by centuries of exploitation.[25] Today, we are challenged to answer the same old questions about ways of living together based on each person's dignity and social justice. A strong symptom of this fact is the recurrent use of the expression "new social contract." One rarely has a specific content for the "new," and this does not even seem to be the main concern, being that the great narratives have lost their enchantment. What is signalized with the expression, above all, is the demise of a certain type of contract and the challenge of seeking out alternatives, perhaps even beyond the classic ideas of contract, not at last because a great part of the Latin American population was left out of this modern social contract, or included in it, in a perverse way. It is also not initially about an academic problem, but about evidences of the reality that are vehemently interpellating the academic world.

Maybe the conception that best articulates the obstacles with the current forms of communal interaction is that of *social exclusion*. Let us look briefly at the concept bringing to the dialogue Paulo Freire's pedagogy, which has as one of its marks the dialectization between that which is permanent and that which changes. The book

Pedagogia do oprimido [Pedagogy of the oppressed] is dedicated "to the oppressed, and to those who suffer with them and fight at their side."[26] In *Pedagogia da autonomia [Pedagogy of Autonomy]* Freire reaffirms his point of view as being that of the "condemned of the Earth, that of the excluded."[27] Freire incorporates this new concept with a surprising naturalness. It can be argued that this new nomenclature is part of an epistemological positioning made effective in the book *Pedagogia da esperança [Pedagogy of Hope]*, when the metaphor of the plot takes on central importance, signaling the need for being postmodernly progressive.[28] That is, society in movement demands a different reading, with new concepts.

Contrary to what happens in *Pedagogia do oprimido*, there is not a concern with definitions in his last book. One can speculate that this is due to, on the one hand, the fact that Freire values a basic continuity in his work, which is given, mainly, by his ethical positioning in favor of "those in tatters" (1972) or of the condemned (1996) of the Earth. On the other hand, the nomenclature seems to have a secondary character in confrontation with the reality of the human beings threatened in their existence, independently of the name that is given to them "from the outside," based on theoretical schemes. The expression *ser gente*, "to be people/to be human," in the last writings seems to indicate a return to what the human being has as most basic and which is connected with his/her dignity and freedom.

One year before the publication of Freire's *Pedagogia da autonomia [Pedagogy of Freedom]* (1996) the collectanea *Pedagogia da exclusão: crítica ao neoliberalismo em educação [Pedagogy of Exclusion: Criticism of the Neoliberalism in Education]* was released in Brazil. It is now evident that the use of the term social exclusion in Brazilian pedagogy takes place in the context of the so-called Washington consensus, which sacramentalized the use of neoliberal policies.[29] Among the themes of the book appear the privatization of education, the World Bank and education policies, the educational markets, and the advance of the new right. In the "Preliminary Notes," the organizer Pablo Gentili calls attention to the fact that these papers "permit characterizing the neo-liberal offensive as a *new pedagogy of exclusion*."[30] Hugo Assmann also uses the concept "exclusion" to refer to the excluding logic of the capitalist market.[31] He understands that exclusion has become a type of *synthesis-word* to refer to the new characteristics of the social inequalities in Brazil and in the world. "Social debt, social apartheid, and similar expressions, do not express the vicious circle of exclusion in the same way."[32] He then lists some characteristics of this phenomenon of exclusion among which to be highlighted is the existence of an enormous contingent of "non-useful [people]" or "unnecessary [people]," the "leftover mass." These are perspectives that harmonize with the thought of Manuel Castells, who synthesizes his idea of social exclusion as meaning a process in which certain groups and individuals are impeded from accessing positions that would grant them an autonomous existence according to the standards of a given context.[33]

Various authors have argued convincingly that, as a structural phenomenon, social exclusion is inherent in the process of capitalist accumulation. Within this perspective, Avelino da Rosa Oliveira concludes his study on Marx and social exclusion affirming that the latter cannot be constituted as a concept capable of representing a new social paradigm. We would not be dealing with a substantive novelty that would indicate the emergence of a new paradigm.[34] The model exclusion/inclusion would be typical of a positivist-functionalist perspective that aims only at correcting the social dysfunctions, rebind the torn ties, supposing the social structure to be untouchable.

José de Sousa Martins starts from the same presupposition that we are not faced with a new dualism, highlighting in his studies that the society that excludes is the same one that includes, in the sense of generating inhuman ways of integration and participation in the same social body. Put in his ironic phrase, "the novelty called social exclusion is its renewed agedness."[35] However, according to him, the definition of social exclusion to identify the social inequalities today would also be revealing one of the new aspects of the class society, that is, that the working class no longer occupies the center of the explanations of the social struggles.

It is important to consider that the concept arose in the North where it refers to two marks of this society: to the loss of the level reached in terms of social and public recognition, and to the threat of nonfulfillment of the promised right to difference. Its emergence is generally linked to René Lenoir's work, for whom the excluded are, in a general sense, the forgotten ones (in the process of progress) or the ones, who due to various circumstances, are not adapted to society, among them the mentally ill, the physically deficient, and the aged.[36]

It is not without reason that Pedro Demo affirms as ironic the "charm of social exclusion" a la English and a la French (style).[37] The concept hides a type of nostalgia for a lost paradise, a feeling that means little to those for whom this reality was never more than a mirage. But it means a lot to someone who sees himself/herself on the verge of "falling" to this other world. Ulrich Beck warns of the risk of the "Brazilianization of Europe," with a rich minority and a poor majority, resulting from an "unorganized capitalism."[38] This expression transmits a feeling of imminent loss of privileges accumulated throughout centuries of capitalist expansion as well as Eurocentrism, from which the other is seen as inferior, and in this new conjuncture, as ever more a threat.

As one perceives, just as the phenomenon characterized as oppression in the decades of the 1960s and 1970s, social exclusion does not refer to something new or uniform. It seems that the generalization of the use of the expression social exclusion in the field of education is due to a series of factors, some of them crossing through ideological fields, which gives the expression an appeal of universality. The decades of the 1980s and 1990s correspond to a multifaceted movement of society with many contradictions. If, on the one hand, there were advances as to neoliberal policies, it was also a period of the promulgation of the new Brazilian constitution, of the restoration of the democratic institutionality in many Latin American countries, and of the election of popular governments. The idea of social exclusion is part of this context and denotes distinctive perspectives of this same reality. On the one side, it signals the existence of what we earlier qualified as pedagogical consensus, which encounters in inclusion an alternative to more radical transformations of the society. On the other side, it points to a field of multiple struggles in the constitution of a new hegemony. The question that presents itself is about the type of social contract that keeps legitimizing inequalities and exclusions, in some cases, true *apartheids* within the countries and between countries.[39]

Among the many criticisms of the modern social contract, there are three that touch on the concept at its core, and through which it is inevitable to pass through, if we intend to look for a re-signification of the concept, which is the intention of this book. One of them deals with the separation of the human being from his/her natural environment, the other deals with the exclusion of the women from the contract, and the third does the same in terms of race. A contract that intended to be universal, ends up in practice being a contract among some white colored men, who, as they do with the women and the people of other colors, exploit nature for their own personal or group gain. Let us look at some aspects of these criticisms, based on books that suggestively qualify the contract as *natural, sexual,* and *racial.*

The Natural Contract

The modern social contract, according to many analyses, deepened and above all legitimized the separation between society and history on the one side and nature on the other. Michel Serres in his *Contrato natural [Natural Contract]* calls attention to this issue in a very challenging way:

> The philosophers of modern natural law sometimes associate our origin to a social contract which, at least virtually, we would have established between us upon entering the collective which made us the persons we are. Strangely mute about the world, this contract, they say, made us leave the state of nature to form society. From the moment of the pact, everything takes place as if the group which signed it, upon taking leave of the world, was no longer rooted in it other than in its history.[40]

Michel Serres' argument is that the modern social contract is insufficient and needs to be complemented by the *natural contract*. According to him, the common man, as well as the one that governs, has forgotten about nature. Our species, the human one, dominated the planet and took possession of its resources. An implication of this is the predominance of short term memory and solutions. That is why, together with the social contract, a "natural contract of symbiosis and reciprocity" should be thought of that would overcome our parasitic view, that is, a relation of one who just takes from the host who provides all.

Modernity and its merely social contract, characterized by Serres as negligence (the opposite of religion), destroyed or lost the links that bound the human to the world. From this, he concludes, arises the need to recover the two laws that sustain this new type of contract. The first one demands that we love one another, those who are near us as well as the whole of humanity. The second requests that we love the world, understood as the local space (the ground on which we step, the air we breathe, the fruit we savor, etc.) as well as the whole Earth. In sum, the contractual obligations would consist in "loving our two parents, the natural and human ones, the soil and the neighbor; to love humanity, our human mother and our natural mother, the Earth."[41]

Michel Serres' concern finds an echo in a series of writings, of which I will mention only a few. Leonardo Boff makes caring—the opposite of the negligence denounced by Serres—the central point for a new ethics that would be capable of re-establishing the broken links of humans between themselves and with the world.[42] Francisco Gutierrez[43] and Moacir Gadotti[44] propose, respectively, an eco-pedagogy and pedagogy of the Earth. The arguments are centered on the necessity as well as the possibilities and strategies to reconnect humans to the natural world of which they seem to have forgotten to be part.

The Conference of the United Nations on Climatic Changes (Copenhagen 2009) revealed to the world the current incompatibility between the standards adopted as criteria for development and for the sustainability of the planet for the medium and long term. If, on the one hand, there is the recognition of the finitude of natural resources and of the foreseeable consequences of certain destructive actions, on the other there is a manifest difficulty of defining goals and measures that would indicate a change of direction.

The Sexual Contract

Carole Pateman analyzes how the discussions of the social contract, even the most progressive ones, do not mention the sexual contract. For her, in principle, the contractual conception reinforces the current polity of private companies and privatization. That is why the idea that the current society emerged from a great contract would rouse so much interest today. She sees the social contract as a story, which is the way human beings seek to give meaning to their existence in the world. As such, it is not just a story among others, but the "most famous and influential" one.[45] That this original social contract is also a sexual contract is a part of the story that was never told. The latter, according to the story, results from the free agreement of free men, being that the women are simply subsumed within this agreement. The theory of the social contract was proposed as an emancipatory doctrine par excellence, promising to construct universal freedom as a basic principle of the modern era. Only, this universal was restricted to men, and to just a few of them.

Pateman argues that the postulate of natural equality alone can assure that the original contract is not really one of slavery. What power do the employees really have in making contracts? The social contract, according to her, was only fiction, but even so, it was a fiction that deeply marked history, giving moral, intellectual, and legal coverage for discriminating against women and for slavery. According to her, the contract of this fraternity had in fact three interconnecting parts: the social contract, the sexual contract, and the slavery contract, these last two never being made explicit. Therefore she warns that when reading the classics of the social contract it is fundamental to read, together with the text, the context in which this story is narrated. She is skeptic as to the possibility of recuperating the concept because of the macho and domination mark that it carries, understanding that its recent use takes place without knowledge of this more specific historical information of the genesis of the theories. However, it does have an instrumental function of agglutinating people and groups around a concept with a strong historical appeal.[46]

The Racial Contract

Just changing the adjective, Charles W. Mills emits an equally well-informed and even more vehement voice in relation to the Racial Contract hidden under the universalizing ideal of the social contract.[47] This contract, according to him, establishes a racial polity, a racial legal system, a racial economy, all under a "neutral" state that guarantees the maintenance of the Racial Contract. This is possible because the signers live within a "structured opacity and blindness," which does not permit racial relations to be seen. All of this, argues Mills, is neither accidental nor an oversight in the application of the social contract, but is part of the structure itself.

The Racial Contract has a spatial reference, which, in turn, is related to *personhood*. Thus, it is "natural" that in a neighborhood or region of "sub-persons" (to be understood as persons for whom a different scale of rights and freedom are used) less investment is placed in education and security or different criteria are used with respect to what is just. Due to these relations and rationalizations the social contract has managed to subsist so well with slavery and with the various empires, all of them originating in Europe, currently being substituted by the United States as the global empire.

The European, white person is defined in contraposition to someone who is inferior. The theory of a good wild person serves, in this way, to place the indigenous peoples on a level between animality and humanity, as beings that are outside of the social contract. The same applies to the mass enslavement of African blacks, being possible that even a defender of individual freedom such as Locke did not see a problem in being a member of a company that transported slaves to the "New World," the "virgin" world to be civilized. In this context, argues Mills, the Jewish holocaust and other atrocities related to race are not an exception or fruits of a sick mind, but result from a Racial Contract assumed openly or in a disguised manner.

According to Mills, the problem is that the questions are not asked and an equality that does not exist in real life is presupposed. That is why the contract theories are also incapable of hearing the voices coming way back from Bartolomeu de las Casas in America up to the anticolonial and antiracist movements of today. But they have always existed and, paradoxically, they also find their support in the social contract. Due to this subversive potential of the social contract itself, Mills agrees neither with a Hegel solution (a superior community that includes individuals) nor a Marx solution (a government of one class) or some flexible type of political postmodernity. He situates his study within what he himself defines as critical modernity, in which one would be placing the Racial Contract in the same space as a historical fact of oppression, discrimination, and exploitation together with the mythical social contract, based on a utopia of equality and freedom. In the end he advocates as a solution the substitution of the social contract with the "Racial Contract" or at least, the complementation of the social contract with the "Racial Contract."

The observations about the *natural contract*, the *sexual contract*, and the *racial contract* reveal how the theme of social contract is placed at the center of the political and social discussions of modernity. They also show that, in the best of hypothesis, if one continues to use the classical terminology, one should not ignore what the social contract has meant for generations of women, for the indigenous peoples exterminated in mass, for the blacks treated as subhumans, or for the millions who barely survive in the midst of badly distributed abundance. At the same time, as we also saw, there was always another story that was silenced and that sought to say that the contract was different. This story continues and we return to it at this moment.

Toward a New Contract

What is "New": From Rockefeller to the World Social Forum

The discussion of the new social contract can be found relatively disseminated within the various movements that, from 2001 on, have found in the World Social Forum, a type of meeting point of peoples and groups who believe that, as the theme of the Forum expresses, "another world is possible." The discussion of the new social contract is associated with names such as Boaventura de Sousa Santos, Noam Chomsky, the mothers of the Plaza de Mayo (Buenos Aires),

Luís Inácio Lula da Silva, among many others situated at some point to the left of the political spectrum.

The concept, thus, seems to have acquired a life of its own, not being strictly connected to the authors known as neo-contractualists in a more restricted academic sense, and serves as a standard in the quest for new forms of social and political organization.[48] It might be a rare case of appropriation, or re-appropriation, by progressive sectors of a concept traditionally more present in the neoliberal discourse. For example, in 1971, David Rockefeller foresaw that the changes that would come with globalization would imply a revision of the social contract. Corporations should act as fast as possible to guarantee the capability of deciding about the content of the new social contract.[49]

Fulfilling Rockefeller's forecast, the following decades witnessed the implantation of a "new social order" commandeered by the exponents of neoliberal conservatism such as Margaret Thatcher in England and Ronald Reagan in the United States. Joseph D. Davey analyzed what this "new social contract" meant in Rockfeller's and Reagan's country between 1973 and 1993 and came to some not too comforting conclusions, as suggested by the subtitle *The American Journey from the Welfare State to the Police State*. According to him, in spite of the increase in the standard of living for the 20 percent situated in the upper part of the social scale, during this period the standard of living of those who are on the other point of the scale deteriorated, with the state using more resources to house the poor in the prisons than effectively in public housing.[50]

In this same political and historical context, we also have a new social contract as opposition to the neoliberal politics of Ronald Reagan. This new social contract would be anchored in a democratic alternative in which there would be greater participation of the workers, of the consumers, and of the citizens in the decisions that have to do with housing, health, and services. It would be based on the market as well as in democratic and public planning. "Democratic planning is the key element in a New Social Contract."[51] This contract would not be written by some specialists but would be forged in the struggle of citizens to be equal partners.

In Brazil the concept has also been widely used in the last decades. Paulo Krischke made an appraisal of these uses and identified the following as being the main ones: first, the social contract as a uniting of forces during the transition from the authoritarian regime to democratic institutionalization; second, the mobilization effort around the

1988 Constituent; and third, as pragmatic and often times sporadic strategies of negotiation. He concludes:

> These (and other) applications of the notion of social contract have fulfilled an important role in Brazil and in Latin America on the way to democratization. Their existence serves to suggest the diffusion and current pertinence of the idea of the social contract in the collective imagination and in the political discourses and practices.[52]

Considered in their entirety it seems that the current discussions about the new social contract have three important characteristics. In the first place, they maintain a contesting tone within the economic globalization commandeered by the transnational companies and the governments and states related to them. Second, the idea of social contract also suggests a propositional moment, almost always coming enveloped in actions, plans, or strategies. And third, the idea is associated with the deepening of democracy through the empowerment of the citizens. These reasons seem sufficient to justify its use.

Following, we place side by side some of the discourses on the new or other social contract. The criterion was again the direct reference to the social contract and the commitment with seeking some type of alternative. It is expected that the contact with authors that explicitly uses the idea of an alternative contract helps to better visualize some theoretical paths that are being forged with the goal of comprehending the pedagogical processes and challenges.

A more encompassing social contract

Boaventura de Sousa Santos understands that the social contract forged in modernity is no longer able to deal with the dynamics of exclusion and inclusion, leaving at the margins of contractuality a large part of the population, in a situation in which they pass directly from pre-contractualism, where even the excluded had the perspective of being included, to post-contractualism, where this possibility of inclusion generally no longer exists.

For him the solution is not in abandoning the idea of social contract. On the contrary, another social contract would be the ultimate demand of the reconfiguration and reconstruction of the space-time of democratic participation and deliberation. It would be a very different contract than that of modernity, as he summarizes in a paragraph that is worth reproducing for the intensity of the colors and the variety of hues with which it is drawn:

> It is, before all else, a much more inclusive contract since it should include not only the human being and the social groups, but also nature. In second place, it is more conflictive since the inclusion occurs through criteria of equality as well as of difference. In the third place, being certain that the ultimate goal of the contract is to reconstruct the space-time of democratic deliberation, this [contract], contrary to what happened with the modern social contract, can not confine itself to the national state space-time but must equally include the local, regional and global spaces-time. And last, the new contract is not fixed on rigid distinctions between State and civil society, between economy, politics and culture, between public and private. Democratic deliberation, being a cosmopolitan demand, does not have its own seat, nor a specific institutional materiality.[53]

A planetary social contract

Another argument stems from the principle that the current social contract is incapable of resolving the problems of communal interaction between the peoples in a globalized world. In a reality in which the modern unity between national state and national society is broken, there is a demand for a new type of regulation of relations between the peoples of the planet.[54]

Of special interest for the discussion of the planetary social contract is the idea that the current globalization signals a passage, situating itself between the political, economic, and social modernity that shows signs of fatigue and an, as yet, undefined postmodernity. More than this, what is called postmodernity corresponds to a multifaceted social construction that finds itself at the center of the debate amidst conflicting forces. In other words, they are conflicting narratives about the situation and the destiny of the world in which we live.

For Riccardo Petrella, the current globalization is a narration of the world and the society that became hegemonic as of the decade of the 1970s due to a conjunction of various factors: (a) the acceleration of the financialization (techno-scientification and dematerialization) of the economy due to the development of the technologies of information and communication; (b) the crisis of the saturation of the Western economy that would have favored and justified the new "Holy Trinity" based on the processes of liberalization, deregulation, and privatization; (c) the loss of credibility in the Soviet-style socialism that was no longer a desirable alternative to the capitalism of the Western market; (d) a new colonialism that opens the whole world to Western capitalism, especially North American.[55]

The narrative of the alternative world social contract would have to confront the following challenges: free itself of the current great narrative that believes it to be the daughter of the marriage between the scientific and the technological revolution that would guarantee it unquestionable legitimacy; develop a science and technology at the service of the collective well being; democratize the access to the gains in productivity, today the property of the holders of the financial capital; overcome the tendency of transforming the person into a "human resource"; confronting the total mercantilization of everything from knowledge to life itself; recuperate the credibility of politics.

This proposal of social contract has as its center the development of a consciousness of the problems that today have planetary dimensions. An example of this is the availability and use of water, a subject that Petrella touches on repeatedly. In spite of the fact that today over two billion people lack this good, the leaders of the developed nations are promoting a polity of privatization of water services. Besides this, local or even regional solutions will be insufficient over the medium and long term to take care of this basic need for survival on the planet.

It is in this sense also that Susan George speaks of a planetary social contract.[56] She identifies four main sets of crisis: environmental crisis, crisis of poverty and inequality, crisis of democracy, and the economic crisis. For her, a planetary contract that confronts these four crises is indispensable to avoid the type of conflicts the world is experiencing today. The greatest problem for effectuating such a contract is the institutional void on a world level. New institutions should be created since the World Bank and the IMF do not have the legitimacy to conduct the process and the quest for alternatives must pass through a more effective participation and organization of civil society. "The point is that we can no longer accept structures where governments and governments alone are represented. The United Nations Charter begins 'We the Peoples of the United Nations' before immediately sweeping them aside: now the people must be brought home and civil society put back in the picture."[57] Porto Alegre is referred to as a model of administration where corruption is practically eliminated through the Participatory Budget Planning.

A new political contract
Tarso Genro emphasizes the necessity of the "political contract," of the recreation of the political apparatus.[58] For him the idea of a new social contract has as a presupposition that the current state and its

traditional political representation are no longer able to mediate the conflicts in the context of the economic globalization and within the new standards of production originating from the scientific and technological development. "Since 200 years, he says, we did not create new institutions, in spite of the profound changes that took place in this period."[59]

Tarso Genro supports the need for creating a "new public non-state space" that would be equivalent to a "new political contract" through which the executive would open itself up to another sphere of decision-making. It would be a way of radically democratizing the state, placing alongside the already existing decision-making sphere, originating from the political representation, a different one originating from a new public space that would permit the permanent and direct presence of the various organizations of civil society. "The political representation would be permanently re-legitimated under democratic pressure and would make decisions with a greater degree of authenticity, through the acting knowledge of the majoritarian social aspirations."[60]

If Tarso Genro proposes that participatory budgeting experience is worn out, it is because he believes in it being surpassed by more permanent and democratized mechanisms of political participation. This participation would not be restricted to budget issues, but would cover other dimensions of public life, finally effectuating the control of the state by society in movement.

The New Contract As A Pedagogical Issue

As happened with the social contract in the time of the classic authors referred to here, so also the new or other social contract emerges together with new or other pedagogical proposals. The next moments of analysis will deal with these aspects. First, the focus will be on what could be characterized as the "pedagogical contract," explicit or implicit within the modern social contract. For the reasons cited earlier, the emphasis will be on Rousseau because of the significance his theory has, in general terms, for pedagogy and particularly for Latin America. The presupposition is that eventual political-pedagogical proposals of another social contract or of a living together that supersedes the idea of a contract will develop together with a critical look at the way today's social contract originated and impregnated educational praxis.

4

Emile and the Limits of Citizenship

As far as I know, no philosopher up to now has been sufficiently bold as to say: up to this point man can go and is not able to go beyond. We do not know what our nature permits us to be; none of us has measured the distance that can exist between one man and another man.

—Jean-Jacques Rousseau

If there were a nation of gods, they would govern democratically. Men are not suited for such a perfect government.

—Jean-Jacques Rousseau

Introduction

Ma'am, will you answer this questionnaire for a research project?
No, I will not answer it.
Why?
Because I am dumb.

This dialogue, between a participant of a research team and a woman who was participating in an assembly of participatory budgeting in a city in southern Brazil, could have occurred any place in the nation or in Latin America. She is one of the people who, as we analyzed in the prior chapter, does not have a place in the social contract. "I am dumb, I have no opinion, I do not know how to express myself, what I have to say does not matter..." At the same time, this woman, as so many others, did not give up on her citizenship. She was at an assembly that was discussing the construction of a gymnasium for the school, resources for the firemen, and a proposal for a road.

The question, in this chapter, is about how this subjectivity of negations is constructed. What would be the *originating evils* of this limited vision and experience of citizenship? What happened that so many people, like this woman, were left at the margin of a contract that is said to be universal? I initially bring reflections about the precariousness of the conditions for constituting an effective citizenship within the state characterized recently as coloniality. There follows an attempt to verify if, at the beginning of the social contract, especially in its pedagogical project, there was something that caused situations such as these to be considered "normal" or "natural." More concretely, the goal is to analyze if there is a connection between this situation and the political-pedagogical vision of Rousseau and its reception and application in Latin America. The working hypothesis is that such a relation exists, although we do not have the intention to establish a "direct line" between two distant and very distinct time periods, much less a simple cause-and-effect relation.

The title seeks to express the problem as well as indicate the argument. Citizenship is placed as a fundamental problem, in different degrees, for the Latin American societies. What is the noncitizen? The image of the savage and the conception of the abstract individual, I argue, can help understand this situation of pre- or extra-citizenship. At the same time, Rousseau embodies another equally important aspect: this same woman who doubts her capacity and therefore does not assume herself as a citizen, on that night she deposits her vote in favor of one of the priorities of her state. In other words, the issue is to see how that same contract that excludes on the basis of race, gender, and goods, as we saw in the previous chapter, can also serve as a platform to demand another contract.

As the goal is to read Rousseau together with Paulo Freire, this chapter begins a dialogue with both of them, trying to understand the relevance and the viability of such an approximation. The emphasis, however, will be on Rousseau seeking to identify what his ideas meant and still mean for education, especially for Latin American education. A more complete mapping out of his reception in our pedagogical context still needs to be carried out. I hope to contribute with some intuitions and questions for the eventual realization of this task.

Citizenship and Coloniality

In the year 1905 Manoel Bomfim wrote what today is a classical book entitled *A América Latina, males de origem [Latin America,*

Original Illnesses]. In it he denounced the parasitism of the dominant classes of Latin America, which, in the republic, perpetuated the same vices of the colony:

> The leadership classes, direct heirs, unfailing continuators of the governmental, political and social traditions of the State-metropolis, seem incapable of overcoming the weight of this inheritance; and everything that that peninsular parasitism inculcated in the character and intelligence of the governing people of those times, here can be found in the new governing classes; (...) the refractory, elements remaining from the parasitic past, revive, proliferate, indoctrinate, orient; and the new nation will never become a nation, rather [will continue being] an ex-colony, which is prolonged through the independent State, against all the laws of evolution, suffocating progress, bound to thousands of prejudices, tethered by the ignorance about conservatism.[1]

The ideas of this excerpt by Bomfim a few years after the proclamation of the Republic of Brazil are repeated in a recent denouncement in the newspaper of a teachers union in South Brazil: "120 years after the end of the Empire in Brazil the political vices remain the same."[2] There follows an analysis of the possible historical causes, which are more or less known by the population, from the persistence of clientelist politics to the corruption that dwell harmoniously together with heated discussions in favor of ethics and with eventual *ethics councils*.

Let us look at another great Latin American educator Simón Rodríguez, known as Bolívar's mentor. In him we have a clear perception that there could be no true independence without the development of good education for the people. In the book where he defends Simón Bolívar, he writes the following:

> The chiefs of the people must be convinced that they will gain nothing without instructing. When this observation is presented to them, some answer that the government is not a teacher—and others that, to form a people centuries are needed. Neither one nor the other reflects enough, and they do not reflect because they scorn the warning.

> Government needs to be a teacher
> and, for the people to form a republic,
> five years are necessary, at most.

And he continues:

> Great projects for ILLUSTRATION at the side of absolute IGNORANCE will always contrast and will never associate themselves—together they

form a SOCIAL MONSTER. Orders to carry out the impossible may gratify in the beginning because of some happy results; however, in the end, they produce *scorn* or DESPAIR.[3]

José Martí also warned that gaining independence could not be restricted to a change in form, but he advocated that true emancipation, above all else, was an issue of attitude and of spirit. Thence the importance he gave to the metaphor of the foundation. The true role of the government in these colonized territories was that of founding nations based on the nature of the peoples of this land. Founding meant opening up space for an irruption—another central metaphor of his thought—of life stifled by the castrating exercise of power by the colonizers. "To become knowledgeable about the country and govern it according to that knowledge is the only way to free it from tyrannies. The European university is bound to give in to the American university (. . .). The world can be grafted into our republics but the trunk will be that of our republics."[4]

The condition denounced by the aforementioned thinkers and by many others who could be listed is described today with the concept of *coloniality*. One of the articulators of the idea of coloniality, Walter Mignolo, distinguishes this concept from colonialism.[5] The latter would be applied to specific periods of dominion, as when the Dutch, the English, the Portuguese, the Spaniards, and other European countries imposed their dominion on other peoples in the name of progress and the Christian faith. *Coloniality,* on the other hand, denotes the underlying logical structure of the economic and political control. It refers to the creation of a way of thinking and acting hidden behind the salvationist discourse of modernity.

The author goes on to explain that this logic operates on four interconnected levels. These are: (a) economic, through the appropriation of the land, the exploitation of manual labor, and the control of the finances; (b) in the political realm through the imposition of authority; (c) in the social field through the control of gender and sexuality; (d) finally, in the epistemological and personal field through the control of knowledge and subjectivity.[6] Within this context a limited citizenship was developed, which both the conservative as well as the progressive politics tend to perpetuate. Pedro Demo classifies the two respective forms of democracy as tutored and assisted. The tutored citizenship is characterized by clientelism and paternalism that have as their goal to maintain the population bound to the political projects of the elite. The assisted citizenship permits the elaboration of the notion of rights, but is basically restricted to the right to assistance tied to a system of state benefits. "It paints over the social marginalization. It does not confront it."[7] It would be what today is being experienced through a great variety of grants and social programs.

Education is enmeshed in this form of subordinate citizenship. In the first place, because the educational policies themselves are part of a set of policies and end up running into difficulties where the confrontation or solution of these problems is outside the realm of education itself. There can be excellent projects for educating the youth, but when many of them feel that their real chances of entering the work market are few, even considering the education they would get, they refuse the "generous" offers.

In the second place it is a problem of the pedagogical field. And as to this we, educators, need to assume the responsibility. There exists a pedagogical coloniality that, as I see it, reveals a *fatalist* attitude Paulo Freire already denounced. A "decolonial epistemic turn"[8] in the field of education would imply understanding the insertion into modernity based on the "wounds" of coloniality and assume theoretical rigorousness.

Among other things, this implies identifying the place from which one is reading the world and carrying out the respective educational action. The fact that the assertion that a neutral education does not exist has become commonplace does not make it less relevant or current. On the contrary, the complexification of social relations and of the meanders of power demand a reading of the world with new resources and methodologies. For example, how does one comprehend the phenomenon of violence that today is present in our schools?

Another point resulting from the prior one has to do with the theoretical construction itself. It is part of *coloniality* to import or transplant theories to interpret our world and orient our practice.[9] I believe this has to do with the construction of another type of the rigorousness in the pedagogical reflection: freed from the canons, dogmas, and imported fashions; and anchored in the pedagogy of the other, which reveals itself mainly in the victims of the triumphant modernity.

The Social Contract and Its Pedagogies: Rousseau and Freire

At least since Plato, the comprehension of education is indissociably connected with politics, so much so that Rousseau will honor the *Republic* as the best treatise on education. "If you want to have an idea of public education, read the *Republic* by Plato. It is not a political work, as those who judge books solely by the title think: it is the most beautiful treatise on education ever written."[10] However, under the surface, there are important differences. For some, education is the extension of the political project, a more or less natural consequence of power relations.[11] F. Cabral Pinto, in turn, argues that Rousseau inverts this instrumental relation, making politics subordinate to the project of constructing the modern, universal man.[12] In my point of view, there is a less linear interpenetration, not one of simple cause and effect, between the two spheres of the constitutions of citizenship and the human in the work of Rousseau. Whichever way, this relation is placed as an underlying issue for the pedagogical approach to the social contract.

In this chapter and in the next, we will carry out an exercise of approximation between two authors situated at the two extremes of the contract. Rousseau develops his ideas on education in the period when modern social contract was generated, and the work of Paulo Freire is situated, likewise, in a time characterized as "paradigmatic transition."[13] This analysis is important in order to identify some points that constitute limits of this social contract, respectively the quest for it to be surpassed by what we earlier called the "new" or "other" social contract.

The first issue to highlight, once more taking up the problematization presented earlier, is that for both of the authors the boundaries between politics and education are very fragile, often indistinguishable. Rousseau elaborated the *Social Contract* together with *Emile*, a gesture that reveals it to be impossible to think of the education of the human being without thinking of society itself, a permanent tension that he describes with these words: "It is necessary to study society through men and men through society; whoever wishes to deal separately with politics and morals will understand nothing of either of them."[14]

On the other hand, we know the arguments of Paulo Freire very well that education does not only have a political dimension; education is always and necessarily political. We become men and women in society within certain political projects that, although never having the power to determine us, do necessarily condition us. Freedom and the respective commitment take place within a history where the limit-situations themselves constitute possibility. In Rousseau as well as in Freire, therefore, the argument of the instrumentalization of education by politics or vice-versa does not hold up.

A second motive for which the dialogue between these two men[15] is so challenging is the fact that they reveal an enormous sensitivity toward the moments being experienced by their societies. Some decades before the French Revolution, Rousseau prophesied: "You believe in the current order of society without thinking that this order is subject to inevitable revolutions and that it is impossible to foresee or prevent what will be in store for your children. (...) We are approaching the state of crisis and the century of revolutions."[16] He foresaw that the great monarchies of Europe were in inevitable decline.

Two centuries later, in the midst of the social movements (student, feminist, popular, among others) at the end of the decade of the 1960s, Paulo Freire opens *Pedagogy of the Oppressed* with words that revealed equal sensitivity to the great changes that were being experienced: "Once more men, challenged by the dramaticness of the current moment, propose themselves as a problem. They discover that they know little about themselves, of their 'post in the cosmos,' and are restless to know more."[17] He presents humanization as the central problem that also passes through the quest for new ways of living in society.

There are also curious coincidences in their biographies. Paulo Freire establishes himself as a world educator in Geneva, Switzerland, where he lived from 1970 to 1979, the same city where in 1712 Jean-Jacques Rousseau was born. The Geneva praised by Rousseau in the dedicatory of *Discourse on the Origin of Inequality*[18] is the same [Geneva] that will ban *Emile*. Both were forced to peregrinate through other countries because of political persecutions, in both cases related to their pedagogical ideals. Although *Pedagogy of the Oppressed* was not burned as was *Emile*, in many places it was equally clandestine reading. This peregrination seems to be a common destiny for people, who shake up life inhibiting beliefs and institutions and who, paradoxically, become witnesses that there are no owners of history nor anyone who can apprehend life indefinitely.

Why Read Rousseau Today?

In the provocative definition by Ítalo Calvino,[19] a classic is a book of which many speak but few read. Rousseau's *Emile* fits this definition perfectly. The size of the volume might explain a little of why it is unknown, but certainly not everything. Other books called classics have the same destiny. It is as if the simple mention of the book gives immediate access to its content. Oh, yes! the *Didatica magna* by Comenius, *Democracy and Education* by John Dewey,...and also *Pedagogy of the Oppressed* by Paulo Freire. Those who read them are surprised to find new layers of meaning in each rereading. Those who had not read them discover that the current pedagogical common thinking is a historical construction, resulting from the often long and arduous clash of theories and practices. They also discover that some of the great human issues, among them pedagogical ones, have an incredible durability.

I do not intend here to present a systematic study of *Emile,* or, more broadly, of Rousseau's ideas.[20] Within the concern with the social contract, what matters is to comprehend how Rousseau's ideas came into our midst and how this helped form a certain political-pedagogical set of images. Above all, it is relevant to see how pedagogy is imbricated with the totality of his political ideas and how these ideas helped to form a set of images of what we are and how we should act.

What makes reading Rousseau so instigating today is that, in the words of Boaventura de Sousa Santos, he criticizes the lights based on the lights themselves.[21] Emile is educated to conduct himself by his reason, to be autonomous, and to not depend on outside opinions. Sophia, Emile's companion, although capable of using reason, is limited in the exercise of this faculty due the feminine "nature," which is not made for these things. Therefore, he fits in very well as a target of the criticisms of modernity. At the same time, Rousseau manifests himself contrary to a cold rationality, separated from feelings and corporality. Referring to the education of youth he warns: "Dress up reason with a body if you want to make it sensitive. Make the language of the spirit pass through the heart so that it [the spirit] can be understood. I repeat, the cold arguments may determine our opinions but not our actions; they make us believe and not act..."[22] His criticism of faith in modern science as being able to produce more happiness for men (*sic*!) goes in the same direction. "But how can it be" he asks in *Discourse on the Sciences and the Arts,*

> that the sciences, whose source is so pure and whose goal is so laudable, should give origin to so much impiety, so many heresies, so many errors, so many absurd systems, so much contrariness, so much ineptness, so many bitter satires, so many miserable novels, so many licentious verses, so many obscene books, and in those who cultivate them [the sciences] so much pride, so much avarice, so much malevolence, so much intrigue, so much jealousy, so much lying, so much depravity, so much slander, so many cowardly and shameful adulations?[23]

The paradoxical character of the life and work of Rousseau perhaps led to the fact that he is one of the thinkers about which the most is written. Although some of the authors might intend to eliminate the tensions, finding a just balance, the argument of Neidleman can also be applied to the pedagogical theory: "Independently of what might have been the fundamental intentions of Rousseau, it is my position that the great political lesson of Rousseau's political theory is in the paradoxes."[24] As an example of this see the two texts placed intentionally as an epigraph of this chapter. On the one side, the affirmation of the immeasurable human potential (who could dare set limits to what the human being is able to do or be?), and on the other, the confirmation that democracy is not a political system made for men and women, unless they are gods.

The paradox that will be of more immediate interest in the analysis that follows has to do with Rousseau's identification with the revolutionary ideals in Latin America. It is about Rousseau as the man of utopia, of democracy and community, the visionary who believed in the immeasurability of human life. On the other side, there is the suspicion that various elements in his theory contributed or were used to maintain the people in a state that Boaventura de Sousa Santos calls "pre-contractual," which is equivalent to the pre-citizenship in societies supposedly founded on some type of contract.

Rousseau and the Spirit of Emancipation in Latin America

An important ramification in the reading of Rousseau identifies him with the utopian current that inspired the revolutions and in the case of Latin America in the eighteenth and nineteenth centuries, the emancipation movements from Spain and Portugal. Emile, Rousseau's fictitious pupil, incarnates the ideal citizen to live within the social contract proposed by him. The form of presenting *Emile*, known as a pedagogical novel, indicates that Rousseau is not concerned with describing society as it is to then insert Emile into it. According to Ulhôa "it is precisely this radical repulsion of any given concession to political realism which builds in Rousseau the possibility of utopia."[25] This would be founded in his radical optimism in relation to human nature and in his no less radical pessimism with regard to society. "Man is born free and all around him he finds fetters."[26] Here is the base issue of the social contract and for which he proposes to present a solution.

This is why Emile is raised alone and the first and greatest concern of the tutor must be to not interfere in his natural development. This, however, does not mean that his final destiny will be like that of Robinson Crusoe, the solitude of an island. The ideal of society that Rousseau proclaims is the one where the citizens are able to have direct participation in the life of the community. The model of democracy is in the simplicity of the peasants regulating the state business in the shade of an oak tree. Contrary to Locke, for whom freedom is founded on the individual right to property, for Rousseau, freedom, accompanied by equality, has a community dimension.[27]

It is not to be considered strange that this Rousseau would have found an echo in the independence movements in Latin America and that his ideas would have been from the beginning in the "crossfire." Although there are different points of view as to the degree and type of influence his ideas had in the struggles for emancipation, there seems to be a consensus as to their presence in these struggles. Richard M. Morse argues that it was about "vaguely rousseaunian inspirations or affinities," sometimes tied to the traditional Iberian populism.[28] This influence would have dissipated after independence, when the effort to mobilize the population was substituted by a conservative ideology of consolidation of some elites.[29]

The pedagogical controversies that reflect divergent political positions are present in the criticism that Franz Tamayo would make of the ideas and ideals of Rousseau, out of Bolivia, where at the beginning of the twentieth century he was working on the creation of a national pedagogy. He classifies Rousseau's ideal of humanity as nothing more than a comedy, "an artificial and false product of the French romanticism," since man and the society proclaimed by Rousseau never existed and never would. The criticism approximates his view of man and society much more to that of Hobbes, reflecting the complex game of influences that had Latin America as the stage. According to Tamayo, if there exists a human ideal, it cannot be based on an impossible and foolish principle of universal peace and concord, but "on the foreknowledge that all of life is a struggle of interests, a struggle on every territory and of all types, in the markets as well as on the battle fields."[30]

On the other hand, the book by Boleslao Lewin, *Rousseau en la independencia de Latinoamerica*, which contains a rich documentation, serves as a reference to exemplify this presence of Rousseau as a utopian thinker and the inspirator of the emancipationist movements.[31]

A significant fact to understand the political climate of the period is the prohibition of the work of Rousseau by the Inquisition, as reaffirmed in this document of August 27 of 1808:

> Know ye that the sovereign pontiffs, among them Clement XI, charged the Holy Office of the Inquisition of Spain to oversee and watch over the fidelity that all the vassals, of any degree and condition that they be, should maintain in regard to their Catholic monarchs... We establish as a general rule that ye should review the propositions which ye readeth and heareth to denounce, without fear, to the Holy Office those which have deviated from this fundamental principle of thy happiness: that the king receives his power and authority from God; and that ye should believe with divine faith what proves without controversy the express texts of Scripture... *For the most exact observance of these catholic principles we here reproduce the prohibition of all and any books and papers and of any doctrine that exerts influence and cooperates in any way to the independence, and insubordination toward the legitimate powers, such as renewing the manifest heresy of the sovereignty of the people, as Rousseau dogmatized in his Social Contract and that other philosophers taught* (emphasis mine).[32]

The fact that the Holy Office had to go public, reaffirming the power of the king as a divine right and denouncing the heresy of the sovereignty of the people, with explicit mention of the *Social Contract* of Rousseau,[33] is, in itself, proof that his ideas were known in some circles causing apprehension and discomfort as they fed the dreams of freedom.[34] See as an illustration, how in a speech on the Constituent Assembly of Bolivia, in 1826, the *Social Contract* served to defend the place of the indigenous people:

> The issue of the social pact is nothing less than the desire of happiness, due to men consenting in forming a public force which will defend all, and in nominating magistrates to guarantee their rights: being that the indigenous do not participate in all the goods of society, the pact with respect to them will be null and of no value. On the other hand, it has been sanctioned that the sovereignty resides with the people and this people are composed of all Bolivians, being that two thirds at least of these are indigenous.[35]

It is also known that Simon Bolívar (1783–1830) had read Montesquieu, Rousseau, and other thinkers of the period.[36] Studies reveal, at the same time, a lack of clarity as to the role and type of state that the liberators were thinking of implanting and what would be the real role of the people that they would carry out in their new nations. According to a quote of Bolívar,

> The federal system, although it is the most perfect and most capable of propitiating human happiness in societies, is, however, the most contrary to the interests of our recently born states. Speaking in general, our citizens still do not have the aptitude to rule for themselves and more broadly, exercise their rights, because they lack the political virtues which characterize the true republican; virtues that are not acquired from absolute governments where the rights and duties of the citizens are not known.[37]

In other words, the same idea of the immaturity of the people for exercising citizenship was used by various generations of dictators and continues to the present in the political action of the majority of those who govern. It is also an echo of Rousseau's expression, cited in the epigraph, that democracy is a form of government for the gods.

In another analysis based on Max Weber, Ricardo V. Rodríguez points out that the emergence of the national state in Latin America took place in a very distinct manner from that of countries where the discussion of the social contract arose with Hobbes and Locke, Rousseau, or even before with Puffendorf and later Kant, since they had not had the feudal experience.[38] The states emerging from feudal contexts would give place to a "contractualist" conception of political power that originated in Western Europe with Thomas Hobbes, John Locke, and Jean Jacques Rousseau. The conception coming from patrimonialism would counter this tradition, without a multiplicity of centers of power that characterized feudalism, but with power centralized in one strong patriarchal authority. Brazil, with an emperor who guaranteed the political and geographical unity, would have been the most typical example of this patrimonialism.

Just as Rousseau's ideas were present within the disputes for the constitution of the Latin American states, they were also not foreign to education. His influence can be noticed from the concern with systems of public education to the elimination of corporal punishment.[39] However, our history shows that the ideas of sovereignty, of equality, and freedom in some way were left behind. The emancipationist movements themselves did not create the conditions for developing the capacities for fulfilling them. In the following section I seek to broaden and deepen this issue from a pedagogical point of view. The intention is not to identify the guilty one (or one more) for our problems, possibly Rousseau, but to contribute to understanding ourselves, on both sides of the Atlantic or in the North and the South, as part of a historical process in which the lack of citizenship is perpetuated and presents itself as a situation to be overcome.

The Emile From Both Sides of the Atlantic

Could the peoples of Latin America be the Emile that went wrong? There have been and continue to be a quantity and variety of rationalizations to justify precisely this, such as climate, race, nature of the people, among many others. That is, they are attempts to attribute the guilt for the failure onto the victims themselves, since one begins with the presupposition that in the contract all have the same freedom and equality.

There is, however, a different reading that gains strength in the anticolonialist studies. Through the universality of the social contract the Europeans become the lords of the world with the right to reduce all peoples to slaves, if not to exterminate them in the name of the superior, white, masculine, and Christian civilization. Although at no moment was there a signed contract, this contract was constructed through papal edicts, in the pacts between the powers, in the discussions about the humanity of the non-Europeans, and in the daily life of the people. The measures to prevent abuse serve only to confirm that the rule was accepted as legitimate.

I seek to show here that the "structured blindness"[40] of the proponents of the social contract, among them Rousseau, is associated with education and that, in Emile, the hypothetical pupil of Rousseau, it is possible to identify characteristics that contributed to providing an excluding and discriminatory education. Let us have a look at the representation of the New World and its inhabitants. The only book that Emile should read in his adolescence is *Robinson Crusoe*, by Daniel Defoe, published in 1719, when Jean Jacques was seven years old. According to Rousseau, this would be the best treatise in natural education ever written, and from there on, it would have a place of honor in Emile's library. It is the only adequate literature because "the most secure way of elevating ourselves above prejudices and organizing our judgments according to the true relations among things is to situate ourselves in the place of an isolated man, judge everything as such a man would himself judge in relation to the utility for him."[41]

One cannot deny that it is a beautiful story that many of us heard in our infancy. At the home of my parents there was an old volume, with some pages missing, which was often told mainly from the pictures, thus often without the details that appear in the text. It is evident that I identified myself with Robinson Crusoe, the hero and adventurer. Today, I leave aside the adventure, the exotic passage through the "Brazils" (e.g., I did not know that he did not like the color of the "Brazilians" since it was an "ugly and nauseating yellow") and the dexterity of the survival tactics in the jungle, to look at a facet of the story that would certainly demand redefining the identifications with the book of my infancy.

Our hero does not take long to discover that he is not alone on the island and so he sees himself confronted with a moral problem of how to act with *caribes*, which later he discovers are *cannibals*. It they kill their adversaries, he, Robinson, could also kill them, but how to kill them if they have done him no harm? Religion helps Robinson at least to leave aside the idea of extermination. However, the reflection on how to get out of there leads him to conclude that it will be difficult to succeed without a savage in his possession. "Besides, I fancied myself able to manage one, nay, two or three savages, if I had them, so as to make them entirely slaves to me, to do whatever I should to direct them, and to prevent their being able at any time to do me any hurt."[42] The circumstances permitted this wish to come true. Robinson narrates with details how he made the captive know that his name was Friday, the day in which he "saved" his life, and that he should call him Master; that this—Master!—would be his name. All worked very well, so much so that there was no more reason to fear "for never a man had a more faithful, loving sincere servant, than Friday was to me; without passions, sullenness, or designs, perfectly oblig'd and engag'd; his very affections were ty'd to me, like those of a child to a father; and I dare say he would have sacrific'd his life for saving mine..."[43]

We know the happy ending of the story, passing through the fact of Robinson becoming governor of the island and coming back with his life made. My interest in reproducing some of the passages of the story was to verify how Emile, evidently identified with Robinson Crusoe, comes to perceive his relation with the world and with the other. Friday will never be an Emile, much less so the dangerous *caribes*. But these are the inhabitants of the "other" (from Emile's point of view) side of the Atlantic and have a not surprising and maybe not accidental similarity to Rousseau's natural man.

This reflection leads to two legendary figures in the play *The Tempest*, by William Shakespeare, that have inspired important reflections about being Latin American and Caribbean. One of them is Ariel, characterized in the play as an airy, harmonious, and poetic spirit, representing the noble sentiments of humanity. Ariel serves as the model in the book with the same name, for the famous exhortation of the Uruguayan José Enrique Rodó to the young Latin Americans. While Caliban would represent the utilitarism of the Americas of the north, Ariel would represent the generosity and the elevation of the human spirit. "Ariel is superior reason and sentiment. Ariel is this sublime instinct of perfectibility (...). Ariel is for Nature the highest crowning of her work (...). Ariel triumphant means ideality and order in life."[44]

The other figure is Caliban who, as the antithesis of beauty and perfection, was retrieved as a creature-symbol of coloniality. The name originates from cannibal whom, in turn, has to do with Carib or the Caribans, inhabitants of the regions today known as the Caribbean. Caliban, a slave of the illustrious tyrant Propero, is a figure with a thousand deformities. A review of prior readings is done by Roberto Fernandez Retamar when he proposes viewing Caliban as the symbol of the exploited people of Latin America. "To take on our condition as Caliban, implies rethinking our history starting from the *other* side, starting from the *other* protagonist."[45] The other side would be represented by Prospero who took the island from Caliban and enslaved him.

Let us observe the density of the characters and worldviews that are revealed in some of their movements. Caliban remembers his encounter with Prospero, his love for Prospero, and, respectively, his profound deception:

And then I loved thee
And showed thee o' th' isle:
The fresh springs, brine pits, barren place and fertile.
Cursed be I that did so.

Prospero then says that he housed him in a cell and treated him kindly until he tried to rape Prospero's daughter, Miranda. To this Caliban responds roguishly that he was sorry he did not do it because in that way he would have populated the island with Calibans. Miranda enters the conversation and says that out of compassion she taught him the language and the meaning of things, since before he was just "babbling something brutish." To which Caliban formulates his fantastic answer, an expression both of submission as well as of resistance: "You have taught me language, and my profit on't / Is I know how to curse. The red plague rid you / For learning me your language."[46]

What do Friday, Robinson Crusoe's servant, and Caliban, Prospero's slave, have to do with Emile, Rousseau's pupil? In fact, very little, precisely because they are his counterpoint. But this was the necessary counterpoint for Western civilization that in the process of becoming aware of itself as an emergent power, needed comparisons expressed in images of the natural man, the cannibal, the good savage, among others.[47] Hèléne de Clastres synthesizes, in this way, this interest that the men of the Enlightenment have in the inhabitants of other places:

> The savages are from now on objects of a discourse which only takes them into account because they are apt for incarnating the idea of a universal nature; when one talks of them one talks immediately of nature and only of nature: wise nature, natural reasoning, opposite of artifices and conventions; but also hard nature, inefficacy and debility of the *natural* right with regard to the *positive* right. This is why the reference to nature permits controversies and also encompasses opposite views of the savages, but in all cases it converts them into a figure of the universal, into a negative. Consequently, the savage serves only to return to those who are civilized the image of what they are not.[48]

The Emile from this side of the Atlantic, therefore, was useful as a means of affirmation of a superior culture, but as a person he was, in the expression of Enrique Dussel, concealed. "America is not discovered as something that resists *distinctly,* like the *Other,* but as the material into which 'the same' is projected. It is not therefore the 'appearance of the Other,' but the 'projection of the Same': 'hiddenness.'"[49] The context has changed, the argumentations have changed, but from this side, the Fridays and the Calibans, as Rousseau reminded us with regard to the poor, they do not need education. "The poor person does not need education (...). Let us choose, therefore, a rich person; at least we will be certain to have made one more man, while the poor person can become a man by himself."[50] Yes, the poor have learned to defend themselves, even if just to survive. As they learned to take care of their education, it is also supposed that the body will have acquired sufficient resistance, and one can dispense with the care for their health and their dwellings.

The Education of the Abstract Individual

A work does not become a reference by chance. There is a complex process of canonization that, in the end, attests to the value of the permanence of the ideas, as Bernardette Baker exemplarily shows when dealing with the reception of Rousseau in the United States.[51] I say this because a work like *Emile* has taken on such a magnitude that any criticism becomes at least audacious, and it is quite probable that in some place there already exist counterarguments. Be that as it may, it should not inhibit us from daring to make readings that mark distinct places of reception of the same work. If before we situated Emile as a work and as a student within the context of images of the Other and about him/her, here the focus will be on some more specifically pedagogical aspects. The guiding question will be the same as already presented earlier, that is, how *Emile,* a basic reference in modern education, is related with the limitation of citizenship.

One of the arguments has to do with the types of education that Rousseau proposes for his student. What justifies education is our ineptness for life. "We are born weak, we need strength; we are born lacking everything, we need assistance; we are born stupid, we need intelligence. Everything that we do not have when we are born and that we need when we grow up is given to us through education."[52] From this follows that there are three masters from which all education proceeds: nature, men, and things. Rousseau then says that, since we have no control over the education of things and much less over the education of nature, what is left is the education of men.

In Emile's education, therefore, Rousseau's every effort is to minimize the role of men (*sic*!) as educators. In Simon's words, "instead of renovating the education that comes from men, Rousseau's plan with Emile consists in systematically substituting the education received from men with an education from things."[53] There are many examples of the distrust of the opinion of others and the corresponding belief that the direct experience with things and facts will form Emile's autonomy. Let us see the case of teaching history: "The worst historians for a young person are those who judge. Facts, facts! And let him judge for himself and so learn to know men."[54]

This has to do with Emile's freedom, which the author himself defines as being watched. The things with which Emile makes contact and the nature that is presented to him are carefully mediated by the tutor. Nothing escapes the attention of the master who watches every step of his pupil, including those in which Emile will have problems, taking from them the due pedagogical advantage. Starobinski says that "Emile is the captive in a refined trap." In his opinion, there is a mistake in most of the readings of Rousseau, in the sense that the readers see in the book an invitation to imitate the spontaneity of the child, when in truth it is about the "exposition of a pedagogi-cal science and of a reflected *technique*."[55] That is, it is a treatise on how the natural being is transformed into a certain type of citizen. The problem, as we shall see in the confrontation with Paulo Freire, is not in working with the limits that the historicity of the human being imposes on us, but in hiding it under the veil of nature or of the truth of the facts themselves. In truth, the adult society, represented by his tutor, exempts itself from the explicit role of direction; this is why it cannot be changed, only negated. The school (for Rousseau, the schools are ridiculous institutions) does not have a place in this world of Emilie since it is part of this corrupt world.[56]

At the same time it must be recognized that *Emile* represents a rupture from a view of the pedagogical subject being centered on the adult, a fact with broad and deep pedagogical repercussions. For Bogdan Suchodolski with Rousseau we have a first radical move-ment in the direction of a pedagogy of existence in contraposition to the pedagogy of essence.[57] Moacir Gadotti points out that the child passes from the condition of being object to being the source of education.[58] And still, Adriana Puiggrós sees in the fact that "Emile educates Rousseau," the foundation for a pedagogical relation that makes it possible for Marx to see in the proletariat the educator par excellence based on their concrete life situation.[59]

Another point in terms of limitation of citizenship and that, in a certain way, summarizes the prior ones has to do with Emile as an expression of an abstract individual. In reality, this child simply appears on the scene, no one knows from where. One only knows that he comes from a rich family, because it is the rich who need education to become men and citizens. His parents do not have names, he is not born in a community, he does not have cousins, uncles, or grandpar-ents, and has no childhood friends. In other words, he lacks human and historical concreteness. However, it is this generic and abstract human being that, according to Rousseau, would be most apt to deal with "the accidents of human life."[60]

This meta-historical being is one of the points on which the criti-cism of Rousseau concentrates. Fontanella, in the comparison with Kant, who does not give up discipline in education, asks if Rousseau is not being exaggeratedly anti-historical.[61] Ulhôa calls attention to the danger of a posture that rejects historical reality, creating an illu-sion that it is irrelevant.[62] Galvano Della Volpe's formulation, based on a Marxist perspective, presents the problem well:

> It is the abstractness of someone who comprehends the constitution of the *person* through an extra-historical attribution of values, and who proposes to separate the human person and his dignity and respective rights from the universal value which only the *person* can in fact attribute. (...) As a result, in a last instance, the extra-historical, original person can only be a *privileged* individual because he is *abnormal,* or abstract, free from what is normal for his species. His original, extra-historical ("eternal"), "natural" *rights* are nothing more than the justification of real, existing *privileges*.[63] (Emphasis in the original)

We must also see in this abstractness of the human the root of his ambiguous position with regard to women. Mary Wollstonecraft, writing in the same century as Rousseau, refers to this incoherency in this manner: "Whoever at some time drew up a more elevated feminine character than Rousseau, even though, in the concrete, he was constantly working at degrading the (feminine) sex?"[64] She attributes this to the personal experiences Rousseau had with women. The current analyses, however, permit one to see how certain forms of conceiving the human being induced and continue inducing the acceptance of certain practices and relations as normal.

There is a universal substratum in the state of nature, but this has been lost in the civil state. In society what are left are "artificial men" and fleeting passions that change according to the times and places. That is why Rousseau takes Emile to study the customs of his time, observe the different ways of governing, and see how women raise their children. Religion itself is understood as a subject of geography. Peoples, depending on their life conditions, invent their ways of naming and worshiping the divinity.

There is, however, an important difference between nature and culture as relates to sex. Confer this intriguing phrase: "The male is only male in certain instances, the female is female for all of life, or at least for all of youth."[65] That is, man is seen essentially as a being of culture and the woman as a being of nature. Even today the reference to becoming a man is still more common than to becoming a woman, leading to the understanding that the construction of the latter is almost an appendix to the construction of the man. This has implications in the education of Emile and Sophia. If the girl can do without education—or at least without a refined education—it is because she is born more or less ready. She is born a woman, with all the necessary prerequisites to be a mother and a wife. The man, on the contrary, is born lacking the formatting for the demands of society.

Up to here we have pointed to some limits of the education of the citizen Emile. The question we need to ask is if obstacles to current citizenship on the national and planetary level are not related to the creation of this abstract individual, disconnected from history, guided from the sidelines, while believing that one is educated objectively by the facts and by things. Besides this, it should be asked whether this individual has developed the gifts of solidarity and caring, necessary conditions for life in society. Without concrete relations of caring for others, Emile could not develop the necessary civic virtues for an active political life. The dependence in relation to the tutor, in the final dialogue of the book, reinforces this suspicion and concern: "Council us," says the now father Emile, "govern us and we will be docile, while I live I will need you."[66]

5

Autonomy Revisited: From Rousseau to Freire

No one is first autonomous in order to decide afterward. Autonomy grows in the experience of various and innumerable decisions that are being taken.

—*Paulo Freire*

Following Freire, we may argue that the central question of education today is what role, if any, educational institutions and practices should play in the constitution of the social pact that articulates democracy.

—*Carlos Alberto Torres*

The Question of the Historical Agency

I imagine that the title of Freire's last book, *Pedagogia da autonomia [Pedagogy of Autonomy]*, came as a surprise for many people. How can one speak of autonomy in the context of the theoretical efforts of the deconstruction of the modern subject, criticized by its abstract and instrumental rationality, for its essentiality, for its autonomy? Is this discussion not dislocated in time and space, that is, a regression in relation to the modernity that one desires to overcome? Could it be that the U.S. publishers were suggesting something more adequate to the present time when they used *Pedagogy of Freedom* as the title of the North American version.

This is not the first time that Paulo Freire surprises his readers. When his *Pedagogy of Hope* was published in 1992, Latin America was just coming out of the so-called lost decade. The world was still experiencing the echoes of the fall of the Berlin wall, whose impact in Latin America, especially among social movements, was not so much a frustration with the dismantling of a determined political model, but above all a loss of space to think of alternatives. A prediction that unfortunately became real, as an internationalized market began to dictate, absolutely, the rules of the good life in every corner of the world. At that moment of the counterflow of the popular movement Paulo Freire said that there was hope, that our role as educators is to take care of that hope, to nourish it, and to orientate it so that it does not lose its way. Today we see how hope that is disorientated, independent of its ideological color, can be dangerous. It can end up as a bomb strapped to the body of a youth, just as it can lead to the aiming of missiles against civilians. For this reason, Paulo Freire did not speak about educating for hope, which exists as an ontological condition, but to educate hope.

If we go back in time, *Pedagogy of the Oppressed* was not less of a surprise, especially for many who discovered this book outside the country or who read it in hiding.[1] Certainly he could have written something more palatable to the dictators or of immediate use for teachers. One only needs to remember that two decades later people still asked if this pedagogy could be "used" in the schools. After all, it was a pedagogy that talked about power, about classes, about a revolutionary vanguard, things that at that time were out of place and even today (or today once again) look strange.

This characteristic way of presenting the themes is coherent with his theory. For Freire, men and women are not beings of adaptation, but due to their double capacity of being with and in the world, they have the possibility of critical insertion in this world. His work exemplifies this: few, in the second half of the twentieth century, better expressed that which many felt and would have liked to have said. In his self-definition, he was a pilgrim of the obvious. At the same time his texts make one feel that there is a movement toward the outside or from the outside, whichever way one wishes, that questions the common sense. His words say what we already know, yet they paradoxically transcend what we know and transcend themselves in the quest for new meanings.

This is why the question of whether Paulo Freire is current or not seems to be displaced. The question should be: how does Paulo Freire help us be (ourselves) people of our time? For example, Paulo Freire did not live the September 11, 2001, experience, which exposed the tensions and precipitated conflicts that show that we are living in a distinct reality from that of the year of his death, in 1997. Could he be current? The answer can be yes or no, or yes and no. He certainly is not current if we look in a simplistic way at the fact that he never dealt with September 11 and the war on terror that followed or if we don't look beyond the written word. He is current if we are seeking a companion to help us face new challenges with audacity and creativity, like he did in his time.

In this sense, the title *Pedagogia da autonomia [Pedagogy of Autonomy]* for a book that deals essentially with the type of knowledge that is necessary for educators cannot be attributed to an oversight. Considering the density of this little book, it might fit better among the books of wisdom than among the scientific books, if one wants or can make this distinction. Five years before his death, he said in an interview that, at seventy-two years of age, he kept thinking of the priorities, "considering the probable time of life that I have."[2] Unfortunately, his prediction that ten years would probably surpass his limits came true. We can see in this choice the lucid intention of an author who desires to be with his times and who, with authority conquered, can use an apparently worn out or badly used word giving it a new life. In this chapter, I intend to do a reading of this concept, associating it, as much as possible, with the prior reading of Rousseau. The premise is that this concept is an important door of entry to understand what happens after *Emile*.

Autonomy and the Pedagogies of Freire

With Freire we learned how to think of pedagogy in the plural: pedagogy of the oppressed, pedagogy of dialogue, pedagogy of hope, pedagogy of conflict, pedagogy of autonomy. Ana Maria Araújo Freire (Nita) gave the suggestive name of *Pedagogy of Indignation* to a posthumous work with texts that had not yet been published upon his death. In other words, indignation, a fundamental human capacity to feel injustices, also needs to be educated. But with him we also learn to doubt an easy plurality. The differences, as warns Pierucci, have their traps, being historically part of the conservative discourse, since under the façade of differences inequalities are easily hidden.[3]

Therefore, Freire talks to us of the tension between unity and diversity. I believe that this principle can also be applied to his pedagogy. There is a diversity of pedagogies, in dialogue and tension, seeking a never static unity. Just as we should understand race, gender, and class as historical production, so also education—as a praxis—is actualized in different ways throughout history.

> To think history is to recognize education as possibility. (...) One of
> our tasks, as educators, is to discover what can be done historically
> in the sense of contributing to the transformation of the world, that
> may result in a "rounder" world, with less edges, more human, and
> in which the materialization of the grand Utopia is prepared: Unity in
> Diversity.[4]

Said in other words, in the various pedagogies we saw someone
who knew how to reinvent himself in and through time. In readings that I was doing of Freire before the publication of *Pedagogia
da autonomia*, I identified three metaphors that serve as a type of
matrix of his work. Playing with words of Freire himself, this Freirean
tripod is characterized as *line (transition)—rupture—web*. Each of
these images has to do with distinct historical experiences that conditioned—not determined—the work of Freire. It is not the case of identifying a first, second, and third Freire, maybe even a fourth. There is
nothing further from the goal than this. The starting point is (a) that
Freire was open to history and is marked by history and that (b) this
is expressed in his work. This review is important to situate the theme
of autonomy as another great axle of his thought.

The first metaphor—*line*—refers basically to the book in which he
presents his proposal for literacy training, situated within a society in
transition.[5] At the beginning of the decade of the 1960s, his reading
of the reality was that there was occurring a transition from a closed
society or an object-society to an open society or a subject-society;
it was also a transition from a man (*sic!*) as object to a man (*sic!*) as
subject. Everything is within a rationale that assumed certain linearity within the happenings. After all, he had been elected nothing less
than the coordinator of the National Literacy Training Program in
Brazil. But already here there were important subtleties, as when he
said, in the midst of the euphoria with changes of all types, that not
all change is transition. Transition, differently from change, implies
the creation of something qualitatively different. The reproduction in
greater scale or in a more accelerated rhythm is still not transition.[6]

There is the untimely coming of the military dictatorships in Latin
America, and with them, profound changes in the life of Paulo Freire,
who seeks political asylum first in Bolivia and then in Chile,[7] before
passing on to the United States and then establishing himself for a
decade in Switzerland. Seen with today's eyes, the accusations against
him are pathetic, but they reveal the climate of the period of this

so-called Cold War. In a denunciation to the auditor of the Seventh Military Region by the Military Promoter of this region, Paulo Freire appears as a dangerous subversive leader:

> all of these last ten denounced formed, under the direction of the denounced Paulo Reglus Freire, the intellectual core of subversion in the Cultural Extension Service, a work Team which was sensitizing the illiterate toward "basic reforms" seeking, with the social hate that they were inculcating in the spirits of these people, to disintegrate the Brazilian social structure at the service of the communization of the people.[8]

This context of political repression and of restriction of rights is also the context of a strong movement of resistance and the construction of what would be called popular movement (or popular movements, in the plural). Expressions of this were the Ecclesiastical Base Communities and innumerable Culture Centers or Popular Education Centers. This is the context in which *Pedagogia do oprimido* emerges, the manuscript being dated 1968 and published in 1970.[9] Clodovis Boff was correct in commenting, in the preface of *Educação Popular*, that Paulo Freire did not invent a methodology and much less a theory.[10] He had the sensitivity and the ability to interpret what was happening. And at this moment, we know, the strong terms were the binomials oppressor-oppressed, or oppression-liberation. The line ruptures. Society not only did not open up but ended up closing itself even more. Because of this there is a need for a new pedagogical articulation. Theoretically there are other challenges, for example, how to combine the Hegelian dialectic of master and slave, translated into social classes, with the idea of dialogue. The question of what is dialogue in a society divided between oppressors and oppressed will be the theme of many debates.[11] At the same time, Paulo Freire does not abandon the idea of transition, that is, of qualitative change, but re-contextualizes and transforms it. History is still a "pro-ject," something that one throws forward, but there is a different reading of the world that informs this project.

The other foundational metaphor of his work emerges in the pedagogical scenario with the *Pedagogia da esperança [Pedagogy of Hope]*.[12] One only needs leaf through a few pages to become aware that the idea of a web has a very great force. Personal life is formed by many threads that end up weaving a web; in education and in society there are many webs that form who we are. We are living in a moment of the weakening of the popular movements and of the coincidental avalanche of neoliberal politics, accompanied by theories of the end of history, of the end of the meta-narratives, of the death of the subject, among other ideas generically covered under postmodernity.[13] Paulo Freire was not alienated from this movement and, in the midst of it, he proclaims that we need to be postmodernly progressives,[14] a contradiction at first glance, but maybe only at first glance.

In *Pedagogia no encontro de tempos [Pedagogy in the Meeting of Times]*, after analyzing these metaphors in more detail, I summarized the picture in the following way:

> A line, a rupture and a web; three images and three ways to see life and education. One does not annul the other, instead broadens and deepens its meaning, showing how the drama of human existence is paradoxically always the same and always different. Maybe this might be a paradigmatic way of understanding education's own paradigms.[15]

In other words, Freire has a theoretical core that permits him to "trans-ition" (be in time and through time), living in his praxis the dialectic between permanence and change.

The reading of Paulo Freire in the perspective of the social contract suggests that *Pedagogia da autonomia* reveals another dimension, which corresponds to the concern with the disappearance of the subject, with the risk of undermining the base for political action. It is a new critical reading of the prior pedagogies that does not negate them, but also does not feel any need to hang on dogmatically to some of the formulations. The difficulty that many academics have with the reading of Paulo Freire and what they characterize as the lack of rigor, in my point of view, has to do with the fact that he founds his rigorousness beyond any disciplines and any determined theoretical body. It is more or less what Peter McLaren writes when studying Che Guevara and Freire: "I am arguing that theory should be organically connected with a vision and practice of revolutionary politics. It should be a theory of flesh and bones."[16] His theory is precisely that.

Pedagogia da autonomia is neither a treatise on autonomy nor a pedagogical manual for the formation of citizens with autonomy. It is the reflection about the "necessary knowledge for educational practice." The word "autonomy," in fact, appears very little in the text. What is implicit is that there is a set of knowledge or competencies that is fundamental for the constitution of autonomy, first for the educators themselves. The educators then, as witnesses in the process of knowing, can help their students to become autonomous.

The Reinvention of Autonomy

When he compares the man ("the human machine") to the animal, Rousseau considers that the essential difference is not in the ideas. Animals must also have ideas, since they are gifted with senses. What constitutes the difference is the human capacity to be a "free agent."[17] It is the capacity to act rationally and freely, from a multiplicity of instincts, which are part of the human nature.

Mainly in his first writings, Freire concerns himself very much with the same issue. What, in the end, make the man and the woman (be) human? Without dealing with this question it would be difficult to think of a pedagogy to overcome so many experiences of dehumanization. His starting point, however, is not the dichotomization between the world of nature and the world humanly created in response to needs, the world of culture. Nature itself does not exist in a more or less pure state. It is always nature permeated by culture; the fact of naming it already is a sign of human interference. What distinguishes the human being is his/her conscience, which permits that one separate oneself from the world of nature and from the world of culture itself to insert oneself in a different, critical way. This is also what makes the human be the agent in this world, which, since it is a world of culture, is a world of history and possibility.

Rousseau and Freire share the interest in identifying and situating the political and pedagogical agent. Educational practice concerned with the transformation of society is definitively linked to the way we position ourselves facing this theme. Abandoning it would mean to abdicate the possibility of seeing the world as a project. In their criticism of the postmodern thinkers, Peter McLaren and Farahmandpur point to the difficulty of passing from isolated cases (anecdotes) to history.

> Postmodernists rarely elevate facts from anecdote to history, a practice which is commensurate with following the latest top-of-the-line designer narratives. At the same time they ritualistically weave together post-Marxist and end-of-history claims into a seamless genealogy in an attempt to mummify historical agency and seal the project of liberation in a vault marked "antiquity."[18]

In this context it is interesting to return one's attention to Freire, because I understand that in him we find the way to reinvent the idea of historical agency, having as a focus the quest for autonomy.

I develop the argument around two axes. The first one is an attempt to see autonomy as an expression of human historicity and later as construction pertaining to intersubjectivity.[19]

Autonomy and Historicity

In Rousseau we saw that Emile did not really have a history. For Rousseau's argument the less he needed to situate Emile in history, the more adequate it would be, since he represented the counterpoint of the corrupt society, to which one day he would have to return. Unfortunately, from what everything indicates, he did not return very well prepared, beginning with the fact that he had to find the best possible place to live, insinuating that all the others were condemned, unfit for life together. In other words, the Emile as a "human agent," that which would make him different from the other animals, did not have much trust in human regeneration. Pestalozzi, a follower of Rousseau, tries to show in *Lienhard und Gertrud*,[20] how a poor, caring, enlightened good mother, beyond instructing the children and saving the husband, can influence a whole community. Education passes from an isolated individual to a community, but, even so, it is still seen as an island.

It is important to look closer at what Rousseau's rationale implies for the education of women, where the naturalization of the conditions of existence becomes even more evident. Book V of *Emile*, which deals mainly with Sophia, causes disenchantment in the reader, especially in today's female reader. Up to here one has accompanied attentively the precious observations of the child's thought, the study of nature, of man, and of his world. Suddenly, at the beginning of this chapter, the following affirmation is disconcerting:

> In everything which does not have to do with sex, the woman is a man: she has the same organs, the same needs, the same faculties; the machine is constructed in the same way, the figure is similar, and, from any angle that we consider them, they only differ between themselves from more to less.[21]

Each one of them, man and woman, contributes for the same objective, but in distinct manners, according to their own nature. The man is strong and active; the woman is passive and docile. Both complement themselves in these roles that nature wisely distributed for good communal interaction. On the subject of gender the revolutionary Rousseau decidedly takes the conservative side. He observes, for example, that one is living in a period of "confusion of the sexes" and recognizes the protest of women,[22] but finds a quite simplistic way of contesting the criticisms. How can men, he argues, be guilty for the situation of women if it is women who create men as well as women?

He, therefore proposes, *without scruples,* a specific education for the women:

> Offer, without scruples, a woman's education for women, make it so that they like the jobs of their sex, so that they be modest, so that they know how to watch over their home and take care of the house; the excessive concern with beauty will disappear by itself and they will only dress themselves with better taste.[23]

The argument that there exist in nature the criteria for determining the differences between the human sexes becomes especially evident when Rousseau deals with feminine reasoning. Sophia should not be an automaton or a servant, "she can learn many things, but only those which are appropriate."[24] As an attentive observer of his society, Rousseau sees that the girls like to play with dolls, especially dressing them up. From thence learning to embroider and to sew is a natural path for their education, while reading and writing are costly tasks.

To today's eyes there are evident contradictions in Rousseau's argumentation. On the one hand, women have their limits fixed by nature; on the other, they need to be carefully controlled to not exceed these limits. The affirmation at the beginning of Emile that no philosopher has dared to measure the distance that goes between one man and another certainly does not count for women. For them there are limits, established by someone who seems to have a privileged view of nature. After all, concludes Rousseau, they will always be subject to masculine judgment.

Different from the reasonable man, capable of abstract rationale who elaborates principles, women's rationing if eminently practical. They are gifted with an "experimental moral," tied to the facts, while to men the capacity to systematize was granted. In another passage Rousseau discusses how men know the ends, but need women to discover the means. The interdependence however is so perfect "that it is with the man that the woman learns what she should see and it is with the woman that the man learns what he should do."[25]

The girls also should be taught according to their age, but always having in view the limits. In the case of religion, as occurs with the boys, one does not expect simple repetition of dogmas, but Rousseau warns that no one would imagine transforming a woman into a theologian. For the home, then, the learned woman is a disaster: "An intellectual woman is the torment of her husband, of her sons, of her friends, of her servants, of everyone."[26] It is not surprising that the destiny of such women is to remain single for their whole life.

This somewhat lengthy excurse on the education of Sophia, representing the education of women within the modern social contract, is relevant in that it brings to light arguments that help to keep citizenship restricted to males, and just a selected group of them, based on the person's conditions of educability. Similar arguments will be found to justify the exclusion of Indians, slaves, and poor people from the educational process.

In Paulo Freire, contrary to Rousseau and also to Pestalozzi, autonomy takes place from the beginning and only as an expression of the historicity of men and women. Autonomy does not exist in the abstract, just as the human being does not exist without being mixed up in history. Utopia, for Freire, does not consist in returning to an ideal past or in the dichotomization between a state of perfection and a current condition to which we are fatalistically imprisoned.[27] He translates this tension that is inherent to utopia in this paragraph, which, because of its expressiveness, I transcribe in its entirety:

> Utopic for me is not the unrealizable, it is not idealism. Utopia is the dialectization in the acts of denouncing and announcing, the act of denouncing the dehumanizing structure, and the act of announcing the humanizing structure. For this reason it is also historical commitment. Utopia demands that one know critically. It is an act of knowledge. I can not denounce the dehumanizing structure if I do not penetrate it to get to know it. I can not announce [something] if I do not know it. But between the announcement and the realization of the announcement there is something that needs to be emphasized and that is that the announcement is not the announcement of a project but is the announcement of a pre-project, because the pre-project becomes a project in historical praxis. Thus, between the pre-project and the moment of the realization or the concretization of the project there is a moment that is called historical. It is precisely history that we have to create with our hands and need to make. It is the time of transformations that we need to be carried out. It is the time of my historical commitment. For this reason only the utopians—and as revolutionary utopians—(who was Marx if not a utopian, who was Guevara if not a utopian) can be prophetic and can be hopeful.[28]

Freire's emphasis on the idea of time stands out. Not all time is a time of transforming action. The Italian philosopher Giorgio Agamben affirms that it is a certain comprehension of time that makes it possible to understand historical action, and this would be the messianic "time that it takes to finish time," placed at the side of "chronos" (the linear time of the watch and of the calendar), with a special density because of the wait. It would be the time that corresponds to the prophet's speaking, that one which, according to Foucault, pronounces the word that does not belong to him.[29] In the case of the Freirean utopian, it is the word that is (still) outside of history as a "possible dream" or as an *inédito viável*,[30] expressions that, to him, had practically become synonyms of utopia.

This historical time, on the one hand, implies conditioning and, on the other, possibility. It is in the tension between these two conditions of human existence that autonomy is carried out. The first of these conditions points to the limits within which each one's life develops. Paulo Freire, as we know, from the beginning distinguished between conditioning and determination. If we were determined, our time would not be a time of history, which, on the contrary, is a time of possibilities, because the limit itself is not felt as a fatality but as a moment of the fulfillment of "being more." "The future," he says,

> is not a historical province beyond today waiting for us to arrive there someday and do this operation of adding this *tomorrow* that *was already done* to the *today,* becoming old and surpassed. (...) In a truly dialectic perspective the dream which moves us is a possibility for which I should fight to realize.[31]

In the language of Agamben, reflecting Walter Benjamin, it is a time, the time of fulfilling the prophecy, invading another time, the time of everyday life within which the future is gestated.

What makes the conditionings to be felt as limit-situations is the human possibility of transcending. Not in the religious sense of a connection with a sacred force, although Freire does not discard this possibility for his own existence, but transcendence in the sense of not adhering to the quotidian, to the world. Men and women are beings who can be with the world and not just in the world; they can distance themselves and, through this movement, identify the possibilities of change.[32]

There not being a predetermined way to be in the world opens up a broad space for what Freire calls the "strategic dream."[33] Dreaming as a political act and as a way of being men and women not only permits, but demands this space of creation and reinvention of the praxis. Considering this characteristic of the opening of the Freirean political-pedagogical project, Balduíno Andreola proposes that stemming from Freire we have the unique possibility of developing a "pedagogy of great convergences."[34]

Within this debate, I highlight two tasks that are required for the development of a pedagogy of a new social contract. One of them relates to deepening the issues in the area of the critical pedagogical theory itself, where movements of reconfiguring traditional categories such as class, race, ethnicity, and gender, among others are taking place. Peter McLaren, for example, seeks to bring back to the progressive pedagogical field, explicitly based on Freire, the idea of social class, always related with other categories that have occupied cultural studies, such as race and gender. According to him, while the intellectuals abandoned the concept of class as an instrument for understanding the world and history, an ever smaller group took over the means of production, making life literally unbearable for the great majority. However, he makes it quite clear that it is not about privileging class relations over those of gender or race, but of understanding their complex combinations. The choice between a culturalist perspective and an economist perspective, according to him, represent a false dichotomy. Identity, difference, and class are categories or relations that interpenetrate within themselves. Freire could be a type of platform of encounters for a renewed and reinvigorated critical pedagogy.

> There is still a reason to hope for a cooperative pedagogical venture among those who support a Freirean, class-based, pedagogical struggle, feminist pedagogy, or a pedagogy informed by queer theory and politics, that may lead to a revival of serious educational thinking in which the category of liberation may continue to have and to make meaning.[35]

This is certainly a challenge for Latin America. According to Carlos Alberto Torres, the notion of pedagogical agent—supposedly the historical agent as well—and its ties to the social and pedagogical structures demand

> an ever more refined thought process to understand the subtleties (within the conceptual construction as well as within the social construction of the historical experience) of the struggle for identity, including the ever more burning concerns within pedagogy, considering the multiple and asynchronous parallel determinations of class, ethnicity, sexual preference, religion, gender and regionalisms.[36]

Due to this, some have found in Habermas a fundamental interlocutor to recreate the base of dialogue for the development of an emancipatory pedagogical theory for our days.[37] Others have returned to the Christian matrix of his thought or rediscovered the Marxian or existentialist influences. All of them correspond to efforts to apprehend the multiple dimensions of experience, an exercise that Paulo Freire pursued restlessly.

The second task is the quest for pedagogical metaphors in fields that have been less explored in education and above all, the dialogue among them for the construction of this "pedagogy of great convergences" in the Freirean spirit of humanization. Here we find quite different thinkers such as Rubem Alves, Leonardo Boff, and Hugo Assmann. What unites them is the quest for new paths for the reinvention of the historical agency based on the metaphors of life. Love and pleasure (Rubem Alves), solidarity and sensitivity (Hugo Assmann), and care (Leonardo Boff) bring to the surface dimensions that sometimes are counterposed to excessively narrow visions of *conscientização*, forgetting the central place that lovingness (*amorosidade*) occupies in his pedagogical praxis and in his life.

For Freire existence is above all the "expanding of life." That is why, in his thinking, there is no dichotomization between vital processes and historical-cultural processes. After all, "it is life that questions itself, that makes itself a project, it is the capacity to speak of yourself and of others who surround you, of pronouncing the world, to unveil, to reveal, to hide truths."[38] This idea becomes even clearer when we read his answer to the question about the conception of freedom that is the basis for his methodology.

> The vital phenomenon, freedom. One cannot speak of life without recognizing the connotation in the experience of being alive, of something of freedom, something that implies movement, not only physical but movement in dispersion, revelation of something. (...) In the vital phenomenon, it is unfeasible to not think of freedom: there are certain movements which a tree suggests to us which are of an incipient freedom. The tree moves seeking light, the sun. It carries out a whole exercise of seeking at a very different level than the five of us here will do to find air. We have a thirst for freedom.[39]

The human being is not bound to the world like the tree, however, on the other hand, that which is most precious to him, freedom, is part of the same vital phenomenon. What these theories present that is new in terms of the discussion of autonomy is that this [autonomy] needs to be seen in the context of this vital phenomenon of which men and women are a part. Remembering Michel Serres' observation in the third chapter, it does not befit us to live as if we were only rooted in history.

As a conclusion, what could remain is the affirmation that we have the conditions to develop more complex constructions of autonomy and human and historical agency based on the dialogue between distinct theoretical perspectives. I believe Freire's work challenges us to this type of rigorousness. The solution is not in creating a great new redemptive pedagogy, but in developing conditions for dialogue between pedagogies that place the promotion of life as their foundation and horizon, with syntheses written in certainties known to be temporary. In this sense the "pedagogy of the great convergences" may be before and above all the convergence of pedagogies for the fulfillment of the human and humanizing vocation of *being more*.

Autonomy and Intersubjectivity

Enrique Dussel identified Paulo Freire as the creator of an anti-Emile.

> When Rousseau defined the agent of the modern pedagogy, he found him in *Emile*, a young man, male, solipsist, without parents or tradition, with a bourgeois *curriculum* to form a technical-industrial spirit which would be able to be the counter point of the *ancien régime*. Freire, to the contrary, in his transmodern pedagogy of liberation, bases himself on a community of *oppressed victims*, immersed in a popular culture, with traditions, in spite of being illiterates, wretched...the condemned of the earth.[40]

In this quote there are various aspects to be considered. The first of them is that, for Freire, autonomy cannot be disconnected from intersubjectivity. In the phrase that possibly is his most famous one in *Pedagogy of the Oppressed*, he said that no one educates nor frees anyone; men and women educate and free themselves in communion, mediated by the world. We are not only social beings, in the sense of being naturally prone to live in society by a demand of the instinct for survival. We have the possibility of communion, which implies communication, which in turn, implies co-intentionality and dialogue.

Autonomy, therefore, does not exist abstractly as someone's property, but it is constructed together with the Other, in community. The Other, in Dussel's understanding, is that person from outside the system who questions, who interrogates. In this sense, the criterion of autonomy within a society is the "community itself of oppressed victims." It is in this community that resides the possibility of change or, in other words, the liberation from the oppressors for the formation of a different community will come from the oppressed. Freire explains how this affirmation has been badly interpreted, especially by orthodox Marxists who believed it to be expressing an idealist position:

> When I say (this) it means more or less this: the oppressor does not have conditions neither to free him/herself nor to liberate the oppressed; it is this one [the oppressed] who, upon freeing him/herself frees the oppressor, frees the oppressor to the extent that the oppressor is prohibited from continuing to oppress. This is the affirmation and there is no idealism in it.[41]

The importance of these affirmations for our theme is that a different base is constructed to think of the relations within a new or a different social contract. The individual exists in a web of relations, within which, in turn, there are distinctions that, when not put into effect, level out the relationships and reduce the political and pedagogical practices to harmonious interactions, to a peace that, using a biblical image, is not embraced with justice.

This issue, as we saw before, was a theme of the discussions of Freire when he affirmed that between oppressors and oppressed there could be no dialogue; what there could exist are pacts in which there could be concordance on strategies of communal interaction. The recent discussions on Marxism and the "rediscovery" of the concept of class can contribute to the advance in the redefinition of autonomy and of the possibility of resignifying the power relations. In these discussions, class is seen as part of a process in which not only are the workers exploited for their surplus value, but all forms of sociability are determined by the logic of capitalist work, including the commercialization of subjectivities.[42]

To comprehend the possibilities of autonomy in the political-pedagogical field demands penetrating the thick game of alliances, of power, of exchanges, of negotiations, and, above all, of exploitation. The creation of a new social contract must have this characteristic of permanent epistemological curiosity in confrontation with the world in which one lives and, as such, will also and above all be a risk, because it does not place itself outside or above history.

> When one assumes any human possibility of being or doing, one necessarily assumes a risk. One of the neatest things for a man and a woman in

the world is to know that a person is a risk. Outside of the risk, there is no artistic, scientific creation, no creation of any sort. Part of every creating movement is the risk of not being, of being distorted in the process.[43]

Freire shares with Rousseau the idea that the inequalities are not natural, but are historically produced. The two centuries that separate them, however, did not go by blankly and Freire incorporates, besides the fruits of the revolution itself that Rousseau foresaw, Marxist analyses and their various practices, the inheritance of existentialism, of the critical theories, among others. From all this originates the understanding that the new will not come from an Emile, protected from a corrupt society, but from those who have been denied their citizenship and their humanity. The Freirean historical agent does not exist a priori, but is constituted in the multiple struggles and marches that the people carry out to conquer their humanity.

It follows from this condition of human historicity that the educator is not a facilitator of the learning process who neutrally organizes the opportunities for teaching-learning. Someone who, like Emile's tutor, manages the pieces backstage. Mainly due to the Rogerian wave of the 1970s, Paulo Freire from early on needs to sustain that education is directive. Being that it is of an intrinsically political nature, it will always be "directed" to a certain project of society and enmeshed with the power relations. The educator is not a facilitator of the learning process, but positions himself/herself as a witness within the process of knowing. He is someone who makes and remakes, in front of the students and with them, the paths to knowledge. In this sense, the educator is also a witness of citizenship, when s/he explains his/her convictions while at the same time placing them under the screen of criticism, his/hers and of the others.

One learns citizenship in praxis, through the marches that men and women have carried out during history in the quest for being more. Today there are many examples of these marches: in schools, in social movements, and in governmental and nongovernmental organizations. As an example of this learning experience of citizenship a pedagogical reading of participatory budgeting is presented in chapter seven. However, before moving on to that, let us have a look at the Freirean notion of *conscientização*.

6

Conscientização: Genesis and Dimensions of Critical Consciousness

The majority of the people passed over this earth sleeping. They ate and drank, but they did not know of themselves. We must now begin a crusade to reveal to people their own nature and to give them, with the knowledge of simple and practical science, the personal independence which strengthens kindness and encourages decorum and the pride of being a loving and living creature in the great universe.

—José Martí

Up to here we have pointed out aspects of the construction of the pedagogy of the modern social contract, contrasting basically Rousseau's and Paulo Freire's ideas. There is a wide lapse of time between these two authors, which cannot be covered here. The basic argument in this book is that in Paulo Freire we have a reference for thinking about education in a different social contract, because he incorporates elements of an emancipatory pedagogical tradition, from Hegel and Marx, passing through John Dewey and through the philosophical currents that impregnated the twentieth century up to the rereading of Christianity promoted by Liberation Theology and other liberation movements in the world. In this chapter we intend to have as the theme for reflection the concept of *conscientização*, which, in turn, is at the center of Freire's pedagogical theory. It is intended as a starting point to outline an itinerary in the complex map of interaction, identifying places and paths for the necessary educational reconstruction in our days.

The notion of *conscientização* is umbilically associated with the work of Paulo Freire, although he does not claim its authorship or any exclusiveness with regard to its use. According to him, *conscientiza-ção* was part of the vocabulary of the Instituto Superior de Estudos Brasileiros (ISEB) [Higher Institute of Brazilian Studies], an entity connected to the Ministry of Culture founded in 1955 with the goal of promoting research and teaching in the social sciences.[1] "As soon as I heard it, I realized the profundity of its meaning, since I was fully convinced that education, as an exercise of freedom, is an act of knowing, a critical approach of reality."[2] It was also a notion that was at the center of the polemics of his works, this being the reason that Freire for a long time did not use the term in his writings. We find it again being used in his last book, *Pedagogia da Autonomia*, when he reclaims *conscientização* with surprising vehemence.

> In the 60's, already concerned with these obstacles, I resorted to *con-scientização* not as a panacea, but as an effort at critically knowing the obstacles, and their reasons for being. Against all the force of the fatalist neoliberal, pragmatic and reactionary discourse, I insist today, without idealist deflections, in the need for *conscientização*. In truth, as a deepening of the *"prise de conscience"* of the world, of the facts, of the happenings, *conscientização* is a human demand, it is one of the paths to put into practice the epistemological curiosity. In place of being *strange, conscientização* is *natural* while being unfinished, it knows it is unfinished."[3]

Freire continues, affirming that the substantive issue of *conscien-tização* is not that the human being is unfinished, but the fact that this not being finished can be recognized as such. This is what differenti-ates men and women as *historical socio-cultural beings,* from plants and animals. People do not exist outside history, being conditioned—not determined—by it and at the same time being able to assume themselves as agents creating history. A symptom of oppression is the submersion of people into a culture of silence, making it impossible for them to say their word. This word, when truthful, is pronounced in the context of praxis, that is, of the reflective action about and in the world. On the other hand, the word that does not generate involved and transforming dialogue is denounced with adjectives as unauthentic, hollow, empty, magical, and naive.

For Freire, a privileged place of critical consciousness-raising are the social movements, more precisely the popular social movements. They provide the glasses through which he gets to know reality, even if the sponsors of the projects and programs in which he worked professionally were government organs, or, later, nongovernmental organizations. A second mark left by the social movements on his works is the dynamicity that these imprinted onto his thought, helping to construct a true pedagogy of movement. Last, and connected to the prior items, Freire's pedagogy is characterized by its innovating character stemming from the margins where one finds energies capable and willing to produce changes.

The Marches: Society in Movement

In the second pedagogical letter, when he refers to the march of the MST (Movimento dos Trabalhadores Rurais Sem Terra [Movement of the Landless Rural Workers]) heading to Brasília, Freire manifests his dream of seeing the country full of marches:

> The march of the unemployed, of those suffering injustice, of those who protest against impunity, of those who clamor against violence, against lying and the disrespect of the public good. The march of the homeless, of the school-less, of those without hospitals, of the renegades. The hopeful march of those who know that change is possible.[4]

Ana Maria Araújo Freire, his wife and work companion in the last years, tells about the emotion of her husband upon seeing the public manifestation that culminated in such a march, at the Esplanada dos Ministérios, in Brasília, speaking in front of the television as if he were there present: "That's the way my people, Brazilian people. This Brazil is everyone's. (...) This country can no longer continue belonging to a few...Let us fight for the democratization of this nation. March, people of our nation..."[5] With these words and gestures Paulo Freire recognizes the social movements as the forces *par excellence* capable of altering situations of injustice constructed throughout history on the basis of interests that came to be naturalized.[6] Next, I intend to identify some moments in the construction of his work based on the relation with the social movements, not without acknowledging that there is a great diversity among them, from ideological perspectives to their strategies of struggle. I argue that these constituting moments of Freire's works can be roughly grouped into three categories, which correspond to the emergence and construction of the grassroots in Latin America, to the elaboration of a global perspective, and to the involvement in the struggle for democratization and human rights in his country. *Conscientização*, as a concept that is not stagnant, acquires new facets as the movement of the society responds to new needs and challenges.

The Emergence of the Popular

The decades of 1950 and 1960 are recognized in popular education as the moment when something new was founded in the Latin American pedagogical panorama.[7] Education comes to be seen as an instrument for the lower classes to occupy a place in society that had been denied them. Paradoxically the society that denied this space recognized that neither economic development nor modern democracy could live together with this enormous contingent of ignorant and illiterate population. Industries needed workers who were at least minimally qualified and the increase in the number of citizens able to deposit their vote, at that time not permitted for the illiterate, was important for the regional and national political disputes.

The populist politics in power at that time consisted in adapting the masses to the structure of society without altering their essence. Francisco Weffort comments that "this was probably their greatest mistake and, at the same time, the greatest virtue of the populists."[8] On the one hand they needed the growth in popular pressure through the mobilization of the masses to guarantee their interests of power and the carrying out of reforms. On the other hand, for this to happen spaces of participation were necessarily created that escaped their control and which represented an awareness raising that went beyond the foreseen parameters.

For this reason Francisco Weffort refers to Freire's pedagogical experience in these first years as an "education movement" integrated into the wider "Brazilian popular movement."[9] In the presentation of the book in which Freire narrates his experience in Angicos, the sociologist weaves the following considerations:

> The presentation of this book seems to us to be a precious opportunity to present some considerations about the Brazilian popular movement. In truth, it would be difficult to treat an engaged thinking process such as that of Paulo Freire's in any other way. His ideas are born as one of the expressions of the political emergence of the popular classes and, at the same time, lead to a reflection and a guided practice about the popular movement.[10]

This same mobilization, in the perspective of the sociologist, had a "congenital weakness" that consisted in the fact that the movements were directly or indirectly tied to the government, not arriving at the point of creating a level of organization that would permit them a

Even though his passage through Bolivia was brief, it leaves in him marks of the strong indigenous presence in that country.[16]

Slowly other actors enter. The fact that the first footnote in *Pedagogia do oprimido* speaks of the social movements around the world seems especially revealing in the sense of indicating the source of inspiration for this pedagogical theory, but also in the sense of signaling the connections between the various movements of the society of that time. Let us see the note:

> The current movements of rebellion, especially those of youth, while they necessarily reflect the peculiarities of their respective settings, manifest in their essence this preoccupation with man and men (*sic!*) and as beings in the world and with the world—preoccupation with *what* and *how* they are "being." As they place consumer civilization in judgment, denounce bureaucracies of all types, demand the transformation of the universities (changing the rigid nature of the teacher-student relationship and placing that relationship within the context of reality), propose the transformation of reality itself so that universities can be renewed, attack old orders and established institutions in the attempt to affirm men as the Subjects of decision, all these movements reflect the style of our age, which is more anthropological than anthropocentric.[17]

In this quote there are five elements that make up Freire's comprehension of the social movements.

1. The movements carry with them a rebellion that stimulates the changes in society. We will find the word rebellion in later writings, already incorporated in his pedagogical reflection in the sense of the need for an education of rebellion and of indignation.[18]
2. The social movements are localized, answering to specific challenges of a class, of a social group, of an emerging social issue, thereby differentiating themselves from an institution. It should be observed that even though the text was written in the heat of the feminist movement there is no explicit reference to the women's struggle. The macho language of these first writings will also be reviewed later due to the criticism of the women.[19]
3. The social movements are at the same time bearers of an essential concern of universal character, that is, the quest for humanization. The indigenous movement of the Andean region and the ecological movement, although struggling on different fronts and using distinct strategies, meet around issues that have to do with all of life on the planet.
4. The social movements are places where men and women are constituted as agents or subjects, as someone who has their say. Becoming an

agent, as part of the process of *conscientização*, happens in the critical insertion into reality in order to recreate it.

5. The social movements of present times indicate, to Freire, the transition from an anthropocentric perspective toward an anthropological one. With this affirmation Paulo Freire begins a discussion about the centrality of culture and the valorization of difference, which seem to be possible only if there is a decentralization, where the human being no longer is the center, but life itself, according to text presented further on in the same book where, based on Erich Fromm, there is reference to the tension between the "biophilic" and the "necrophilic" movement as bearer of possibilities for a humanizing education.

The passage through the World Council of Churches is without doubt a decisive mark in Freire's career and was a conscious option on his part. At the end of the decade of the 1960s he was already sufficiently well known to be able to opt for a relatively comfortable academic career in an institution of international renown. The invitation of the World Council of Churches, however, gave him, at that moment, the space he needed to test his ideas in confrontation with other realities.[20] His relation with the Liberation Theology movement also becomes paradigmatic for the connection of these two areas of knowledge in Latin America.[21] The one as well as the other stem from the concrete reality of the people who believe, who learn and who teach.

The Reconstruction of Democracy

Returning to Brazil in 1979, after fifteen years of exile, Paulo Freire finds a different reality in the sense that the popular social movements had disassociated themselves from the state, counteracting it in the struggle for workers' rights through the unions, for human rights and for democratization, for public schooling, for land, and other citizen rights. At the same time, as democracy is re-conquered, they come to have a propositional role and become protagonists in the struggle for public policies. The Brazilian Constitution of 1988 incorporated many of these proposals through the action of the Forum of Popular Participation in the Constituent.[22]

Giovanni Semeraro points out that one is dealing with the change from the paradigm of liberation to the paradigm of hegemony.[23] The direct confrontation with the state was no longer important. What was important was the occupation of spaces in civil society that would guarantee the construction of a project with a popular character. In the political-pedagogical discussions, the concepts from the Gramscian vocabulary become common, such as civil society, unitary school, organic intellectual, historical block, among others.[24] It is also in this period (1980) that the Workers' Party is created, of which Paulo Freire is one of its founding members, and which comes to represent the expectations cultivated throughout two decades of the silencing of the movements, often in clandestineness.

In this period important leaders were formed, both in the area of the unions as well as in the area of the Ecclesiastical Base Communities. The president Luiz Inácio Lula da Silva[25] and the writer Frei Betto are eloquent examples of the formative force of the social movements of that period. Herbert de Souza, Betinho, led a pioneer campaign against misery and hunger in the country.

In the prior years Paulo Freire had insisted on the idea that peda-gogical action is not neutral, but is always also political action.[26] At the moment when the movement allies itself and in many cases fuses with a party, and when this party, in not rare occasions, governs itself by hegemonic political logic, the question becomes prominent about what to do with the power. It is necessary, according to him, to rein-vent it: "Well, if we have a political option of commitment with the working class, we have a dream, a utopia. My dream is not to simply take power: but the reinvention of power. Taking power can imply the ideological reproduction of the old authoritarian power. But, yes, it is necessary to reinvent it completely in a democratic way."[27]

Conscientização, as we have seen, is not created through teaching about it or though textbooks lessons about reality. For Freire it is con-stituted in the concrete lives and struggles of people. Being part of life while they act upon their word it is also polymorphic and its appre-hension as a concept implies looking at the process from different perspectives. Here we highlight some of them—the political, the epis-temological, the ethical, and the esthetic dimensions, respectively.

Dimensions of *Conscientização*

The range of the concept of *conscientização* certainly contributed to the equivocations in its comprehension, which Paulo Freire, at one moment, seems to have given up combating, opting for a strategic silence that permitted directing the focus to beyond the explanation of a concept. At the same time, the concept remains an important place in which to articulate the various dimensions of the Freirean pedagogical thought. Ana Lúcia Souza de Freitas identified three dimensions, relating them with central themes of Freire's work: hope as a challenge for the political dimension; curiosity as a challenge for the epistemological dimension; and joy as a challenge for the esthetic dimension.[28] To these three dimensions cited we add the dimension ethics, safeguarding the importance of still other dimensions such as the existential-dialogcal and the social-communitarian ones that likewise would merit highlighting.

The Political Dimension

One of the marks of Paulo Freire's work is the categorical claim that education is a political action. The supposedly neutral practice could be defended by two types of people: the naive, who have not awakened to the fact that history is not predetermined and that their lives do not move in a fatalist way toward a destiny; and the astute, who with their astuteness justified their privileges, hiding them underneath the mantle of myths: that the existing social order is God's will, that it could be much worse, that the poor are lazy, among others.

The risk of affirming that education as *conscientização* is always political becomes clear in his interrogation by the military in 1964, which would culminate with a brief period of prison followed by fifteen years of exile. In many ways the investigators sought to make him "confess" that his method of literacy training was above all a method of "politicization," understood by them as a positioning in favor of communism. It is important to remember that the world of the Cold War was divided into two blocks and that it was only five years after the Cuban Revolution. Although they were wrong about the supposed indoctrination of the literacy training method inaugurated in Angicos, a small city of Rio Grande do Norte, the inquirers were correct in their suspicion that when men and women assume their roles as agents of their history, this history can take unforeseeable directions, in this case, certainly different from those tied to the interests of the governing classes.

For Freire the politicity of education has to do mainly with the comprehension of history as possibility. Freire counters the discourse of the *end of history,* which, according to him, is part of an ideology that calls itself postmodern and denies the human being his/her capacity of *emerging* as agent and remaking his/her world. Being possibility, history does not advance in a linear way, but is constructed among the contradictions of the real society. We can see an example of what it means to live these contradictions when he is called to head the Education Department of the Municipality of São Paulo. There are various testimonies where he complains of an inoperative and insensitive bureaucracy when facing the needs of the schools of the municipality, but we also experience, at the same time, his untiring struggle to change the face of these schools.

Also, the political dimension of *conscientização* presupposes a permanent reading of the world. When affirming that this precedes the reading of the word, Paulo Freire is indicating that we are constituted as women and men based on the comprehensions of the reality that we are forming from the time we are born through a complex set of lenses that we inherited and that, at the same time, we reconstruct in an always original way. If we cannot deny the formative character of the experiences, we need to also recognize that this formation does not happen in a mechanistic way. It is up to the educator, being a political agent, to help identify the great generating themes that, in their time, are placed as limit situations for humanization.

The recognizing of education as a political fact implies recognizing changes in the comprehension of power and in the political use of power in these decades. With the end of military regimes there emerges a range of political actors that make the political spectrum much more complex than what was taught in many textbooks of reality analysis. The words of Carlos Rodrigues Brandão translate very well the current state of the issue: "In an almost natural way this appreciable polysemy makes appear vulgar a game of opposites such as: State x civil society, dominant elite x subaltern people, dominant culture x dominated culture, alienated x *conscientizados*, etc."[29] Paulo Freire's last writing reflects, as pointed out previously, this construction of the society less as a bipolarity and more as a web.

This does not mean that Freire does not recognize the existence of social classes, sexism, racism, and other forms of domination. What changes is the type of reading of this same phenomenon. Asked about his position regarding the future of the class struggle, he divides his response didactically in three parts: (a) that it is necessary to negate the discourses of a reactionary ideology that tries to paralyze history and the action of men and women as agents of history; (b) that unfortunately there continues to happen exploration and consequently social classes, although they present themselves in a distinct way in different places and times; (c) that the forms of struggle also change.[30] A conscientizing education is one that is able to read the emerging possibilities.

The Epistemological Dimension

One of the most important insights of Paulo Freire's thought has to do with the testimonial role of the teacher in the process of teaching-learning. Considering that education is, according to him, a theory of knowledge put into practice, the legacy left by the educator for his or her students will be, above all, the attitude they cultivate toward knowledge. Teaching means redoing, in front of the students and with them, the act of getting to know, the beginning of which already took place in the preparation of the class or seminar. Part of the process of *conscientização* passes through promoting what Freire calls epistemological curiosity, which is the deepening of the natural curiosity with which each human being comes to the world. And this is not transferrable in the form of content, but needs to be testified in dialogue.

The process of becoming knowledgeable is not an abstract exercise, distant from the real conditions of existence. Being that consciousness itself is always a consciousness of some specific situation or reality, teaching in the void does not exist. At the same time Freire's perspective of knowledge is also critical with regard to a strict utilitarian conception, according to which the only knowledge that has value is that which has some immediate application. If the mistake in the first is to cultivate curiosity as a virtue in itself, the second impedes the possibilities of the student to situate himself or herself as a historical agent.

> It is in this sense, among others, that radical pedagogy can never grant any concession to the artifices of neoliberal "pragmatism" which reduces educational practice to the technical-scientific training of the students; to *training* and not to *education*. The necessary technical-scientific education for which the critical pedagogy fights has nothing to do with the technicist and scientificist narrowness that characterizes mere training.[31]

Coming to know is related to the transforming praxis of the human beings upon the world in which they live. *Conscientização*, being a deepening of the awareness raising in the direction of a growing state of being critical, cannot be conceived separated from praxis. Paulo Freire argues, from his first writings, that a proof that one is thinking correctly is thinking one's own practice, submitting it always to new judgments. It is the confrontation with the practice, with its contradictions and complexities, that introduces doubt and opens up space for new questions.[32] The *bureaucratization of the conscience* can affect the thinking of the left as much as the thinking of the right of the political spectrum. In the case of the left, with which Paulo Freire identifies himself, it means nothing less than the stagnation of the revolutionary process.

Because of all of this, *conscientização* is also a painful birthing process. In this case there would be no palliatives such as exercises or medications for the women who go into labor. Freire uses the metaphor of Easter to explain the *rebirth* implicit in this process of getting to know, which takes place in the permanent dialectic of dying and being born. In this sense, it is very different from the conversions that take place in political-religious groups where rebirth means taking on a new identity that is closed to new questionings. Rebirth, in this case, means taking on the risk of the awareness of the nonconclusion of the individual and collective life plan.

This knowledge, as pointed out in various moments throughout this book, always takes place in the relation. Even in the solitude of his or her office, the educator is involved in a dialogue with himself or herself, with others, and with the world. In the opening of the book *À sombra desta mangueira*,[33] Freire speaks of the dialectic relationship between solitude and communion, both confirming each other mutually in the process of being in the world and of getting to know. "Coming with such deliberateness to experience solitude, emphasizes my need for communion. While I am physically alone, that is when I perceive the essentiality of *being with*."[34]

The Ethical Dimension

Conscientização is supported on a solid ethical foundation. Freire defines his ethic as a universal ethic of the human being in contrast to an ethic of the market, which sees the human being as a part of the cogs in the production and consumption of goods.[35] The basis of this ethic is found in humanization as a process that takes place in history and manifests itself in different ways, but, nonetheless, is a phenomenon that has to do with all people. The universality is expressed precisely in the historical and cultural diversity. The being human, however, cannot be taken as evident, since men and women live in a permanent tension between humanization and dehumanization.

Being more as a vocation for humanization does not refer to a state of being, but to a persevering and constant conquest, as much in the daily living of each individual as well as in the history of nations. At the end of the decade of the 1960s he writes on the first page of *Pedagogia do oprimido:* "Once more the men, challenged by the dramaticness of the current hour, propose to themselves that they themselves are the problem. They discover that they know very little of themselves, of their 'position in the cosmos,' and are restless to get to know more." And he continues in the next paragraph: "While the problem of humanization has always, from an axiological point of view, been men's central problem, it now takes on the character of an inescapable concern."[36]

The dehumanization does not only affect the oppressed, those who have been robbed of their freedom to seek to *be more*, but also those who do not allow that this movement of humanization is fulfilled in others. That is why Freire insists that social injustice has a structural dimension and true change implies as much in the change of the individual conscience as of the social structures that promote injustice, although not in a mechanistic way.

Freire considers himself a utopian thinker in the sense of believing that *conscientização* has an important role in producing another reality. Utopia, for him, is the dialectization of the denouncement and announcement acts: denouncement of the factors that oppose themselves to humanization and the announcement of new possibilities. That is, *conscientização* means to not only have knowledge of the reality that is oppressing, but also to become aware that a process of liberation is possible while there is concrete involvement for the transformation of this reality. Since this process takes place within the contradictions of history, the new reality will not emerge out of nothing, from one moment to the next. From this Freire coined the expressions "untested feasibility" [*inédito viável*] and "possible dream" to express, at the same time, that no one creates a new world in a magical touch, but that this desired world will also never happen if there is not the first step today and the second tomorrow for its construction. Waiting with hope is an active and propositional waiting.

The Esthetic Dimension

"The necessary promotion from naiveté to criticality can not or should not be done distant from a rigorous ethical education always at the side of the esthetic education. Decency and beauty go hand in hand."[37] These words from *Pedagogia da Autonomia* reveal Paulo Freire, in his maturity, confirming the inseparability of the *good* from the *beautiful* in educational practice. Nowhere in his works do we find a systematic theoretical elaboration of his comprehension of esthetics, but it is manifest in at least three ways throughout his writings.

Beauty has to do in the first place with the dreams and the world projects that one cultivates and extends to the way one fights for them. "One day, he said, this country will become less ugly. No one was born to be ugly. This country will be more beautiful as the people struggle with joy and hope, [...] what changes is the way of fighting."[38] A less ugly country is a country with less injustice, a better country for all the citizens. The fact that he uses the term beauty instead of prettiness[39] signals his intention of not associating the beautiful and the esthetic with some elitist style, with the taste of erudition. Esthetics can be in all places where one is permitted to live a decent life: it is the beauty of the body, of the school, of the cities, of nature, in sum, of the world.

Esthetics has to do with joy that Paulo Freire does not disassociate from seriousness. For example, the fact that a school is a place of serious work does not mean that it cannot be a joyous place. This is not about a naive happiness, but a joy that needs to be conquered in the struggle because it is born from hope. "There is a relationship between the joy that is necessary for the educational practice and hope. It is the hope that the professor together with the students can learn, teach, become disquieted, produce and together, equally, resist the obstacles to our joy."[40] We could say that just as hope, with which the human being is born, needs to be educated, just so joy needs to be cultivated.

Esthetics is yet revealed in his way of writing. Thiago de Mello, the poet who wrote the poem "Canção para os fonemas de alegria [Song for the phonemes of joy]" went through Freire's work seeking metaphors that reveal Freire's concern with maintaining a coherence between a discourse about beauty and presenting a beautiful discourse, capable of impregnating the word with a magical, transformational power. He said, in a poetic dialogue:

> Paulo Freire has a liking for metaphors and that is good, since it permits him to *walk through the streets of history,* to see and hear clearly the *rich contours of the peasant's talking, free of the angular corners which hurt us.* Paulo is owner of a talk which leads us to think. It is his courageous way of loving. He arrives and animates us: *time is foundational, the untested is feasible,* and he encourages us against *spiritual weariness, the fear of adventure, the empty hope,* because he learned that from this weariness grows a *historical anesthesia.*[41]

To Conclude

Even after more than a decade since the death of Paulo Freire, one still feels the strength of his ideas and here and there practices and projects emerge trying to reinvent him. With his death a great void was created, which has come to be filled by an infinitude of words and voices. We are confronted today, in reality, with multiple Freires and I believe it makes no sense to try to place oneself as the guardian of what would supposedly be the true Freire.

First, because he himself was fully aware of the contradictions in his life, due to the simple fact of living in a society full of contradictions, where the opportunities and the life conditions are extremely unequal. The coherence that he preached, without moralisms or fatalisms, had to do with a position of denouncing these conditions and announcing, in the praxis (word-action), new possibilities of constructing individual and collective existence. Second, because few like him knew how to recreate themselves, in practice and in theory, within the movements of history. His pedagogy of the oppressed turned into a pedagogy of hope, of autonomy, of indignation among others named by him or by those that were inspired by him to show another side or a different dimension of the educational practice directed toward *being more*. The *being more* never designated a determined way for the human being or the limits of what this could be, but pointed to the incompleteness of life as a space for fulfillment.

Maybe for some the name Paulo Freire has become a brand, a type of a trademark to guarantee credibility or legitimacy, from names of schools to quotes in academic papers. But, for the great majority of those who occupy themselves with his thinking and his works, Freire symbolizes the possibility of thinking of what he called "untested feasibilities." This quest for the untested feasibilities or for the "possible dream" can happen in the daily life of the classroom, in the management of schools or of the teaching systems, in work with public health care, in social movements, and anyplace where one accepts the premise that the future does not need to be the repetition of the present and that education has a role in projecting and constructing this other future. *Conscientização* is this faith in transforming power of the word connected to action. The word, when united with action, has an almost magical power. Thiago de Mello said this in a very beautiful way in his *Canção para os fonemas da alegria [A Song for the Phonemes of Joy],* referring to the man who has learned to read:

because uniting pieces of words
little by little one unites clay and dew,
sadness and bread, yoke and humming bird,
and one ends up uniting one's own life
in one's broken and shared breast
when finally one discovers in a burst of light
that the world is also one's own...[42]

7

Citizenship Can Be Learned: Participatory Budgeting as a Pedagogical Process

I think that we cannot propose to be a team that collects demands. For this purpose the community knows how to organize and does it with the mechanisms it has always used. Now, the important thing in this process is actually to arouse the citizens.

—Íria Charão, Coordinator of the Participatory Budgeting
in Rio Grande do Sul/Brazil

Education, Citizenship, and the Public

Citizenship is only possible insofar as what is public exists as a space of collective construction, of common good. It is the conditions of citizenship that provide the measure of democracy. As Peter Burke reminds us, "Although citizenship need not entail democracy, democracy does entail citizenship; to assert this is to claim that the value of democracy is grounded in citizenship."[1] This consideration is relevant because insofar as democracy has become an almost universally accepted value, the debates on citizenship, respectively, the difficulties of experiencing citizenship also are expanded. We have examples of these debates, in topics on radicalization and furthering of democracy, especially through a mechanism of direct citizen participation, and on the strengthening of civil society or of the nonstate public sphere.

In chapter two we pointed at the two characteristics that Hannah Arendt identifies in the concept of what is public, respectively, to be able to be seen and heard by all, and constituting a world common to all and distinct from the particular place of each person. These characteristics of what is public, which Hannah Arendt pointed to, have several implications for education. One of them concerns the condition of *being seen and being heard*. This condition refers us to what Paulo Freire called the *culture of silence* and that currently is given other names, some of them related to the notion of social exclusion, such as disqualifying people or making them "invisible." These are ways of putting people "in their place." Not outside the system, but integrating them in a perverse and subaltern manner. *Saying one's own word* is precisely to bring back the possibility of participating in the deliberations that take place in the public sphere.

Hanna Arendt's observation that what is public implies *creating a common world* with a horizon of *permanence*, of future, has great relevance and actuality for education. In another text, on the crisis in education, Hanna Arendt argues that the parents' loss of authority has to do with the refusal to take responsibility in this world to which the child was brought. It is as though parents have told their children that they are really not at home in this world and so wash their hand regarding their future. The philosopher's argument is that adults must take on the responsibility for ensuring a world in which the novelty that comes into this world at each birth and with each generation can emerge. It is like the mother who takes care of the child in her womb, hoping that it will be born strong and healthy. The conservative character of education lies paradoxically in recognizing that no matter how revolutionary, the world of the adult is always an old world from the point of view of the new generation.[2]

Acknowledging the other is part of the creation of this world. It is a paradox that in a world in which, according to Richard Sennet, we live under the tyrannies of intimacy, we also experience the "fall of the public man." He explains that the *ideology of intimacy* confounds political categories with psychological categories and advocates that the city is actually the place where strangers interact and for this they have to create an "institutionalized civility." According to him there would be truth in the vision of the social as an esthetic life that guided the classical image of *theatrum mundi*. Social relations are esthetic relations, because they find their roots in children's games that are only possible when the latter can act according to rules and conventions that do not depend on a person's immediate desires.[3]

Among the various initiatives to constitute what is public is the experience of participatory budgeting, which we will analyze in the following paragraphs from a pedagogical point of view. Here we provide data and reflections based on two distinct experiences: one of them performed in the state of Rio Grande do Sul, and thus covering a wide geographical area; the other in the city of São Paulo where the process integrated children and youths.

Pedagogical Mediation in Participatory Budgeting

We may be surprised as educators, at seeing business managers referring to their companies as "learning organizations," physicians facing therapy as a learning process and communicators discovering the pedagogical potential of their work. Actually, education is always mixed with life. One learns because life, as Hugo Assmann says, likes itself.[4] This goes for all living beings, but especially for human beings. If, throughout history, there have been times of narrowing, in the sense of limiting education to certain times and spaces, currently there is a movement to recover it as a broad process of socialization, humanization, and recreation of life.

In what follows the objective is to spell out aspects of pedagogical mediation within participatory budgeting in the state of Rio Grande do Sul, and in the Children Participatory Budgeting in the city of São Paulo. The assumption is that in participatory budgeting we have a privileged space to observe participatory social processes that can lead to producing another social contract. The latter involves, innovatively, some of the topics suggested in the description of the scenario, ranging from the daily struggle for survival to the role of the state.[5] This is proved by the fact that many researchers who were paying attention to what was happening in Porto Alegre have turned their attention to other places in the world, where similar experiences are being carried out.[6] Boaventura de Sousa Santos, one of these attentive observers, thus describes the reason for this interest:

> Today, disseminated throughout the world, there are many concrete political experiences of the democratic redistribution of resources obtained from mechanisms or the participatory democracy. In Brazil experiences in the participatory budget must be highlighted in the municipalities under the administration of the PT,[7] namely, with particular success, in Porto Alegre. Although these experiences are, for now, on a local level, there is no reason not to extend the implementation of the participatory budget to the governments of the states, or even to the Union government. Indeed this must be urgently done in order to fulfill the objective of eradicating patrimonialist privatization of the State for once and for all.[8]

This Porto Alegre experience began in 1989 and was spread to the state in 1999, with the electoral victory of the Popular Front coalition of political parties led by the Workers' Party (PT). This is the context of the study out of which originate the reflections in the present chapter. Emphasis will not be on presenting specific data, but on building arguments and formulating questions that can guide the search for new information and the systematization of the data aimed at education for a new social contract.

Participatory Budgeting As a Place of Learning and Teaching

What could distinguish participatory budgeting as a place of learning? First of all it is a participatory process that involves the "hard core" of government planning.[9] It is one thing to be invited or called to participate in school building renovations or in cleaning up a river, but quite another to have the possibility of opining and helping decide on priorities for government investment. The Pluriennial Plan of the state government defines the issue in the following terms: "This participation of the agents can no longer be limited to operationalization, to implementing the tasks, but to a participation which assumes the existence of active agents in the decision making process of what to do, in defining where one wants to go, in formulating strategies to achieve these objectives."

According to this vision, the budget is not a set of lifeless numbers, but concerns the life of people, communities, and state. Governor Olivio Dutra, during whose term in office this process began in Porto Alegre (1989) and in the state of Rio Grande do Sul (1999), expressed his vision of a budget in these words, during a participatory budgeting meeting:

> The budget is not a fictional or merely technical paper, or simply carrying out a legal formality. The budget, thus constructed, involves life. The life of people and their communities, their state (...) The Participatory Budget is not a ready or finished recipe, it is an open, rich, instigating, provocative process; in a positive sense it provokes us to becoming participants, it provokes to being protagonists in politics, and no longer the object of other people's politics. And politics in the sense of building the common good, not in the partial, party politics sense, which is also rich, and it is important for each citizen, man and woman, to have their party connection, their ideological position. The politics that we want to work on, respecting the party and ideological

identities is the politics that allows the confluence of differences, that can join the local demands to the demands of our region, where not only do we have our municipality, our community, but other municipalities, other communities, and that will also join these local, regional demands to the demands of an entire state...[10]

Another characteristic that distinguishes participatory budgeting as a major political and pedagogical fact is its outstanding level of organization and the involvement of a large number of people. In 1999, 179,055 people in all of the state of Rio Grande do Sul; in the year 2000, 280,000; in 2001, more than 400,000; and in 2002, 333,040. If the percentage of the entire population (of approximately 9 million) is still low, it is certainly a significant number of men and women in a state involved in the same discussion.

The people who spend their time (most meetings are on Saturdays or in the evening) and money (on tickets and other expenses) clearly do not see learning as the purpose of their participation. The answer concerning the motivation to participate can be classified in three categories: (a) a sense of the urgency of changes (e.g., "Contribute to making a better and fairer state"); (b) an expectation of influencing decisions (e.g., "For the opportunity to participate in applying public resources"); (c) for the possibility of creating another relationship with power (e.g., "Political conviction concerning the need to build a new relationship between the public power and the common citizens, organized or not"; "To contribute my capacity to the expression of desires of the community").

The coordinators of participatory budgeting, in their turn, during the meetings reiterate the three basic elements that guide this process, which are: (a) popular and direct citizen participation in government; (b) social control exerted by the community on public management; (c) the possibility of inverting priorities in public investment, directing the resource to the public policies on health, education, agriculture, prioritizing the funding of small and medium sized businesses. Nobody goes to an assembly proposing some topic or content to be taught, and in the end no one will ask the classical question about lessons learned today. The issue of learning is on another, less visible level, which is just as important.

This educational dimension is very clear to the participatory budgeting coordinator in the state, as per the citation in the epigraph. Íria Charão knows that the communities have their ways of getting organized to present their claims for work to be done, and that a simple survey of needs and demands might very well be implemented through other mechanisms, for instance, questionnaires or consulting local and regional leaders.[11] Behind participatory budgeting proposal is, according to her, the conviction that it is a way to awaken and learn citizenship, practicing it through a modality of consultation that enables breaking with the historical patterns of the Brazilian clientelistic and paternalistic political culture.

"What does one learn in participatory budgeting?" The research team asked hundreds of people this question, wrote down the conversations, taped videos that were mostly transcribed, and handed out questionnaires. The answers, with variations, belong to the following categories: (a) broadening and building knowledge; (b) the discovery of the strength and power that are the result of participation; (c) the process of producing a consensus or of decision-making; (d) the importance of unity of the collective and of solidarity. A brief comment follows on each of the items mentioned.

Broadening and Building Knowledge

To the participants in the participatory budgeting meetings, it appears clear that it is impossible to really exercise citizenship without an adequate level of information to generate knowledge. The meetings are a place where knowledge on many different issues of public life circulates at several levels. It is a space for creating and using knowledge as a collective instrument of intervention in society; a possibility of seeing that knowledge is not fated to be merchandise for consumption and personal benefit. Roughly speaking, we can distinguish three types of knowledge.

Knowledge about the budget

Budgets are usually a space reserved for a relatively restricted circle. The arguments to reserve this space, as the participatory budgeting participants know, involve a technical sophistication that is unattainable for most people in dealing with this complex and excessively large reality. A councilor refers to the possible learning in this way: "I learned what a public budget is, which until then was a subject limited to a few government executives who, in their offices, distributed the resources, and the people who did not know anything about the subject did not have any possibility to question this, and when they did, they were overwhelmed with technical terms until they gave up." Another participant remarks: "I learned that other people's problems may be worse than mine. I learned that despite the flexibility of the levels of understanding and individual participation, the synthesis of the process is very rich and dynamic, and that the collectivity knows a lot more than the technocrats and elites think."

One learns to see that the budget is not a stand-alone fact. Based on the budget, one has access to the "innards" of power. "I learned," says another councilor, "that participatory budgeting is much more profound and efficient than I had thought. I learned more about budget law and about the structure of the state government." Several mention that they learned how government is organized and how and on what the resources are spent.

The myth that the budget is a reality that is beyond the people's ability to understand also collapses. At assemblies, it is noteworthy how naturally one deals with figures that begin to represent roads and schools, the possibility of planting and selling one's crops. After the explanation given by the participatory budgeting coordinator in the Caí River Valley region, about one hundred kilometers from the state capital, one of the delegates makes an evaluative remark on the resources foreseen for the region: "Well, what is important for us to understand about all this? The state will invest 41 millions. Here in this region we will receive 1 million 831 thousand *reais*,[12] in other words, if one takes the 41 millions and shares it among the 22 regions in the state, we have a good proportion…" Another delegate informs how a municipality in the region deals with obtaining financing: "Pareci Novo has a program in which 3 per cent interest is charged from farmers per year, and now it has money in hand, if I'm not mistaken, 300 thousand *reais*. This means that there is no need for subsidized interest."

What happens is a demystification of the numbers, which begin to make sense insofar as relations are established between, for instance, the cost of a school and that of a sports gymnasium, between what one invests in transport and in culture in the state, between the availability of resources for investment and the service of the debt.

Knowledge of the local and regional reality

Here appears to lie one of the strongest points of learning in participatory budgeting. There are assemblies where true local and regional X-rays are performed. A farmer who advocates rural credit says the following about his reality, which goes beyond the frontiers of the place where he lives: "One sees the abandoned houses, with the weeds taking over, and the children who have gone to the city seeking a better future, increasing unemployment and other social injustices here in the city…" Like in a puzzle, the pieces begin to fit together: rural and urban, roads and education, telephone and culture. Not even the need for research and dependency on multinational companies are left out of the picture that is being drawn:

> it is not surprising that 90% of the people present here are from the rural milieu…There is the issue of the laboratories: it is unacceptable that it should take 21 days for the report to arrive on material sent to the laboratory to UFRGS (Federal University of Rio Grande do Sul) or FEPAGRO (State Foundation of Agricultural and Livestock Research). Research has been neglected, we depend on the large companies, such as multinationals…We did nothing against citrus canker, nothing against something that concerns defending our product, earning our living, and that is work that has to be done by research.

Research, however, while not ignoring the complexity of the laboratories, is reminded not to belittle the knowledge that is found in the community itself. In the case of citrus canker, the same farmer reminds that one should not forget something "simple and run of the mill," such as orange juice itself, which "may be enough to kill bacteria."

At another meeting, a councilor begins to build a map of regional crops, attempting to find mechanisms to work together and perform exchanges. "It is known that Caí has strawberries, here in Montenegro we have tangerines, in Feliz there are strawberries. So the families want to get together and establish a strawberry processing plant…" Local production is valued, but one tries to learn from experiences that worked in other places.

Discussion of the local and regional reality allows entering another level of knowledge of society, that is, its organization and functioning. Using terminology from his milieu, the farmer discusses how the prices of oranges he produces have a lot to do with the road on which produce is sent to be sold, with the international market, with payment of the state and country debt, with the production structure, and with relations to power and research in citrus fruit production. The daily issues and the world connect.

In order for this discussion to be held based on data, the coordinators must concern themselves with supplying information that will support the argumentation, without detracting from the process. It would be interesting to verify, for instance, the level of information on the region, and on the region's position in the country and abroad favored by participation in participatory budgeting. Could there possibly be a challenge to the academics of the different regions in the sense of providing subsidies for discussions? Or are the academics paying attention to the emerging needs in terms of the generation of new knowledge?

Participation and Power

Participation in participatory budgeting shows the strength that arises from uniting around common objectives. This is expressed in answers to the questionnaire, with sentences such as these: "I learned that every person contributes to improvement." Or: "I learned several things, including the force of such a process." Or: "I did not learn, I only confirmed my convictions about the population's capacity and will to contribute."

Analyzing the words and expressions most frequently associated with participation, we can establish some relations. First, participation is associated with the desire and prospect of change. This is recorded in expressions such as: "Because it is through the assemblies that we can change the directions and destiny of our state"; "Breaking with the practice of elaborating public budgets"; "Because we have to change Rio Grande..."; "The need to change the way resources are allocated..."[13]

Participation is also associated with rights and duty. Let us illustrate this with a few answers: "I want to exert my rights as a citizen"; "Enforcing our rights to participate and decide about our own resources"; "It is my duty as a person in favor of the struggle for a better distribution of resources to the true priorities."

It should be asked to what extent these rights and duties are already part of the culture of most communities in Rio Grande do Sul, which, in the opinion of Fischer and Moll,[14] due to the peculiarities of their historical formation, would have constituted a sort of *public social sphere* "beyond or despite the state." The strength of this movement would be expressed in the two thousand community schools organized by 1938 (the year when they were nationalized) and a complex, broad network of organizations connected to churches and clubs (for singing, target shooting, bowling, and many others). Iria Charão, the participatory budgeting coordinator, corroborates this hypothesis:

> The more polemical the subject of participation becomes, which is treated very heatedly and even questioned, because it is a loss of power, the more the public assemblies grow. Decentralization, the opening of power in my understanding as a militant who has been involved in social movements for almost forty years, brings back the tradition of community life, which is that of Rio Grande do Sul. Independent of where people are, community life is important, and we see this in the different regions of the state. People mobilize for their regional vocation, and here we have the largest participation in the Middle Upper Uruguay, which is a region of small farmer.[15]

Finally, participation is associated with the idea of influencing decisions, especially as regards the use of public resources. The participants say: "It is an opportunity to participate in decision-making"; "It is necessary to emancipate the people, to create autonomy and direct participation in decision making"; "For the opportunity of being able to participate in applying public resources."

In these responses the desire is seen to conquer spaces and power, reflecting the exhaustion, or at least the fatigue of a participatory model based on the traditional forms of representativeness. This still exists, but it goes through other channels: workers' unions, residents' associations, NGOs, and so on. The difference is that here there is an almost immediate calling to account by those who participate in later stages. "In my position as union leader, besides representing my class, I am participating so that we will achieve something further together, not only strengthening us, the farmers, but also de municipality of Ipê." In other words, it is a mixture of a new form of representativeness with direct participation.

The Negotiation of Consensus

Participatory budgeting proposes to be an instrument of the executive power for listening to the communities, for rendering accounts, and community inspection and enforcement of the action of the state. One of the most frequent criticisms leveled at participatory budgeting is that it is rather a game of manipulation than the exercise of a dialogue among partners. In this context it is not possible to perform an analysis of this question, but a serious involvement in the process requires permanent attention to some issues: What interests are present and prevail throughout the systematization process? How does one deal with the asymmetry of power when on the one side is the weight of the executive and on the other, the citizen, often alone? The participants have diverging opinions on these issues, although the idea that participatory budgeting is a space where one is heard and valued predominates.

The concept that appears to correspond to what occurs in participatory budgeting is "cultural negotiation," especially because it takes into account that an educational relationship is also always a power relationship.[16] During the meetings information (data on the place and the region), points of view (based on personal and professional experiences), values (what is considered a priority), methodologies (ways of doing and deciding things) are negotiated. Let us see how this happens in the participation of a female teacher in an assembly in Montenegro:

> I would like to refer to all comrades who defended agriculture, full support to agriculture, except that agriculture can not be separated from the issue of water, just as we talk about tourism. Here we have the Caí River, which bathes the entire region, we have the streams, all of them dying. So, when one thinks about agriculture, which is sustainable agriculture, one must also think about protecting the sources where our water comes from…

After that, the same participant goes on to talk about the topics of education and income generation.

The intervention mentioned earlier occurs at a time when priorities are being advocated, with a strong tendency, in this case, to agriculture. The teacher did not challenge agriculture, which appeared to be a legitimate priority in a region where most people have connections with work on the land. According to one of the participants, agriculture "is present in possibly 9 out of 10 hearts at this plenary." The teacher's discourse acknowledges this priority, but, at the same time she expands and challenges the other participants to look at it in a broad context of needs, one of which is the issue of water. There were no other manifestations in favor of "water," but it is to be assumed that a seed was planted there, which may grow, together with the fulfillment of the other priorities, since water involves multiple factors.

Beginning with apparently disconnected statements, suddenly consensus and decisions begin to arise, with a high degree of agreement. This is because during the process, negotiations occur with a view to achieving the best possible result for one's place and region. During one of the meetings we observed how three different, but always "connected," blocks were formed. One group sat on the chairs, in the room, and participated, listening and speaking; another group, further back and standing, relatively "switched off" from what was happening at the front, plotted possibilities, while some of them drank beer. Another group, even outside the room, was still listening in another way and making other adjustments. It was quite clear, however, that nobody considered this assembly, on a hot Saturday afternoon, as a simple pastime.

The collective discussion about priorities and needs allow creating a new consciousness that goes beyond the limits of the current municipalities, or of the districts within the municipalities. A delegate defined this possibility as follows:

> I think that this is the time for us to reposition. I am from São Sebastião do Caí, he is from Barão, he is from Capela de Santana...We have to take the following position: we are all the Caí Valley family. We are going to get together more frequently, drink *chimarrão*[17] together more often, visit around, and then we will articulate to determine what is most important for the region. We have to stop thinking about the municipality individually.

This is in agreement with the vision of Iria Charão, in a statement after an assembly in the municipality of Portão:

> Now we are going to have delegates and they do not go there only to defend the school, they go there to deal with the problems of the region. They will stop gazing only at their navels and have to think regionally, where there will be diagnoses, scientific indexes, and sometime they will have to give up something. They will learn in practice that they have to make choices for the collective good and for the larger number of people who will benefit from a given investment.

When Children Discuss the Budget

In the municipality of São Paulo, the *OP–Criança* (Children's participatory budgeting) was implemented during the Marta Suplicy administration (2001–2004).[18] A characteristic of this project was that it was school-based, a fact that contributed to high rate of participation in assemblies.[19] Four hundred and eighty-three schools were involved and 153,168 children and youths participated in the assemblies.[20] The methodology was based on the *from/with* developed by the Spanish educator César Muñoz, which combines the principle of beginning *from* the children's reality and being *with* them in what he defines as the "light" presence.[21] Two groups were established to carry out the proposal: the *Grupo Motor* (Motor Group), composed by adults, which was committed to following the process and creating conditions for it to work; and the *Grupo Faísca* (Spark Group), formed by children, adolescents, and youths, mostly between the age of eleven and fifteen years, who are to get their classmates involved, sensitize them to the proposal, explain, and participate in conducting the process. There was process of preparation for both groups.

The objectives of *OP-Criança* of São Paulo combined concern about school and city management, as follows:

a) To increase the participation of children and youths in the democratic management of school;
b) To integrate the contributions of *OP-Criança* with the Political-Pedagogical Project of schools and with the municipal policy, emphasizing education as a right of children and youths;
c) To articulate the actions of *OP-Criança* with those of the participatory budgeting of the city of São Paulo;
d) To provide spaces and opportunities for mutual continued education among children and adults, emphasizing the participation of children and teenagers;
e) To stimulate the creation of organs to represent children and teenagers, and strengthen the already existing ones;
f) To define priorities, in the universe of social policies, from the perspective of children and adolescents;
g) To potentiate budget resources in the actions in which children and youths are the privileged and immediate participating public, with a view to realistically sizing the proposals presented and to meeting the established priorities.[22]

Contributions "From Below"

Insofar as spaces for the participation of children and youths are opening up, their contribution with their life experience to society is also recognized. The following contributions to society can be highlighted from the experience of *OP-Criança* in São Paulo:

Small things

In the book *The God of Small Things*, Arundhati Roy tells the story of two children who try to reinvent a world inside the world in ruins around them. A world that managed to escape the furious eyes of the Great God and where a Small God laughed foxily and escaped from the "Worse Things" that were always about to happen.[23] Looking at the priorities voted in the *OP-Criança* of São Paulo, we do not find large works such as establishing an industrial district, building tunnels, or opening new avenues for automobile traffic. On the other hand, it should be remarked that the São Paulo children's reading of their world corresponds to an unfragmented and self-centered vision of reality.

For the schools, the most voted projects were those for placing a roof over sports courts, establishing or expanding science laboratories, renovating the building, and internal security. The first priority, according to the children themselves, has to do with the fact that the school is often the only place for leisure. The request for science labs is related to their desire to discover and invent. The school renovation is because they want to study in a pleasant, beautiful place. Internal security is because of the experience that the school is invaded by violence, by organized crime, and by drug trafficking. As to the city, the priorities voted were leisure areas, public safety, job generation programs, paving streets, and building amphitheaters for cultural and artistic activities, all of them attuned to the world in which they live.

Bringing the school and community closer to each other
One of the problems in Brazil is the articulation between school and the community. Schools must be "protected" by high walls and closed off behind gates that only open to let the students in during the class hours, and schools and communities mutually ignore the problems that they often have in common. In the São Paulo experience we found the following report as an example of building a relationship of trust between the school, the family, and the community:

> The OP-Criança enabled many dialogues between the family and the schools: many proposals made by the children mobilized their parents, called their attention, and they wanted to know, understand, and also discuss what was being proposed. Through the children they discovered a new way of exerting citizenship.[24]

Questioning the school and the family
The children's participation makes them more attentive to what happens around them, at school and in the family. They also begin to observe the authoritarian attitudes of the principal or that the teachers have not kept up with developments. At the same time, they present greater solidarity in solving the problems. The words said by a girl, Suziane, are an example of this criticism and of the hope for change:

> I only think that the teachers still felt sort of...like, some teachers took an interest in our ideas. Now, there are others who couldn't care less. They are only interested in teaching their class and, like, going away. There are teachers who are like that, this is the reality, but slowly we are taking over this space, because this has just begun. It is

a beginning, so far, I know that I am leaving school next year, but it will continue, and a time will come when, besides us, all students will have an active voice at school, see? We are not the only ones who are going to be there.[25]

Another student Evelin criticizes the principal for not accepting the children's proposals. In her opinion, if the principal opened up to the children's ideas, many things at school would change for the better. In these criticisms, the sense of maturity of the children is remarkable. They challenge the adult world and academia to rethink the drawers in which they place the children according to their level of development, more or less associated with age.

Exerting a joyful democracy
In the adult world, politics has become the activity of a quasi-caste of professionals who alternate in power. The population follows the movements of these players through the media, generally very unenthusiastically. Political life is perceived as a necessary evil. The children teach that it no longer has to be so. In the words of Gislaine: "We discovered that we can have fun, that we can play, and at the same time learn how to exert democracy, how one exerts citizenship."[26] In other words, the children do not dichotomize between the earnest world and joy, fun. In this sense, Paulo Freire used to speak of joy as a necessary ingredient to educational activity, because it is linked to hope as an essential condition to understand history as a possibility. For him a critical attitude does not develop outside the relationship between ethics and esthetics. Decency and beauty side by side.

This joy can also be found in many of the participatory budgeting assemblies, among adults. In some places, the assemblies are like social meetings where *chimarrão* circulates, or where friends and acquaintances can enjoy their beer in a corner of the room where the meeting is being held. The festive atmosphere apparently helps create the necessary conditions for good discussions. One of these conditions is to perceive oneself as part of a community that seeks solutions for its problems. The clash of ideas and the conflict among the proposals bears more fruit in an atmosphere of basic solidarity.

Change in the concept of curriculum
Since many participatory budgeting experiences are directly associated with the involvement of schools, one should think about its implications in the school curriculum. Participatory budgeting studies

reveal how the community manages to use it to study their economic and social reality. The fact that one place requests a health clinic, and another a laboratory for the school leads to major discussions on the difficulty of the region and on priorities. From an objective point of view concerning the needs, the choice between alternatives of this kind may appear pointless. It should however be remembered that the origin of participatory budgeting itself has to do with public resources, which are at the same time scarce and badly used.

In the state of Rio Grande do Sul we have testimonies by teachers who transformed the issues into a topic for debate in the classrooms. Quite often, the schools were present at the meetings, even if voting was only allowed for those above the age of sixteen years. One teacher, in a symbolic gesture, poured out before the assembly a box of copies of the letters written to the authorities requesting the expansion of the school building. The children and youths participated in this movement that allowed teachings that are not in the schoolbooks.

In the case of the city of São Paulo participatory budgeting was considered a basic factor in structuring the curriculum. Based on the Freirean pedagogical approach, the process began with reading the reality for, then, elaborating strategies to interfere in it. The first movement consisted in understanding the reality of the school using various instruments for collecting and analyzing the data. Then it was extended to the neighborhood and the city.

Some Learnings and Questions

The main objective of this exercise, as indicated by the subtitle, was to apply a "pedagogical ear" to participatory budgeting as education for citizenship. Therefore many of the participants' own words were transcribed. In concluding, I gather some of the learnings and questions in three topics, corresponding to the political, pedagogical, and ethical dimension.

A Participant Society

Participatory budgeting is, on the one hand, part of a long process of struggles for popular participation, because, ever since the 1960s and 1970s, participation was the theme and banner of many groups that fought for a political project built from the grass roots up. It was a movement centered on the popular classes, whence were to come the true alternatives for society.[27] Suffice it to recall the CEBs (Base Ecclesial Communities) and the many groups and centers of Popular Education.

This original ideological motivation is not completely absent in the current discourse and reflection on participatory budgeting, but new elements were added.[28] Participation is now presented in a broader manner: very different people and groups are challenged to interact participating in the discussion of priorities for the state and for the destination of resources. The interview of a mayor who did not belong to the state government party provides an example of this expanded vision of participation:

> I think that increasingly citizens must be aware of their responsibility in the social and political process. So, in discussing the budgets we can, possibly, have different positions. No matter. It is a way of building citizenship, and, therefore, based on building citizenship, there is the building of a consciousness of each person's responsibility in the process.

Advocacy of participation, however, is not exclusive to the left.[29] In conservative proposals it is also seen as necessary to promote development that is differentiated and able to compete in a globalized market. There appears to be a consensus that centralization cannot produce ways of being distinctly present either in the market or in society. For this reason it is necessary to situate participation within a project of society, as in the case of participatory budgeting, in a proposal to build another society.

A Learning Society

Participatory budgeting signals how society can change into a living organism that learns. It is possible, tentatively, to spell out some conditions for this learning society to be formed and to function:

- The existence of a process such as participatory budgeting is not the result of chance or of a spontaneous movement of people and groups. It is also not sufficient to want to do it, or to have the political will for it. Both conditions are necessary, but not enough to render the process feasible. It is necessary to have a strategy, with clear rules and defined roles, for the process to become feasible and legitimate. One of the strong points of participatory budgeting appears to be that these rules can be changed as a result of participation. A councilor says: "What we can do there (in the council) is to modify these criteria, if the council believes it should do so. We are here talking with you, so that we will have a foundation to be able to present a position later on…" Among the participants there was a great will to appropriate a process that many considered impossible to understand. "We do not have this knowledge. This (…) will occur over the years." Distinct levels and spheres of responsibility and knowledge are thus recognized.

- A learning society occurs when differences are respected. They can be linguistic differences (in some regions it was necessary to have translation from Portuguese, German, or Guarani); differences in the economic situation (the businessman and the employee may talk at the same assembly); differences in level of schooling (at the meetings there are illiterates and people with graduate degrees); different cultural situations (the meeting of rural and urban, different religious traditions); generations (youths, adults, and elderly using the same space). Asked how one learns in participatory budgeting, one of the councilors summed it up as follows: "In dialogue with those who are different, in clashes, in decision-making and especially in building together."

- One learns because one believes in the possibility of change—that there will be improvement at the individual and collective levels. A teacher says: "I want to leave a message to our children, to our students. This lesson is that believing and participating makes a difference. Today it is just beginning, it is tiny, but it will take over this state…" She knows that it will be difficult for this participatory process to literally take over the entire state. It matters that it has begun. It remains to be seen whether participatory budgeting can, as suggested by Paulo Freire, educate the hopes of thousands of people that participate in it, so that this hope does not become confused or transforms itself in despair. A society in the process of learning is materialized in the actions of daily life being built step by step toward a utopian horizon, which itself is permanently being reconfigured.

- The participatory budgeting meetings are not thought of as moments for fraternizing. There is a clear aim to obtain benefits for one's town, municipality, and thus for oneself. Even so, despite the side conversations and agreements of groups and debates, an atmosphere of interaction that is far from indifference toward the other can be built. One realizes that the residents of other neighborhoods or places have a face and a name.

- It may be that one of the most visible and emphasized aspects learned in participatory budgeting is the possibility of expressing oneself, of saying what one has to say. On answering questions about citizenship, the possibility of expression is widely highlighted: "To have the freedom to opine, above all responsibly, but always to opine." "Citizenship is the expression of individual and collective interests of people who are subjects of their destiny." "Having rights to speak and decide."

A learning society would also be that in which there is a broad possibility of having one's say and of being heard. "Having one's say" was to Paulo Freire the same as being a subject: on saying what one had to say, the world begins to be transformed, in an exercise of autonomy and creation. Vigotsky's reference to his experiments with children also goes for the adult world: "The more complex the action required by the situation and the less direct the solution, the greater the importance of speech in the operation as a whole. Sometimes speech is so essential that, if its use is not allowed, small children are not able to solve the situation."[30] Maybe one has not really understood what it means to speak in public about the local school, the roads, the financing of production, and other issues present at participatory budgeting meetings.

A Solidary World

Solidarity has become a mandatory topic, as a counterpoint to the widely denounced social exclusion, in a reality in which sensitivity about dealing with other people's suffering tends to be blunted. In education, Hugo Assmann said the following about the challenge: "The creation of languages and theoretical-practical fields of solidary sensitivity, in short education for persistent solidarity presents itself as a prospect for the most advanced emancipatory social task."[31]

For the aims of the arguments in this chapter, two major paradigms can be identified in using this concept. One of them is a primarily anthropological-sociological paradigm, in which human interaction is emphasized in the search for a more egalitarian and fairer society, even if it has very different, or even opposite ideological nuances. Another paradigm of solidarity attempts to include the relations that extrapolate the strictly human and social universe. This is a solidarity that is at the same time personal and cosmic, in a consciousness of profound interdependence of the entire universe.

Participatory budgeting may be the place to learn an ethics of solidarity or of care, without which there will not be a social contract, whether old or new. The social tie, as Rousseau already said, does not break only by noncompliance with agreed rules, it also breaks in the heart.[32] Solidarity, as I see it, is above all another way of seeing the world, of being with others, of being in and with life. A Colombian theologian and educator (Peresson) defines it as the tenderness (*ternura*) that is effective and collective. This idea is pertinent for our discussion because: (a) it brings back the concept of tenderness, an idea that has a tradition in Latin American thinking from José Marti to Che Guevara, and (b) it places human relations on a level of social effectiveness, of public policies; it proposes that lovingness and tenderness are not restricted to the intimacy of private life, but should (also) be on the political level, the collective level. In participatory budgeting this is found in the fact that it is also a social and community event, where one meets and makes friends; one drinks a tea with neighbors and acquaintances from other places in the region; where, around a beer, priorities are discussed and, in doing so, one strengthens or reestablishes the "social tie" beginning with common concerns.

Finally, a concern that arises in *OP-Criança*. It appears that we, the adults, actually know very little about what it means to be a child and a youth, in these times. Even further, we feel that the very theories of childhood and youth that guided parents and educators are in a crisis in the same proportion as the parameters to understand the adult world. This could perhaps be a good beginning in the process of listening to us more earnestly and more lightly, also between the generations, to build a society that has place for all. A society that, as Gabriel García Márquez said, is within reach of the children,[33] and that would certainly also be a better society for all.

8

Pedagogy of the New Social Contract: A Few Agendas

Living together cannot be reduced to an organic symbiosis nor to a juridical-political contract. Nor to life according to nature, or birth, or blood or soil; nor to life according to convention, contract or institution.

—Jacques Derrida

What Shall I Do With This?

This question is, to a certain extent, inevitable and two-sided. On the one hand, it helps keep up a necessary level of practicality and operationality in our reflections and discussions, and does not dichotomize theory and practice. On the other hand, it may also help activism to continue asphyxiating educational practice. Actually, theory and practice form a dense web, in which passage from one to the other is neither automatic nor evident. I understand theory as the speech that is born from practice, which, conscious of itself, feels incomplete. It is the time of astuteness in the practice one wishes to have recreated. Both linearity from theory to practice and from practice to theory decharacterize what Paulo Freire considers praxis.

The following exercise, therefore, does not intend to "draw" pedagogical conclusions. Pedagogy, as a type of practice, was present since the beginning of the work. When I mentioned the history of the cigarette butt and shared the experience of the doctoral seminar on globalization in Germany in the chapter on the scenario, I spelled out a pedagogical intention of reading the world, which I would like to have kept up throughout the text. In closing, it is appropriate to trace a few contours that allow one to continue reflection, hopefully better equipped. It is as though we were standing before a picture with many colors, trying to identify a few shapes. That is why they are open agendas, presented as propositions, not as theses.

First, however, a few more notes on the set of knowledge that we call pedagogy. I believe that there are good reasons to localize this knowledge in a plural space, where several languages intersect. Pedagogy has to do with science, with research based on methodological strictness. From Comenius, who tried to "read" the laws of teaching and learning in nature, until the different paradigms and procedures of research today, there has been an effort to construct a place for the studies on education besides other sciences. Educational practice has also been historically associated with art. "Therefore, since education is an art, it is almost impossible for it to be successful, since the contribution needed for its success does not depend on anyone."[1] Art has to do with creation, with beauty, with the search for new forms, with the unusual. Durkheim,[2] therefore, situates pedagogy between science and art, as "practical theories." Finally, teaching and learning are situated in a misty place, like magic and spells. "The wizard is the one who looks for the forgotten song," says Rubem Alves.[3] Being an educator, in this sense, is essentially to help each man and woman meet their vocation. The educator uses his words to give birth to worlds and create projects. Science, art, and magic or witchcraft: the pedagogy of a new social contract will probably be formulated in a polyphonic language, by recognizing the complexity of teaching and learning that, as part of life, are constantly breaking out of the frame and crossing frontiers.

A New Paideia: The Question of Pedagogical Mediation

Proposition 1: The presence of pedagogy in the social processes and movements, where there are experiences that point to what we here call the new or other social contract, is essential to potentiate these practices as formative spaces of citizenship and as a possibility to reinvent education at school.

Sometimes one has the impression that pedagogy has been trapped in school and that there occurs a discussion that does not touch the lives of people not directly linked to this institution. The isolation of faculties of education from other faculties appears to be a symptom of this fact at an academic level. But it need not be so. After an assembly, asked about what she thought of participatory budgeting as a pedagogical process, a participant opined that many things could be changed. One of them is the position of the official table that separates the coordinators from the people, thus revealing the intuition that the pedagogical processes are mixed with power relations. Reinventing education in the Freirean sense includes issues such as this one, which, apparently an unimportant detail, exposes a type of political-pedagogical relationship that contradicts what is said at the microphone.

In participatory budgeting we also see how pedagogy may become the place of commitment for specialists from other fields of knowledge. This occurs in two senses. A pedagogical look will soon perceive the need to provide information that would allow covering other levels of understanding. When speaking of the agricultural vocation of a region, it may be important to have specialized knowledge that, on beginning a dialogue with the knowledge of the people from that place, generates another type of knowledge. It is not a matter of denying one or the other kind of knowledge, but to favor that, in dialogue, both become transformed, that both be overcome dialectically. School, in turn, can make use of the topics discussed at the assemblies as the generating themes. In this way there would be greater closeness between the school and the community, based on issues of reality itself. It is worthwhile mentioning that many young students are present at the assembly. Educators have to take care that this participation will not only be about the vote to build a sports gymnasium or to purchase a laboratory, but that it may have repercussions on the curriculum, on daily life at school. In another sense, pedagogical listening means opening oneself, as educators, to other areas to build knowledge concerning the social processes and movements. The input of sociologists, political scientists, philosophers, communicators, and professionals from other fields of knowledge may give greater consistency to the movement, but indirectly it will serve to reinvigorate pedagogy, making it a permanent partner in the discussion of social and political projects.

It may be necessary to recover, in education, the Greek idea of paideia, which intended to comprehend the integrality of life within the *polis*. It was not just another dimension of life, but the structuring factor of community life itself.[4] This is a matter of opening and expanding the idea of education that was constituted in the course of modernity, often transforming it into training for the technical competencies required by the market. Hans-Jürgen Fraas comments on how the German word "Bildung" (literally, *making a figure*), which originated in the medieval mystique with Meister Eckhart (*ca.* 1260–1328), where it meant communion with God through being dressed up with the image of Christ, slowly acquired an operational character. During the Renaissance, it began to express the idea of conscious and intentional activity to form a figure based on raw material that had to be cut and polished.[5] Then one begins to ask the state to educate these men who are able to meet the competencies that the new world required. Comenius sees the perfect school as "a workshop for men,"[6] where time, course subjects, and method are disposed in such a way that all can learn everything. Outstanding in this concept is the active role of man (sic!) as a modeler and craftsman, and the school as the place where this modeling is performed. The *Ratio Studiorum* of the Jesuits, and the *Didatica Magna* of Comenius, both landmarks of the beginning of modern pedagogy, are examples of how one must "con-figure" this modern man, with time and tasks defined in detail.

The new paideia should perhaps begin with de-formation in the sense of de-education, a figure that Carlos Rodrigues Brandão proposes to characterize the educators of today. It is neither the formation in the sense of modern "Bildung," nor the Rousseau-type self-education, much less the discriminatory *paideia* of the Greeks, but a kind of unformatting:

> In her work, in her/field of science and reflection, the reality of her world of life and thinking and action, a teacher is not an uninformed person. She is a "de-formed" person. Without a definitive form, without forms. Without bandages on her heart and in her imaginary. Always able to learn more, know more and be wiser. Knowing that the more her knowledge grows and the more it is integrated and re-integrated at increasingly elaborate levels of herself, this knowledge is one among others, among many.[7]

What I am proposing is that education should allow itself at least some degree of institutional "de-formatting," and thus becoming free to seek new paths and new places to perform its task of humanization. This does not mean to diminish or deny the role of the school, but to situate it within the broader formative processes of life, where this institution certainly will retain its relevance while having to redefine its specificity. Participatory budgeting, analyzed in the previous chapter, is one of these emerging scenarios in which, in the expressive words of Brandão, "life is fulfilled as knowledge."[8]

Latin America As a Place of Pedagogical Production

Proposition 2: *Latin America has become a place of pedagogical production, especially through the movement of popular education, with Paulo Freire as one of its great protagonists. The challenge is set to rebuild the pedagogical memory that has been covered up by the transplantation of theories and practices.*

Latin America presents itself as a real enigma, which, not rarely, devours whom it believes to have found the magic key that provides access to its mysteries. When the Eurocentric globalization appears to take over the world, the indigenous movement gains strength in several places on the continent, and the first president hailing from the conquered people is elected. In religion, the underground presents a vast wealth of experiences invisible to the ecclesiastic world and to the official statistics. The movement of popular education continues to reveal pedagogical practices of resistance and reinvention of what is social, unknown to the schoolbooks.

Therefore, perhaps, Britto García is right when he says that Latin America is an incommunicado continent.[9] We know little about ourselves and a lot of what we know about ourselves, or others know about us, comes through what others say about us, from specialists on Latin America at centers that are usually located in the North. According to a survey by the aforementioned author, in the United States there are about two hundred centers specialized in Latin America, while in Central America, in South America, and in the Caribbean there are at most twenty of these centers. Certainly there are distinct interests that promote these studies, but they indicate above all our fragility in naming our world.

Already in the writings of José Martí, in the second half of the nineteenth century, one finds this concern about knowledge of Latin American reality, using vibrant metaphors. *Nuestra America* appears as a place that has been stopped, forbidden from being and saying. As in the depths of a dormant volcano, the moment of eruption is being prepared, when the best of each of the peoples who live here will be brought together to form this new homeland and humanity, under the motto: "Universe = the diverse in one." In a conversation with Nicolas Heredia, on the eve of the war in 1895, the latter reminded Martí that in Cuba the favorable atmosphere imagined by the revolutionaries did not exist, to which Martí is said to have answered: "But you are talking about the atmosphere and I am talking about the subsoil."[10]

This lack of communication goes for all fields of knowledge and not least for pedagogy. We know how the Latin American pedagogical thinking is dependant on theories from outside, which, even before taking root, are exchanged for others. José Martí, living in New York, did not close himself off from the novelties he was experiencing, but advocated that they should be grafted onto a trunk that will be that of our republics. Although he did not leave a systematic pedagogical theory, his writings on education reveal his pioneer work in the sense that he saw the Latin American and Caribbean reality as a place for strategic production. Where this concern becomes very clear is in the children's magazine, *A idade de ouro [The Age of Gold]*. There Martí exemplifies what children should learn, how they should be taught, and what purpose was to be served by their education. In the first issue of *A Idade de Ouro*, Martí thus presents the purpose of the magazine:

> For American boys to know how one used to live and how one lives today in America and in other countries; and how so many things are made of crystal and iron, and steam engines, hanging bridges, and electrical light; so that when a boy sees a colored stone, he will know why the stone has colors, and what each color means.[11]

Children should not see anything, touch anything, and think about anything they were not able to explain. Martí sees children as those who "know how to want," the quality that makes them the hope of the world. Children know many things and the magazine should be a means for them to tell what they know. That is why he encourages them to send letters, even if there are spelling mistakes. The boys of America should learn to say what they think, and say it well.

Although we do not find, in Paulo Freire, an explicit reference to José Martí, possibly due to the Brazilian tradition of looking toward the Atlantic, his work reflects the same concern about not copying a literacy method among the many available. The point of departure for the educational practice, according to him, cannot be any other than the cultural and social reality of the person being educated. The investigation of the thematic universe to identify the generating themes in which, in turn, words "pregnant of the world" would be identified for the process of teaching literacy," is based on the assumption that an illiterate person does not live in a cultural void or in a state of absolute ignorance. The alphabet is part of the world to which the person who is being educated has a right, but which will only make sense if it is "grafted" onto their world of concrete life as yet another instrument to deal with his reality.

Here we are dealing with a picture that requires a plural pedagogical theory, whose articulation occurs, beginning with the insertion in the matrix formulated by the absences and emergences, by the pedagogical knowledge covered or silenced, and by voices that appear as survival, resistances, and as a desire to reinvent the possibilities of life. Paulo Freire's pedagogy is a good example of a pedagogy formulated within a cosmopolitan rationality, but rooted in the reality of the popular classes. New criteria are proposed to what is understood as coherence and rigorousness, escaping the dualist traps that require choosing between terms that do not exclude or oppose each other, such as culturalism and structuralism, between biology and history, and others.

Dissonant Metaphors: A New Rigorousness

Proposition 3: *Education for another social contract presupposes the dialogue between dissonant metaphors seeking a more complex pedagogical vision, within a new understanding of rigorousness.*

The pedagogical discourse is essentially metaphoric. We very naturally use terms such as formation, construction, negotiation, exchange, maieutics, synergy, cultivation, or culture. Here I take support from Hugo Assmann's idea in the sense that we must be attentive to reinterpreting or re-signifying the old metaphors and incorporate new ones from new and old fields of knowledge, especially on the frontiers of those fields.[12] Today, as pointed out several times in this book, the challenge appears to go through a new reading of the metaphors of culture and history, accused of being mentalist or culturalist by some, and of the metaphors of life or nature, some of them associated with developments in the field of informatics, accused of fleeing from the real conflicts of society.

Dialogue, if it can occur, will come from recognizing that we do not have full knowledge either of the historical processes or of the natural evolutionary ones, and much less their interrelationships. How could we relate chaos and disorder to historical projects, the unexpected to the planned, the cosmic and planetary destiny to the destiny of the individual and the community, adventure with calculating risk? How do we move between desires and frights, between dream and reality? Hugo Assmann, for instance, sees in the concept of autopoiesis the example of the transversatility needed to reconfigure the epistemo-logical scenario, since it is a theory "that made its peace with biology and evolution, and besides this, perceived the mistakes of historicism, but at the same time intends to avoid falling into the full naturaliza-tion of history."[13]

In order to enable this integration of complementary and dissonant metaphors, it is necessary to reflect on the idea of rigorousness. For Boaventura de Sousa Santos, the break between seeking the truth and seeking the good was a fateful event for modern science, leading to the absolutization of the rigor of truth, and thus compromising the possibility of understanding the complexity of the world. "The rigor of truth," he says, "has become the truth of rigor and the truth of rigor ultimately boycotted the rigor of truth."[14] I believe that the way Paulo Freire did pedagogy may help think about this issue. I tran-scribe a passage from another text where I discussed this topic:

> First of all rigorousness always comes in the context of politicity and ethicity. It is useless to have rigor, humanly, if this is at the service of domination, possibly making it more efficient. Rigorousness has to do with the development of the critical capacity, with the assumption of life as a project, with the universalization of the possibility of "being more."

In another sense, the rigorousness in Paulo Freire focuses atten-tion not on a theory that has to be understood for its value in itself, but on a limit-situation that is becoming an object of "epistemologi-cal curiosity" and of "methodological rigorousness" of educators and people who are being educated. He bears testimony to this in his way of working on issues that are presented to him. First the topic is made manageable. Just as a soccer player, when he receives the ball, tries to make it "round" to continue playing, Paulo Freire approaches or comes lovingly near the theme. The object is not an enemy who must be defeated, but a challenge with which one wages a struggle that is at the same time harsh and pleasurable. The approach is then made from several angles, in a probably more transdisciplinary than interdisciplinary exercise, since the frontiers between disciplines are of minor importance. The logic is no longer that of the disciplines that require a strict application of the method or of curiosity, but it is the limit-situation itself transformed into an object of knowledge that requires as much rigor as possible, including that of repositioning of the relationship between means and ends, releasing the means from prison, when they become an end, and thus often into obstacles to understanding reality, and freeing them mainly for a curious relationship with the world.[15]

As previously mentioned, the thinking and pedagogical practice of Paulo Freire have an articulating logic that enables dialogue among the different ones. He had the courage that Brandão speaks of, when referring to the new forms of knowledge: "Before anything else, it is necessary to have the courage to look with other eyes and discover interlinkages, interconnections and intercommunication of energies, senses and meaning where, before, there seemed to be only separations and oppositions."[16] It is the logic of the connective boy, as he said of himself. However we should take heed of the warning given by Brandão himself, that one must consider the distance there is, at one end, between a festive type holism which, based on the lack of critical imagination, connects to everything and, at the other end, the difficult work of seeking profound interlinkages between sciences, forms of knowledge, rationalities, and sensitivities.

The Unhiding of the Market As an Ethical System

Proposition 4: The pedagogical action within the new social contract must prioritize joining efforts to unhide the market, as an ethical system, and creating effective strategies to develop a life ethics capable of sustaining a new social contract.

I borrow the idea of the market as an ethical system from John McMurtry, who made an exhaustive historical study of the process through which the market stops having an instrumental function to transform itself into the frame of reference for human action, and overwhelmingly, into the educational practice. This issue is particularly important within the discussion of the social contract, because it expresses the side of the contract that has become hegemonic over these centuries.

According to John Locke, one of the authors who wrought the idea of social contract, and together with Rousseau, one of the most influential sources of modern education, human rights and each person's freedom originate in private property, whose preservation is the main function of the state. Locke's argumentation follows more or less these steps.[17] God gave the Earth to all men, however this same God considered it right to use and appropriate this common good, and this is a private and individual process.[18]

Despite the limitations set by Locke for this appropriation, the moral road was open for the accumulation of property and capital that followed. Since all are free, owners of at least their working capacity and endowed with rationality, the conditions are given to establish contracts. This theoretical principle about the market, as we know, flagrantly contradicts what is experienced. In fact, in the First World the number of workers registered by their employers, that is, who have assured labor rights, is diminishing; a large part of the working population does not have any power for free negotiation (the unemployment rate varies from 10 to 20 percent in developed countries and reaches up to 60 percent in countries such as Nicaragua); the force of the unions tends to diminish because of the competitiveness of the internationalized market. In a context of growing social exclusion for many, not even consumer freedom remains.

McMurtry advocates that the market has become an ethical system, dictating the standards of behavior and creating the rules for awards and punishment. Those who behave according to the demands of this market—individuals and countries—are given a happy life. The others, endowed with the same liberty and rationality, did not know how to make use of their chance. This self-referred system (it now does without Locke's *Deus ex-machina*) began to use life (people and nature) as part of a self-perpetuating gearing. This is accentuated with a financial market that works separately from the real economy, as a ghost seeking easy profit. McMurtry summarizes this self-referred process in the equation: money > more money > more money.[19] This equation is transformed into others, such as: money > merchandise (knowledge, education) > more money, or else: money > means of destruction > more money.

In this context, Tarso Genro[20] asks whether we are not really in a blind alley, considering that the supremacy of countries such as the United States itself is a situation of "artificial privilege," largely based on volatile capital, and which, to maintain itself, needs to demand more sacrifices from peoples who are already overburdened with the payment of their debts, and whose resources are melting away, through the exploitive rates of interest, for a capital avid for quick, safe profit. Confirming Genro's concern, speculator George Soros says, talking about his country, the United States, that the established absolute leadership should be preserved, both in economic and military matters since competition is the rule of the game.[21] One item of information suffices to have an idea of the values involved and the gap that separates rich countries from the others: the amount of agricultural subsidies in the developed countries was three hundred billion dollars a year, approximately six times the value of all of the development aid from rich countries to the poor ones.[22] Is there competition? Noam Chomsky denounces this contract controlled by the market as a joke, since for anyone who has to lease out their work, in fact there is no choice. In more civilized times, he says, this was commonly know as "wage slavery."[23]

McMurtry calls this the death circuit, to which he opposes a sequence in which money would be replaced by life as the basic ethical value. He presents two formulae, one representing an elementary form of life (e.g., foods) > life (survival); and another representing life in its human expression, proper (life) > means of living (e.g., education) > broader life (e.g., expansion of the spheres of life). The goal is to realize the "civil commons," which he defines thus: "It is society's organized and community-funded capacity of universal accessible resources to provide for the life preservation and growth of society's members and their environmental life-host."[24]

Despite the criticism that could be made in terms of spelling out how this new ethics would develop, there is in his ideas an undeniable contribution to the development of what Paulo Freire advocates as "a universal ethics of human beings"[25] and Enrique Dussel calls "ethics of life," founded on approaching the victims as a radical alterity to the system that oppresses and excludes.[26]

Strengthening and Democratization of the Nonstate Public Sphere

Proposition 5: Education in the new social contract promotes strengthening of the nonstate public sphere through the development of new forms of participation in recreating power.

When analyzing the minor citizenship in Brazil, Pedro Demo says that "in terms of citizenship, society is founding, never the state. The state enters the process as the needed instrumentation."[27] The affirmation of organized civil society as a space for the gestation and strengthening of citizenship has been a constant in recent discussions with very similar languages: the *citizen public sphere* (Habermas), *nonstate public sphere* (Boaventura de Sousa Santos, Tarso Genro), *the civil commons* (John McMurtry).

It is paradoxical that the hope of change is situated in a place that is currently so fragile. In Latin America, says Diego Palma in an analysis that seems to be as true today as a decade ago,[28] one has gone from an analysis that concentrated on the structure to an analysis that privileges the subjects, sometimes to the point of not recognizing any conditioning. This tends to generate what McLaren and Farahmandpur call "self-limited radicalization of the public sphere," which would stop seeing the state as an agent that could promote the structural reforms. In practice, they observe, the power of capitalism increased as the left embraced a discourse of fragmentation.[29]

Noam Chomsky makes a strong argument about he indispensable role of the state in the economies that developed, or in the sectors of the North American economy that became competitive on the international market, on the contrary of what one advocates for the Third World:

> Capitalism is great for the Third World countries—we love it when they are inefficient. (...) There is not a single economy in history that developed without extensive State intervention, such as high protectionist tariffs and subsidies, and so on. Indeed, all the things that we *do not allow the* Third World were the *pre-requisites* for development in other places.[30]

In other words, there is no contradiction between a strong nonstate public sphere and a competent, strong state.[31] The experience of participatory budgeting seems to point in the direction of a mutual constitution in a dialogue. That is why it is so important that participatory budgeting not be transformed into just another government program or into a simple political arm for the expansion of power, but that it continues to maintain and expand the capacity for self-regulation.

In this there appears to be a confluence with other social movements whose objective is to expand democratic spaces, sometimes without the claim of taking power, as in the case of the *Zapatistas*, in Chiapas (Mexico). Their objective, as we know, is to conquer conditions to be integrated with dignity, for what they are. It is not, therefore, a mere adaptation to the existing system, but the possibility of creating the conditions for its transformation toward a society into which everyone has room.

Here I highlight two challenges for education. The first of them would be to transform education into a public issue, breaking with the limits that insist on keeping it as something in the private sphere, increasingly mercantilized. On not establishing education as a decidedly public issue, the discussion on funding, for instance, usually occurs in a void, restricted to technicalities about funds and not inserted into policies with a density of citizenship.

The second challenge concerns the discussion of the subject or of the historical agency. It appears that now we are able to see the subject, neither as mere illusion or ghost, nor as a fixed and predetermined essence or substance. Dussel argues that subjectivity must be redefined in a complex, fluid way, not missing the diversity of places of enunciation, and thinking about them under a tension of mutual co-constitution.[32] This subject does not exist before and outside the social process, but is constituted within it, in the movement and as a movement. That is why, in the analysis of Jung Mo Sung, the subject is also never fully realized within history. The subject happens in resistance to dehumanization, in marches and struggles waged by men and women to conquer dignity.[33]

Memory, Utopia, and Technology: An Education Worthy of its Time

Proposition 6: In order to be worthy of its era, education in the new social contract must integrate the historical memory, the utopian vision, and the technology of its time; and above all cultivate the capacity to ask questions.

Reading Rousseau and Paulo Freire shows people who were current in their times. Both place the pedagogical discussion in the context of the major issues of the time in which they lived. In this sense, as mentioned elsewhere, the question about their actuality, today, is to a certain extent irrelevant. The question must be how they, as men who in their time were people of their time, can help us to be also people of our time. In the expression used by Paulo Freire, to not be "exiled" from our time. A century before Paulo Freire, in an article published in *La América*, in which he advocated establishing electricity schools in the countries of Latin America, José Martí expressed the same concern, on stating categorically that "the divorce between the education one gets at a time and in its time is criminal." And he went on to say: "Educating is depositing in each man all of the human works that preceded him: it is to make of each man the summary of the living world, until the day in which he lives: it is to place him at the level of his time, so that he will be able to float above it and not to leave him under his time ; it is necessary to prepare man for life."[34]

For education to be worthy of its time, it is not enough for it to be current with the technologies, to adapt to its time. In the passage of *Emile*, in which Rousseau discusses literacy, he says that he was very reluctant to mention this topic in a book on education. In this case, if Emile learns to read a bit earlier or a bit later, if he learns from method A or B, is a pedagogically secondary issue. What is forgotten in the discussion, says Rousseau, is that any method will do, insofar as one has aroused in Emile the wish to learn. Also for Paulo Freire, learning to read never was (only or mainly) a technical matter, but above all the moment of a cultural and political action.

For an education to be worthy of its time, therefore, it is not enough to exchange blackboard and chalk for a power point, in what some call "high tech colonization," in an industry that has a turnover of millions of dollars in research and production of teaching equipment.[35] It must learn to deal with the questions of its time. Before this, it must help identify these questions and be instrumentalized to seek answers.

This involves both memory and the development of a utopian vision. In the former case, we know how much we lack a pedagogical memory in Latin America. It is necessary to make a huge effort for the recovery or unhiding of a history that is not told in the books. Paradoxically, this memory will only form against a utopian horizon that wishes it to be told.

In this sphere, two topics emerge for discussion on the social contract and its pedagogy. One of them concerns the anthropological foundation of the new social contract. We saw how the classical contractualists began with a vision of the state of nature to identify "human" characteristics that would provide support for the interaction of individuals and communities. Francis Fukuyama asks whether the advances of biotechnology might not be leading us to a "post-human" future, due to the possibilities we have not only of adapting to different cultures, but of genetic modifications with much more profound ethical and political implications.[36] Or, as Habermas puts it, "the unquieting phenomenon is the vanishing of the limits between the nature we *are* and the organic disposition which we give ourselves."[37] What would the social contract be in this post-human future in which, for instance, parents would be able to predefine some traits they wish for their children?

Another topic concerns the way in which we insert our educational practices into a scenario of growing complexity and permanent change. I see that a possibility of dealing with this issue is to expand Paulo Freire's idea that the reading of the world precedes the reading of the word in the sense that the former is constitutive of any act of education. In other words, educating is (always) "con-figuring" the world, using multiple languages and tools. This implies placing reading of the world as part of the educational practice, independently of the field of knowledge or context, with the challenge of seeing ourselves more and more as a single "community of destiny."[38]

Still Emile? The Tension of Permanencies and Changes

Proposition 7: Education after Emile is paradoxically still Emile's education.

After Emile is a broad pedagogical space-time, and in this topic the intention could not be either to take inventory of the diversity of existing productions, nor of restricting the post-Emile pedagogy to Paulo Freire. The fact of taking Rousseau and his idea of contract as a reference points above all to the possibility that pedagogy recreates itself in the context of a new ethics/esthetics of living together, that it cannot be a repetition or intensification of the present, nor a creation from nothing. Paulo Freire knew how to live in practice and articulate in theory, as few educators did, the creative tension between permanencies and changes. According to him, just as there are permanencies in changes, there are changes in permanencies. The challenge then, is not in choosing between permanence and change, but in placing them dialectically in a creative tension to provide the possible conditions for the emergence of what he calls transit, in which changes acquire a qualitative character.

In a way, as say Antonio Magalhães and Steven Stoer, we are and probably want to be "proudly the children of Rousseau."[39] On writing this, the Portuguese educators are fighting the constant effort to reduce education to "performance," belittling its formative and self-formative character that still finds in Rousseau one of its sources of inspiration, as we saw, not without contradictions. Where would Rousseau be today? Here I spell out three places where the inspiration of the Geneva philosopher can be felt:

An unconforming education: A marked trait of Latin American pedagogy is its unconformity, its instituting character. In the last decades, this trait was especially present in popular education, a pedagogical practice that is, by nature, an iconoclastic education and that is held preferentially at the margins of what is instituted.

This pedagogy drinks from autochthonous sources, but also is part of a line that has a major source in Rousseau. The latter, as we saw, does not do an adapted or domesticated pedagogy. He dreams of another society, and another education, and sets his "hands to the plume" to create it. Retrospectively, we can, today, identify many weak points and many mistakes in his project of society and of formation. But, in his time, he dared to create a non-place (a utopia), whence to do his pedagogy. The problem lies in trying to transform this non-place again into a safe, perennial home. This pilgrim education, which crosses geographic and symbolic borders, is the heir to Rousseau.

This unconforming education may be everywhere, but it is on the margins that it appears to have its original *habitat*, because society reinvents itself based on concrete needs. The nobles and the clergy burned Rousseau's books because they felt the threat that the well-educated citizen Emile and citizen Sophia could represent for the regime of privileges that supported them. Martí was killed fighting for the emancipation of Cuba, and became the great inspiration for the Cuban revolution. Paulo Freire was forced into a fifteen-year exile where, paradoxically, his ideas found much fertile ground in the liberation movements that were spreading around the world.

Other pedagogical subjects: The panorama of education now reveals a huge complexity. In placing Emile as the educator of Rousseau himself, the doors are opened for other understandings. For instance, Marx may later say that who should educate the educator is a social class, the proletariat. Today maybe we could see this subject, not in a fixed place, but woven into the very movement of society.

Rousseau is there where one discovers and invents new Emiles and new Julias who educate us, the educators, and researchers. Who knows, this time we will want our educator to be Friday and not Robinson. As Enrique Dussel would say: the anti-Emile of Freirean pedagogy is not the lone hero, but a subjectivity built by the intersubjectivity of the community of victims of a society that is no less perverse than in Rousseau's time.[40]

Other rationalities: From the middle of the lights, Rousseau makes reason itself and his reasons a subject of debate. He fights the myth that reason must be cold, soulless, and bodiless. This type of reason, if it exists, is lame because it lacks a leg. He writes these beautiful words in the letter of Mylord Edward.

> A hale heart is, I confess, the mouthpiece of truth, the one that has felt nothing does not know how to learn anything, he only floats from error to error, only acquires in vain, wisdom and sterile knowledge, because the true relationship of things with man, which is its main science, always remains hidden to him. But to not study also the relationships of things among themselves, in order to better judge those that it has with us, means to limit oneself to the first half of science.[41]

Today we go back to valuing the second half of science. The students' reaction shows that school today is not a much more desired place than in Rousseau's times. Pestalozzi, in the steps of Rousseau, was to denounce the schools as machines to torture bodies and asphyxiate the minds of children. From a solution to the problems of society, school tends to become increasingly part of the problem, when not their sources according to some critics. There are rationalities (and sentimentalities) that resist being imprisoned and standardized. It could be said that Rousseau is present when and where one seeks to see learning as the great possibility of our becoming human, in all of its range and radicalness. And this is much beyond what one seeks to do in most schools of today.

If the rationalities are distinct between persons and cultures, they also are plural in the person himself. One of the fascinating aspects of Emile is the daring to imagine the education of a person, in all areas, from birth to the age of twenty years. In our eyes, used to the segmentation of life, this appears impossible. Rousseau challenges us to see the child in the child and the man in the man, but also the man in the child and the child in the man. For him, happiness is built today, but its reference is lifetime. "Youth is the time to study wisdom; old age is the time to practice it. Experience always instructs, I admit this; but it is only useful to the period of time one has before oneself. Is it at the moment when one must die that one must learn how one should have lived?"[42]

Beyond the Contract

Proposition 8: The education of the new social contract must be situated in the search for a living together that is beyond the standardization and contractual legality.

The social contract, for being a contract, is necessarily reflected in a set of norms, written or not, to regulate life in common, from work relations to trade between countries. The struggle for a new social contract is the struggle for these relationships to have new criteria and parameters, based on principles of justice and solidarity. But there are issues of interaction that go beyond the level of what is legal, of the contract. That is what Derrida refers to in the text chosen for the epigraph. Living together implies transporting oneself beyond the nature-culture, organic symbiosis-laws dichotomy, based on which the possibility arises of meeting the other.

Independently of the discussion about really how much in fact we are able to or have to interrupt relations with history or culture and nature, as Derrida suggests, the issue discussed concerns a level of relationship that does not fit exactly into one or the other category (nature and culture) and that receives different names, but with a very similar sense. Rousseau talks about compassion as the basic feeling to be cultivated by Emile insofar as he knows the world with the inequalities created by men. Compassion, although implicit in human relationships, cannot be the object of contracts. Paulo Freire presents lovingness (*amorosidade*) as a condition for dialogue. The law may prescribe respect, but love is outside the scope of what is legal. According to Hugo Assmann and Jung Mo Sung, the great challenge today is to develop, together with technical competence, solidary sensitivity (*sensibilidade solidária*). The name Leonardo Boff gives to a new form of relating with others and with the world is care (*cuidado*). José Martí talked about the tenderness (*ternura*) that would melt the blood clotted in the veins of Latin America. These are expressions that indicate an ethics prior to and beyond the social contract, indicating the temporary character and contingency also of any new contract. Paradoxically then, the education of the new social contract is also education beyond the social contract itself. It is the recognition that *being more* will continue as a search, as a dense and intense waiting in action. "I will not wait for you in pure waiting / Because my time of waiting is a / time of doing (...)."[43]

Notes

Introduction

1. "We must place the future, like the unborn child in the womb of a woman, within a community of men, women, and children, among us, already here, already to be nourished and succored and protected, already in need of things for which, if they are not prepared before it is born, it will be too late" [Margaret Mead, *Culture and Commitment* (Garden City: Natural History Press/Doubleday, 1970), p. 76].
2. *Concientização* will be used in its Portuguese form due to the difficulties of finding an adequate translation.
3. Research on this topic as well as part of the writing of this book was carried out at the Latin American Studies Center (UCLA) as a visiting scholar (2002). The present book is an extended version of Danilo R. Streck, *Educação para um novo contrato social* (Petrópolis: Vozes, 2003). It has been translated into Spanish [*Educación para un Nuevo contrato social* (Buenos Aires: Stella, CELADEC, La Crujía, 2005)] and German [*Erziehung für einen neuen Gesellschaftsvertrag* (Oberhausen: Athena, 2006)].

I Daily Life, Globalization, and Education: Educational Practice and the Reading of the World

1. Octavio Ianni, *Teorias da globalização* (Rio de Janeiro: Civilização Brasileira 1996), p. 113.
2. See also Peter McLaren in the interview with Lucía Coral Aguirre Muñoz, "The Globalization of Capital, Critical Pedagogy, and the Aftermath of September 11: An Interview with Peter McLaren," *The School Field* vol. XII, no. 5/6 (2001), pp. 109–156; and J. Petras and H. Veltmeyer, *Hegemonia dos Estados Unidos no novo milênio* (Petrópolis: Vozes 2000). In another article, McLaren and Ramin Faramandpur put it this way: "To call globalization a form of imperialism might seem a rhetorical exaggeration. But we believe that this identification is necessary because the term *globalization* (italics in

original)) is calculated by bourgeois critics to render any radical politicization of it extreme. The ideology of this move is invisibly to enframe the
concept of globalization within a culturalistic logic that reduces it to mean
a standardization of commodities (i.e., the same designer clothes appearing
in shopping plazas throughout the world" ("Teaching against Globalization
and the new Imperialism: Toward a Revolutionary Pedagogy," *Journal of
Teacher Education* vol. 52, no. 2 (March/April 2001), p. 138).

3. Peter McLaren and Ramin Farahmandpur, "Freire, Marx, and the New
   Imperialism: Toward a Revolutionary Praxis," in Judith J. Slater, Stephan
   M. Fain, and Cesar A. Rossato (eds.), *The Freirean Legacy: Educating for
   Social Justice* (New York: Peter Lang, 2002), p. 37. See also Michel Hardt
   and Antônio Negri, *Empire* (Cambridge: Harvard University Press, 2000).
   These authors argue in favor of the concept of empire as a new face of capitalist domination. For a critical discussion of the ideas of Hardt and Negri
   based on a Latin American perspective, see Atílio Boron, *Império e imperi-
   alismo: uma leitura crítica de Michael Hardt e Antonio Negri* (Buenos Aires:
   CLACSO, 2002).
4. Nicholas C. Burbules and Carlos Alberto Torres, *Globalization and
   Education: Critical Perspective* (New York, London: Routledge, 2000),
   p. 27.
5. See Juan Ramón Capella, "Globalization, A Fading Citizenship," in ibid.,
   pp. 227–252.
6. Ibid., p. 243.
7. See Jill Blackmore, "Globalization: A Useful Concept for Feminists
   Rethinking Theory and Strategies in Education," in Burbules and Torres,
   Globalization and Education, pp. 133–156.
8. Ibid., p. 142.
9. I am referring to the text of Susan Robertson, Xavier Bonal, and Roger Dale,
   "GATS and the Education Service Industry: The Politics of Scale and Global
   Reterritorialization," *Annals of Congress of Comparative and International
   Education Society* (University of Central Florida 2002) . The authors identify four important categories for commerce in education: (a) offer to the
   outside—distance education, didactic material, specialized services that
   can cross borders of the signatory countries; (b) consumption outside the
   country: students can study in other countries; (c) commercial presence:
   international investors can open institutions in another country; (d) physical
   presence of people: possibility of people traveling between countries to offer
   educational services.
10. Jean-JacquesRousseau, *Emílio ou Da Educação* (São Paulo: Martins Fontes,
    1995), p. 91.
11. For a contrasting view on Angicos and Washington, see Moacir Gadotti,
    "Paulo Freire and the Culture of Justice and Peace: Perspective of Washington
    vs. the Perspective of Angicos," in Carlos Alberto Torres and Pedro Noguera
    (eds.), *Social Justice Education for Teachers: Paulo Freire and the Possible
    Dream* (Roterdam: Sense, 2008), pp. 147–159. The author uses the two ter-
    ritories as metaphors of distinct paradigms of civilization. "Even analyzing
    dialectically—unity and the opposition of contrary forces—these two points

of view are fundamentally irreducible, like war and peace, military and uto-pian power, fundamentalism and dialogue" (p. 148).

12. Paulo Freire, *Pedagogy of the Oppressed* (New York: Herder and Herder, 1972), p. 61.

13. Burbules and Torres, *Globalization and Education*, p. 10.

14. Robertson, Bonal, and Dale, in "GATS and the Education Service Industry," develop the notions of "space and scale" as a way to understand the decision displacements in education policies. They argue that there is a complex rela-tion between territories and scales (local, regional, national, international, global regions) and that globalization could thus be understood as the com-plex processes involving movement and fixation, scale and space.

15. Carlos Alberto Torres Novoa, "Grandezas y miserias de la educación lati-noamericana del siglo veinte" *Paulo Freire e a agenda da educação latino-americana no século XXI* (Buenos Aires: CLACSO, 2001), p. 196.

16. See Néstor G. Canclini, *Culturas híbridas: estrategías para entrar y salir de la modernidad* (México: Grijalbo, 1989).

17. Allan Luke and Carmen Luke, "A Situated Perspective on Cultural Globalization," in Burbules and Torres, *Globalization and Education*, p. 286.

18. Fazal Rizvi, "International Education and the Production of Global Imagination," in Burbules and Torres, *Globalization and Education*, p. 223. One understands the relevance of this concern based on the fact that almost half of the college students of Malaysia study in Western universities (p. 206).

19. See Danilo R. Streck, "Revisitando a educação como ação cultural" [Revisiting education as a cultural action], *Pedagogia no encontro de tem-pos* (Petrópolis: Vozes, 2001).

20. The detailed analysis by Douglas Kellner of the tumultuous North American presidential elections of 2000 confirmed the good quality of the information of a great part of the newspapers, magazines, and the Internet, when com-pared to television, which, however, continued being the great constructer (in this case, distorter) of public opinion. See Douglas Kellner, *Grand Theft 2000: Media Spectacle and a Stolen Election* (Lanhan, Boulder, New York, Oxford: Rowman & Littlefield, 2000).

21. Nicholas C. Burbules, "Does the Internet Constitute a Global Educational Community?" in Burbules and Torres, *Globalization and Education*, p. 329.

22. See Robertson, Bonal, and Dale, "GATS and the Education Service Industry," 2002.

23. Blackmore, "Globalization," p. 135.

24. The argumentation about Latin America is based on the analysis by Lourdes Benería, "The Foreign Debt Crisis and the Social Costs of Adjustments in Latin America," in John Friedmann, Rebecca Abers, and Lilian Autler (eds.), *Emergences: Women's Struggles for Livelihood in Latin America* [UCLA Latin American Studies 82 (1996)], pp. 11–27.

25. See Charles W. Mills, *The Racial Contract* (New York: Cornell University Press, 1997).

26. Benedita da Silva, "Race and Politics in Brazil," in Larry Crook and Randall Johnson (eds.), *Black Brazil: Culture, Identity, and Social Mobilization* (Los Angeles: UCLA Latin American Center Publications, 1999), p. 21.
27. Kellner, *Grand Theft 2000*, p. 152.
28. Arundhati Roy, "The Algebra of Infinite Justice," *The Guardian*, November 3, 2001.
29. Douglas Kellner, "Theorizing September 11: Social Theory, History, and Democracy" (www.ucla.edu/faculty/kellner/kellner.html) bases himself on the assumption that those who say September 11 changes everything are correct. He then shows the problem with some theories that try to explain the world: Fukuyama (the end of history); Samuel Huntington (a conflict of civilizations that end up being translated as the east-west conflict); Benjamin Barker (McWorld x Jihad, presenting a simplified view of Islam). He adopts the theory of Calmer Johnson (2000) of "blowback," that is, that the problems are basically a reaction to an equivocal North American politics. September 11 is also the end of the neoliberal fantasies that the market resolves everything. He cites as an example the support of the government for the airline companies, the public responsibility for security, and so on.
30. Noam Chomsky, *Chomsky on Miseducation* (Lanham: Rowman & Littlefield, 2000).
31. See Eduardo Galeano, "The Theatre of Good and Evil," in Roger Burbach and Ben Clarke (eds.), *September 11 and the U.S. War: Beyond the Curtain of Smoke* (San Francisco: City Lights Books, Freedom Voices, 2002).
32. Ibid., p. 11.
33. Kellner, *Grand Theft 2000*, pp. 136–143, made an analysis of the "Bushspeak," alluding to the "doublespeak" of Orwell, in which the word means the opposite: peace means war, freedom means slavery, and so on.
34. David Potorti,"Coming to a Mall Near You," in Burbach and Clarke, *September 11 and the U.S. War*, p. 99.
35. Ibid., p. 100.
36. Arundhati Roy, "War is Peace," in Burbach and Clarke, *September 11 and the U.S. War*, p. 107.
37. Burbach and Clarke, *September 11 and the U.S. War*, p. 55.
38. Roy, "War is Peace," p. 102.

2   The Latin American Pedagogical Labyrinth: A Popular Education Perspective

This chapter is based on a paper presented at the National Association Research in Education (ANPED—Associação Nacional de Pesquisa em Educação), and published in the association's journal: Danilo R. Streck, "A educação popular e a (re)construção do público: há fogo sob as brasas?" Revista Brasileira de educação 32 (2006), pp. 272–284.

1. See Walden Bello, "Fighting for the Future," in Roger Burbach and Ben Clarke (eds.), *September 11 and the U.S. War: Beyond the Curtain of Smoke* (San Francisco: City Lights Books, Freedom Voices, 2002), pp. 141–145.

2. Boaventura de Sousa Santos, "Seis Razões para Pensar," *Revista Lua Nova—Revista de Cultura e Política* 54 (2001), pp. 13–23.

3. See Raúl Zibechi, *Territorios de las periferias urbanas latinoamericanas* (Buenos Aires: Cooperativa de Trabajo Lavaca Ltd., 2008).

4. Ibid., p. 109.

5. Maria da Glória Gohn, "Movimentos sociais, políticas públicas e educação," in Edineide Jezine and Maria de Lurdes Pinto Almeida (orgs.), *Educação e movimentos sociais: novos olhare* (Campinas: Alínea, 2007), p. 37.

6. As observed by Ricardo Forster, *El laberinto de las voces argentinas: Ensayos políticos* (Buenos Aires: Colihue, 2008), p. 99: "Their [the social movement's] presence has simply been deactivated; their voice has been returned to the silence of those who lack protagonism, of those who are simply objects of commiseration and charity, but no longer of expectation or fear, owner of the spoken word fertilized by memory and resistances."

7. Alcira Argumedo, *Los silencios y las voces de América Latina: notas sobre el pensamiento nacional y popular* (Buenos Aires: Colihue, 2004), p. 184.

8. Ernesto Mays Vallenilla, "El problema de América," in Leopoldo Zea (comp.), *Fuentes de la cultura latino-americana III* (México, DF: Fondo de Cultura Economica, 1993), p. 425.

9. Hannah Arendt, *A condição humana* (Chicago: The University of Chicago Press, 2004), p. 211.

10. Valburga Schmiedt Streck, "Narrativas de gênero em famílias das camadas populares," *Ciências Sociais—UNISINOS* 40 (2004), p. 254.

11. Margarita Bonamusa, "Qué es la sociedad civil? Uma mirada a Colombia," in F. J. Londoño et al. (eds.), *Sociedad civil, control social y democracia participativa* (Bogotá: Fundación Friedrich Ebert de Colombia, 1997), p. 78.

12. See Boaventura de Sousa Santos (org.), *Conhecimento prudente para uma vida decente: "Um discurso sobre as ciências" revisitado* (São Paulo: Cortez, 2004).

13. See Raúl Leis, *La sal de los zombis* (Lima: Tarea, 1986).

14. *Apud* Enrique Dussel, *1492 O encobrimento do Outro (A origem do "mito da Modernidade")* (Petrópolis: Vozes, 1993), p. 19.

15. Alexandro Moreno Olmedo, *El aro y la trama: episteme, modernidad y pueblo* [Valencia (Venezuela): Centro de Investigaciones Populares (CIP)—Universidade de Carabobo, 1993], p. 37.

16. Argumedo, *Los silencios y las voces de América Latina*, p. 181.

17. Bartomeu Meliá, *Educação indígena e alfabetização* (São Paulo: Loyola, 1979), p. 20.

18. Argumedo, *Los silencios y las voces de América Latina*, p. 146.

19. Cristina Tramonte, *O samba conquista passagem: as estratégias e a ação educativa das escolas de samba* (Petrópolis: Vozes, 2001), p. 35.

20. Gregorio Weinberg, *Modelos educativos em la historia de América Latina* (Buenos Aires: AZ Editora, 1995), p. 70.

21. Vanilda Pereira Paiva, *Educação popular e educação de adultos: contribuição à história da educação brasileira* (São Paulo: Loyola, 1973), p. 62.

22. José Martí, *Nossa América* (São Paulo: Hucitec, 1983), p. 197.

23. Ibid., p. 183.

24. Moreno Olmedo, *El aro y la trama*, p. 461.

25. Mario Peresson Tonelli SDB, *Educar para la solidariedad planetaria: enfoque teológico-pastoral* (Santafé de Bogotá: Indo-American Press Service Limitada; Libreria Salesiana, 1994), p. 114.

26. Paulo Freire, *Pedagogia do oprimido* (Rio de Janeiro: Paz e Terra, 1981), p. 93. It is interesting to notice that the English version of *Pedagogy of the Oppressed* (New York: Herder and Herder, 1972), p. 76, does not include the last sentence: "not ending, therefore, in an I-Thou relationship." Note also that Freire still uses the masculine "men" to designate male and female, which he will revise in future writings.

27. Moacyr Scliar, *Saturno nos trópicos: a melancolia européia chega ao Brasil* (São Paulo: Companhia das Letras, 2003), p. 17.

28. Ibid., p. 244.

29. See Octavio Ianni, *O labirinto latino-americano* (Petrópolis: Vozes, 1993).

30. Rosa Maria Torres (Org.), *Educação popular: um encontro com Paulo Freire* (São Paulo: Loyola, 1987), p. 74. In another place, the definition is broadened, this time with an explicit reference to the school: "I understand popular education as an effort to mobilize, organize and train the popular classes; scientific and technical training. I understand that in this effort one cannot forget, that *power* is necessary, that is, it is necessary to transform this organization of the bourgeois power that is present, so that one can make school in a different way" [Paulo Freire and Adriano Nogueira, *Que fazer: teoria e prática em educação popular* (Petrópolis: Vozes, 1989), p. 19].

3   The New Social Contract: A Brief Map for Educators

1. See J. W. Gough, *The Social Contract: a Critical Study of its Development* (Oxford: Clarendon Press, 1936), especially the chapter "The Theory of the Social Contract Being Attacked," where the author presents a description of the questionings of this theory from Hume to Hegel and Comte.

2. Gough, after a long historical analysis of the social contract, concludes that one is forced to admit that the political obligations are not a real contract but they are similar to a contract. The expression social contract, if preserved, should be interpreted as an abbreviation to idea of political obligation, as an analogy to the contract.

3. Boaventura de Sousa Santos, "Reinventar a democracia: entre o pré-contratualismo e o pós-contratualismo," in Agnes Heller et al. (orgs.), *A crise dos paradigmas em ciências sociais e os desafios para o século XXI* (Rio de Janeiro: Contraponto, 1999), p. 34.

4. Carole Pateman, *The Sexual Contract* (Stanford: Stanford University Press, 2001), p. 1.

5. According to Michel Serres, *O contrato natural* (Rio de Janeiro: Nova Fronteira, 1991), p. 57, the social contract can be interpreted as the emergence of societies: "As mythically as we might expect, the social contract marks the beginning of societies. Due to these or those needs, some men

decide, one day, to live together and they associate; since then we no longer know how to live without each other. When, how and why this contract was- or was not—signed, we do not know, and without a doubt, will never know. It does not matter."

6. Apud Paulo J. Krischke (org.), *O contrato social ontem e hoje* (São Paulo: Cortez, 1993), p. 64.

7. Ibid., p. 65.

8. Jean-Jacques Rousseau, *Do contrato social; Ensaio sobre a origem das línguas; Discurso sobre a origem e os fundamentos da desigualdade entre os homens; Discurso sobre as ciências e as artes. Um discurso sobre as ciências e as artes*, Vitor Cívita (ed.) (São Paulo: Abril Cultural, 1983), p. 22.

9. Jean-Jacques Rousseau, *Emílio ou Da Educação* (São Paulo: Martins Fontes, 1995), p. 7.

10. See Humberto Maturana, *Emociones y lenguaje en educación y política* (Santiago: Dolmen, 1997).

11. About this issue, see also Alessandro Ferrara, *Modernity and Authenticity: A Study of the Social and Ethical Thought of Jean-Jacques Rousseau* (Albany, N.Y.: State University of New York, 1993). This author discusses a basic paradox of these theories, namely that such a state of nature would not include faculties requiring the existence of society, such as language or needs beyond a basic level of existence. On the other hand, there is still the need to differentiate men and women from other animals. In other words, the state of nature is a kind of limbo, if not an impossibility.

12. Julia Simon sees in this an unresolved dilemma of modern education that has its origins in Rousseau. She deals with this in the chapter "The Dilemma of Public Education: Individual Rights and Civic Responsibilities," *Beyond Contractual Morality: Ethics, Law and Literature in Eighteenth-Century France* (Rochester: University of Rochester Press, 2001).

13. See Rousseau's comment on the conquest of America in the *Contrato Social [The Social Contract]*: "How can a man or a nation make him or itself lord over an immense territory and deprive the whole human gender of it, if not by punishable usurpation, this being why they take away from the rest of the humans the shelter and the foods that nature gave to all in common?" (*Do contrato social*, p. 38).

14. Miguel Arroyo, "Educação em tempos de exclusão," in Pablo Gentili e Gaudêncio Frigotto (comp.), *A cidadania negada: políticas de exclusão na educação e no trabalho* (Buenos Aires: CLACSO, 2000), p. 245.

15. See Ítalo Calvino, *Por que ler os clássicos* (São Paulo: Companhia das Letras, 1993).

16. This is about transparencies that are placed one on top of the other, one with the layout of the streets, another with the localization of the institutions, and so on.

17. See Danilo R Streck, *José Martí & a Educação* (Belo Horizonte: Autêntica, 2008).

18. Domingo Faustino Sarmiento, *Educación Común* (Buenos Aires: Ediciones Solar, 1987), p. 39.

19. Richard M. Morse, *O Espelho de Próspero- Culturas e Idéias nas América* (São Paulo: Companhia das Letras, 1998), p. 13.
20. Ibid., p. 51. Abelardo's tradition, in turn, continued in the Anglo-Saxon world and is manifested in the binary and excluding argumentative form. See the article by Vítor Westhelle "Entre Américas: convergências e divergências teológicas" [Between the Americas: Theological Convergences and Divergences], unpublished. Based on Morse, he highlights the cosmopolitan character of the recent Latin American theology, derived not from a false universalism but founded on the regionality as being indicative of a true cosmopolitanism.
21. Morse, *O Espelho de Próspero- Culturas e Idéias nas América*, p. 78.
22. Ibid., p. 162.
23. See Rodolfo Kusch, *América Profunda* (Buenos Aires: BONUM, 1986).
24. Ibid., p. 11.
25. See Walter Mignolo, *La Idea de América Latina: La Herida Colonial y la Opción Decolonial* (Barcelona: Gedisa, 2005).
26. Paulo Freire, *Pedagogia do oprimido* (Rio de Janeiro: Paz e Terra, 1981), p. 7.
27. Paulo Freire, *Pedagogia da autonomia: saberes necessários à prática educativa* (São Paulo: Paz e Terra, 1996), p. 16.
28. See Paulo Freire, *Pedagogia da esperança: Um reencontro com a Pedagogia do oprimido* (Rio de Janeiro: Paz e Terra, 1992). On this topic, see also Danilo R. Streck, *Pedagogia no encontro de tempos: ensaios inspirados em Paulo Freire* (Petrópolis: Vozes, 2001).
29. See Pablo Gentili (org.), *Pedagogia da exclusão: crítica ao neoliberalismo em educação* (Petrópolis, RJ: Vozes, 1996). On neoconservatism and neoliberalism in the United States, see Peter McLaren and Nathalia Jaramillo, *Pedagogy and Praxis in the Age of Empire: Towards a New Humanism* (Roterdam: Sense, 2007).
30. Gentili, *Pedagogia da exclusão*, p. 9.
31. See Hugo Assmann, *Metáforas novas para reencontrar a educação: epistemologia e didática* (Piracicaba: Editora UNIMEP, 1996).
32. Ibid., p. 214.
33. Manuel Castells, *Fim de milênio* (São Paulo: Paz e Terra, 1999), p. 98.
34. Avelino R. Oliveira, *Marx e a exclusão* (Pelotas: Seiva, 2004), p. 146.
35. José de Souza Martins, *A sociedade vista do abismo: Novos estudos sobre exclusão, pobreza e classes sociais* (Petrópolis: Vozes, 2002), p. 14.
36. See René Lenoir, *Les Exclus* (Paris: Sutil, 1974).
37. For a discussion of this topic, see Pedro Demo, *O charme da exclusão social* (Campinas: Autores Associados, 1998).
38. Ulrich Beck, *Was ist Globalisierung? Edition Zweite Moderne* (Frankfurt am Main: Suhrkamp Verlag, 1998), p. 32.
39. Boaventura de Sousa Santos' commentary summarizes the problem as follows: "At the level of presuppositions, the general regime of values does not seem able to resist the growing fragmentation of society, divided into multiple *apartheids*, polarized along economic, social, political and cultural axes. Not only does the struggle for the common good lose meaning but the struggle for alternative definitions of what is the common good also

lose sense. The general will seems to have been transformed into an absurd proposition. In these conditions some authors even speak of the end of society" ("Reinventar a democracia, p. 41).

40. Michel Serres, *O contrato natural* (Rio de Janeiro: Nova Fronteira, 1991), p. 47.

41. Ibid., p. 62.

42. "What matters is that a new *ethos* be constructed that would permit a new communal interaction among the humans and with the other beings of the biotic, planetary and cosmic community; one which would propitiate a new enchantment confronted with the majesty of the universe and the complexity of the relations which sustain all and each one of the beings" [Leonardo Boff, *Saber cuidar: ética do humano—compaixão pela terra* (Petrópolis: Vozes, 2000), p. 27].

43. See Francisco Gutierrez e Cruz Prado, *Ecopedagogia e cidadania planetária* (São Paulo: Cortez, 1999).

44. See Moacir Gadotti, *Pedagogia da terra* (São Paulo: Petrópolis, 2000).

45. Pateman, *The Sexual Contract*, p. 1.

46. According to a dialogue with Carole Pateman in April of 2002, at UCLA (University of California, Los Angeles).

47. He uses Racial Contract (capital letters) to designate the de facto contract and "racial contract" (with quotation marks) to designate a theoretical construct equivalent to a new contract.

48. These references are situated, although indirectly, within the "resurgence of the ideal of the contract" at the end of the second half of the twentieth century. Paulo Krischke relates this resurgence to a set of crises associated with the end of the Welfare State, of the soviet style socialism, and of the authoritarian regimes of the end of the century. In the discussion there are name such as John Rawls, Robert Nosick, David Gauther, C. B. McPherson, ranging from neoliberals to neo-marxists. See Paulo J. Krischke (org.), *O contrato social ontem e hoje* (São Paulo: Cortez, 1999).

49. According to a citation from *Wall Street Journal* by Joseph D. Davey, *The New Social Contract: America's Journey from Welfare State to Police State* (Westport, CT: Praeger Publishers, 1995), p. xvi.

50. Ibid., p. 160.

51. Martin Carnoy, Derek Shearer, and Russel Rumberger, *A New Social Contract: The Economy and Government After Reagan* (New York: Harper and Row, 1983), p. 232.

52. Krischke, *O contrato social ontem e hoje*, p. 17.

53. Santos, "Reinventar a democracia," p. 60.

54. This argument is elaborated by Ulrich Beck, who explains how in this second modernity new relations of power and competition are configured, between national units on the one side and between transnational identities, actors, and processes on the other (*Was ist Globalisierung?*, p. 46).

55. Riccardo Petrella, "A urgência de um contrato social mundial face aos desafios da globalização atual: mais além das lógicas bélicas," in Cecilia I. Osowski e José L.Mello, *O ensino social da Igreja e a globalização* (São Leopoldo: Editora Unisinos, 2002), p. 20.

56. Susan George is vice president of the ATTAC (Association for Taxation of Financial Transaction to Aid Citizens), with headquarters in France. See Susan Georg, "Clusters of Crisis and a Planetary Contract," in Roger Burbach and Ben Clarke (eds.), *September 11 and the U.S. War: Beyond the Curtain of Smoke* (San Francisco: City Lights Books & Freedom Voices, 2002), pp. 155–158.
57. Ibid., p. 158.
58. Tarso Genro was elected twice as mayor of Porto Alegre for four year mandates, in 1992 and in 2000.
59. Tarso Genro, *O futuro por armar: democracia e socialismo na era globalitária* (Petrópolis: Vozes, 1999), p. 34.
60. Ibid., p. 62.

4   Emile and the Limits of Citizenship

1. Manoel Bonfim, *A América Latina—males de origem* (Rio de Janeiro: Topbooks, 1993), p. 327.
2. *Extra Classe*, SINPRO/RS, 2009.
3. Simón Rodríguez, *La Defensa de Bolívar: El Libertador del mediodia de America y sus compañeros de armas defendidos por un amigo de la causa social* (Caracas: Universidad Nacional Experimental Simón Rodríguez, Editora Rectorado, 2006), p. 192.
4. José Martí, *Educação em nossa América: Textos selecionados*, edited by de Danilo R. Streck (Ijuí: Editora Unijuí, 2007), p. 53.
5. Walter Mignolo, *La Idea de América Latina: La Herida Colonial y la Opción Decolonial* (Barcelona: Gedisa, 2005). See also Aníbal Quijano, "Colonialidade do poder e classificação social," in Boaventura de Sousa Santos and Maria de Paulo Rodrigues (eds.), *Epistemologias do Sul* (Coimbra: Almedina, 2009), pp. 73–118.
6. Mignolo, *La Idea de América Latina*, p. 36.
7. Pedro Demo, *Cidadania tutelada e cidadania assistida* (Campinas: Autores Associados, 1995), p. 7.
8. Mignolo, *La Idea de América Latina*, p. 58.
9. "They will tell us: **What can we do then?** Put aside simulation; renounce the appearance of the sciences and endeavor in the science of the realities; work, work, work, and in the concrete case, close the books and open the eyes…about life." Words of Franz Tamayo, defending a national pedagogy in Bolivia in 1910. [Franz Tamayo, *Creacion de la Pedagogia Nacional* (La Paz: Biblioteca del Sesquicentenário da República, 1975), p. 27.]
10. Jean-Jacques Rousseau, *Emílio ou Da Educação* (São Paulo: Martins Fontes, 1995), p. 12.
11. "For the classic authors, the issue of education was never separated from the issue of power. *Paideia*, pedagogy and politics always walked hand in hand. Education—from Plato and Aristotle to Jean-Jacques Rousseau, John Dewey and Paulo Freire, to mention only a few—has been considered an extension of the political project" [Carlos Alberto Torres, *Democracia,*

educação e multiculturalismo: dilemas da cidadania em um mundo global-izado (Petrópolis: Vozes, 2001), p. 252].

12. F. Cabral Pinto, *A formação humana no projecto da modernidade* (Lisboa: Instituto Piaget, 1999), p. 123.

13. This idea was developed in Danilo R. Streck, *Pedagogia no encontro de tempos [Pedagogy in the Encounter of Times]* (Petrópolis: Vozes, 2001), especially in the first chapter, where an analysis is made of Paulo Freire based on three foundational metaphors in his pedagogy: the line (transition), the rupture, and the plot.

14. Rousseau, *Emílio ou Da Educação*, p. 309.

15. The use of the masculine is intentional to signal the dimension of gender, especially as relates to the canonization of authors considered classics. Thus, Olympe de Gouges, who in 1791 wrote the "Declaration of the Rights of Women," was forgotten by history and by pedagogy. See Gabriela Bonachi and Angela Groppi, *O Dilema da Cidadania* (São Paulo: UNESP, 1995).

16. Rousseau, *Emílio ou Da Educação*, p. 248.

17. Paulo Freire, *Pedagogia do oprimido* (Rio de Janeiro: Paz e Terra, 1981), p. 29. The first two paragraphs of the Portuguese version, from where this quotation is taken, are not included in the English translation [*Pedagogy of the Oppressed* (New York: Herder and Herder, 1972)].

18. "May you last forever, for the joy of your citizens and the example of the peoples, wise republic and happily constituted" [Jean-Jacques Rousseau, *Do contrato social; Ensaio sobre a origem das línguas; Discurso sobre a origem e os fundamentos da desigualdade entre os homens; Discurso sobre as ciências e as artes. Um discurso sobre as ciências e as artes*, edited by Vitor Cívita (São Paulo: Abril Cultural, 1983), p. 221].

19. See Ítalo Calvino, *Porque ler os clássicos* (São Paulo: Companhia das Letras, 1993).

20. For an introduction to Rousseau and his pedagogy, with special emphasis on the reception of his ideas in Latin America, see Danilo R. Streck, *Rousseau & a educação* (Belo Horizonte: Autêntica, 2008).

21. Rousseau, therefore, could explain better than any other the tension between regulation and emancipation, the principles that are in the origins of modernity and are constitutive of the social contract. See Boaventura de Sousa Santos, *A crítica da razão indolente: contra o desperdício da experiência* (São Paulo: Cortez. 2000), p. 129.This is also the opinion of Carlota Boto, *A escola do homem novo: entre o Iluminismo e a Revolução Francesa* (São Paulo: Editora da Universidade Estadual Paulista, 1996), p. 26, for whom "Rousseau, journey companion in the illuminist movement, could not be confused with the movement."

22. Rousseau, *Emílio ou Da Educação*, p. 442.

23. Rousseau, *Do contrato social*, p. 376.

24. Jason Andrew Neidleman, *The General Will is Citizenship: Inquiry into French Political Thought* (New York: Rowman & Littlefield, 2001), p. 50.

25. Joel Pimentel de Ulhôa, *Rousseau e a utopia da soberania popular* (Goiânia: Editora da UFG, 1996), p. 13.

26. Rousseau, *Do contrato social*, p. 22.

27. "The paradigm of modernity is very rich and complex, as susceptible to pro-found variations as to contradictory developments. It is established on two pillars, that of regulation and that of emancipation, each one constituted by three principles or logics. The pillar of regulation is constituted by the prin-ciple of the State, formulated essentially by Hobbes, by the market principle, developed mainly by Locke and by Adam Smith, and by the principle of com-munity which dominates the whole political and social theory of Rousseau" [Boaventura de Sousa Santos, *A crítica da razão indolente: contra o des-perdício da experiência* (São Paulo: Cortez, 2000), p. 50]. Raul Pont sees in Rousseau the expounder of the egalitarian liberal chain of thought, in the same way as Locke would be for the proprietary chain of thought. See Nilton Bueno Fischer and Jacqueline Moll (eds.), *Por uma nova esfera pública: a experiência do orçamento participativo* (Petrópolis: Vozes, 2000).

28. Richard M. Morse, *O Espelho de Próspero- Culturas e Idéias nas Américas* (São Paulo: Companhia das Letras, 1998), p. 92.

29. A second flourishing of Rousseau's ideas occurred during the populist decades (1920–1960) when the incipient industrialization and urbaniza-tion generated expectations of inclusion and participation, respectively of co-option by the dominant class. This observation is especially relevant for our study of the approximation between Rousseau and Freire, considering that it was in the decade of the 1950s that Paulo Freire began his trajectory as educator among the population that migrated to the city seeking better living conditions and among the peasants.

30. Tamayo, *Creacion de la Pedagogia Nacional*, p. 54.

31. The author collects information from various countries in an audacious and ambitious project. The study terminates abruptly upon the recognition of the vastness of the task: "Maybe in a somewhat unexpected way the study of the influence of Rousseau in the independence of Latin America ends here—for erudite reasons" [Boleslao Lewin, *Rousseau en la independencia de Latinoamerica* (Buenos Aires: Depalma), 1980, p. 157]. This recognition is an interesting stimulus for continuing the task.

32. Ibid., p. 32.

33. It is not suggested that *Emile* was politically and religiously less "danger-ous." Proof of this is that it was prohibited by the Parliament of Paris, according to the decree of 6.9.1762, and the edition burned publicly. One of the most fought against points is the discourse of the savoyan priest in which Rousseau directed very hard criticisms against the Church of his time.

34. For an analysis of Rousseau's influence on Artigas, see Carlos Andrés Montalvo, *Rousseau y el contrato social oriental* (Montevidéu: s.n., 1989).

35. Lewin, *Rousseau en la independencia de Latinoamerica*, p. 124.

36. A study by Carla Hesse presents a listing of the editions of Rousseau's works, and it is interesting to note that between 1789 and 1800 there appears no edi-tion in Portuguese or Spanish. To be highlighted are Paris and Switzerland, with editions also from Holland, Germany, and England. This fact seems to confirm Morse's hypothesis with respect to the vagueness in the reception of Rousseau's ideas. Carla Hesse, *Revolutionary Rousseaus: A Study in Dissemination and Reception* (European History & Culture Colloquium, 2002).

37. Simón Bolívar, "Proclamas y discursos del Libertador" apud Nikolaus Wertz, *Pensamiento sociopolítico moderno en América Latina* (Caracas: Editorial Nueva Sociedad, 1995), p. 39.

38. See Ricardo Velez Rodríguez, *Estado, cultura y sociedad em la América Latina* (Santafé de Bogotá: Fundación Universidad Central, 2000).

39. See Gregório Weinberg, *Modelos educativos em la historia de America Latina* (Buenos Aires: AZ Editora, 1995), especially chapter 4, "Emancipación."

40. On the issue of "structured blindness," see Charles W. Mills, *The Racial Contract* (New York: Cornell University Press, 1997).

41. Rousseau, *Emílio ou Da Educação*, p. 233.

42. Daniel Defoe, *Robinson Crusoe* (London: J. M. Dent. 1994), 163.

43. Ibid., p. 170.

44. José Enrique Rodó, *Ariel* (Buenos Aires: Sopena, 1949), p. 120.

45. Roberto Fernandez Retamar, *Caliban: Apuntes sobre la cultura en nuestra América* (México, D.F.: Editorial Diógenes, 1974), p. 35.

46. William Shakespeare, *The Tempest*, edited by Virginia M. Vaughan and Alden T. Vaughan (London: Arden, 2000).

47. Emanuelle Amodio, *Formas de la Alteridad: Construcción y difusón de la imagen del indio americano en Europa durante el primer siglo de la conquista de América* (Quito: Ediciones Abya-Yala), 1993, makes an interesting study about the images of the Indian and their diffusion during the period of the conquest of America, relating these images with conceptions of the Other in the form of mythical figures that were already developing throughout the Middle Ages, generally in semihuman forms. Her perspective is that "the Other is constituted as a mirror of the humanity of the subject. Its negativity lays the foundation for the possibility of the *I*." This being a universal phenomenon, all societies would be, to a greater or lesser degree, necessarily ethnocentric.

48. Hèléne de Castres, apud González Monteiro de Espinosa y Marisa González Monteiro de Espinosa, *La Ilustración y el hombre americano. Descripciones etnológicas de la Expedición Malaspina* (Madrid: Consejo Superior de Investigaciones Científicas, 1992), p. 13.

49. Enrique Dussel, *1492: El encubrimiento del Otro: El origen del mito de la modernidad* (Santafé de Bogotá: Antropos, 1992), p. 51. In the same line of thought, Vítor Westhelle analyzes how from the theological point of view it can be affirmed that "there is no sin south of the Equator." It is as if the peoples that live there are out of the range covered by the idea of good and evil. See Vítor Westhelle, *Voces de protesta en América Latina* (Chicago: Lutheran School of Theology at Chicago, 2000) specially the chapter "El tamaño del Paraíso; o, por qué no existiría el pecado al sur del Ecuador? [The size of Paradise ; or, why sin would not exist south of the Equator?]"

50. Rousseau, *Emílio ou Da Educação*, p. 31.

51. Bernardette Baker, "(Ap)pointing the Canon: Rousseau's Émile, Visions of the State, and Education," *Educational Theory*, vol. 51, n. 1 (2001), pp. 1–43.

52. Rousseau, *Emílio ou Da Educação*, p. 8.

53. Julia Simon, *Beyond Contractual Morality: Ethics, Law and Literature in Eighteenth-Century France* (Rochester, N.Y.: University of Rochester Press, 2001), p. 44.

54. Rousseau, *Emílio ou Da Educação*, p. 314.
55. Jean Starobinski, *Jean-Jacques Rousseau: a transparência e o obstáculo* (São Paulo: Cia das Letras, 1991), p. 223.
56. Rousseau, *Emílio ou Da Educação*, p. 12.
57. See Bogdan Suchodolski, *A pedagogia e as grandes correntes filosóficas: a pedagogia da essência e a pedagogia da existência* (Lisboa: Livros Horizonte, 1984).
58. See Moacir Gadotti, *História das idéias pedagógicas* (São Paulo: Ática, 2001).
59. See Adriana Puiggrós, *Volver a educar: el desafío de la enseñanza argentina a finales del siglo XX* (Buenos Aires: Companía Editora Espasa Calpe/Ariel, 1995).
60. Rousseau, *Emílio ou Da Educação*, p. 15.
61. Francisco Cock Fontanella, "Ensaio de pedagogia comparada: Jean-Jacques Rousseau (1712–1778) x Immanuel Kant (1724–1804)," *Comunicações* vol. 7 (2000), p. 113.
62. See Ulhôa, *Rousseau e a utopia da soberania popular.*
63. Galvano Della Volpe, *Rousseau and Marx* (London: Lawrence and Wishart, 1978), p. 30.
64. Maria Luiza Ribeiro Ferreira, *Também há mulheres filósofas* (Lisboa: Editorial Caminho, 2001), p. 107.
65. Rousseau, *Emílio ou Da Educação*, p. 496.
66. Ibid., p. 680.

5   Autonomy Revisited: From Rousseau to Freire

1. See Ana Maria Araújo Freire (org.), *Pedagogia da libertação em Paulo Freire* [*Pedagogy of Liberation in Paulo Freire*] (São Paulo: Editora UNESP, 1999). The book, organized on the occasion of thirty years of *Pedagogy of the Oppressed*, contains many testimonies of encounters with this central text in the work of Freire.
2. Edson Passetti, *Conversação libertária com Paulo Freire* (São Paulo: Imaginário, 1998), p. 46.
3. See Antônio Flávio Pierucci, *Ciladas da diferença* (São Paulo: Editora 34, 1999).
4. Paulo Freire, "Anotações sobre unidade na diversidade," *Política e educação* (São Paulo: Cortez, 1993), p. 35.
5. *Educação como prática da liberdade* was published in 1967 and presents in detail the original process of literacy training. The text was based on his academic thesis and was finished in Chile. In English, *Education as Practice of Freedom* was published together with *Extensão ou Comunicação* [*Extension or Communication*] in *Education for Critical Consciousness* (New York: Seabury Press, 1973).
6. Paulo Freire, *Educação como prática da liberdade* (Rio de Janeiro: Paz e Terra, 1980), p. 46.
7. About his exile in Chile, see Augusto Nivaldo Triviños and Balduíno Andreola, *Freire e Fiori no exílio: um projeto pedagógico-político no Chile*

[*Freire and Fiori in Exile: A Pedagogical-Political Project in Chile*] (Porto Alegre: Ritter dos Reis, 2001).

8. *Jornal Utopia* Informativo do Centro Paulo Freire [Paulo Freire Center News Bulletin] 5 (Nov./Dec. 2001).

9. For biographic and bibliographic data on Freire, see Moacir Gadotti, *Paulo Freire: uma biobibliografia* (São Paulo: Cortez, 1996); Ana Maria Araújo Freire, *Paulo Freire: uma história de vida* (São Paulo: Villa das Letras, 2006); Danilo R. Streck, Euclides Redin, and Jaime J. Zitkoski, *Dicionário Paulo Freire* (Belo Horizonte: Autêntica, 2010).

10. Paulo Freire e Adriano Nogueira, "Apresentação" *Que fazer: teoria e prática em educação popular* (Petrópolis: Vozes, 1989).

11. Benedito Cintra, *Paulo Freire entre o grego e o semita* (Porto Alegre: EDIPUCRS, 1998), when reviewing the topic, proposes a return to the Semitic perspective of the other as an absolute, which places the subject beyond the dichotomy of "antagonism" and "non-antagonism." Based on Levinas, he invites reading the theme of democracy in Paulo Freire from the point of view of the "Infinite desire of the other."

12. See Paulo Freire, *Pedagogia da esperança: Um reencontro com a Pedagogia do oprimido* (Rio de Janeiro: Paz e Terra, 1992).

13. For an analysis of the criticisms of Paulo Freire from the postmodern point of view, with the respective attempts at answers, see Peter Roberts, *Education, Literacy, and Humanization: Exploring the Work of Paulo Freire* (Westport, Connecticut: Bergin & Garvey, 2000).

14. Freire, *Pedagogia da esperança*, p. 81.

15. Danilo R. Streck, *Pedagogia no encontro de tempos: ensaios inspirados em Paulo Freire* (Petrópolis: Vozes, 2001), p. 30.

16. Peter McLaren, *Che Guevara, Paulo Freire, and the Pedagogy of Revolution* (New York: Rowman & Littlefield Publishers, 2000), p. 103.

17. Jean-Jacques Rousseau, *Do contrato social; Ensaio sobre a origem das línguas; Discurso sobre a origem e os fundamentos da desigualdade entre os homens; Discurso sobre as ciências e as artes. Um discurso sobre as ciências e as artes*, edited by Vitor Civita (São Paulo: Abril Cultural, 1983), p. 243.

18. Peter McLaren and Farahmandpur, "Critical Pedagogy, Postmodernism, and the Retreat from Class," in Dave Hill, Peter McLaren, Mike Cole, and Glenn Rikowski (eds.), *Postmodernism in Educational Theory: Education and the Politics of Human Resistance* (London: Tufnell, 1999), p. 185.

19. "The conception of autonomy present in this work is tied to *cooperative independence,* which the involved agents, *problematized by authorities,* are capable of carrying out; it is tied to the capacity of assuming positions of solidarity and collective construction which attend common goals, with the necessary mediation of individual elaborations" (emphasis in the original) [Gomercindo Ghiggi, *A Pedagogia da Autoridade a serviço da Liberdade: diálogos com Paulo Freire e professores em formação* (Pelotas: Seiva, 2002), p. 120].

20. See Johann Heinrich Pestalozzi, *Lienhard un Gertrud* (Bad Heilbrunn: Klinkhardt, 1993).

21. Jean-Jacques Rousseau, *Emile ou Da Educação* (São Paulo: Martins Fontes, 1995), p. 490.

22. Ibid., pp. 548, 500.
23. Ibid., p. 514.
24. Ibid., p. 501.
25. Ibid., p. 520. For a more detailed elaboration of this subject, see Danilo R. Streck, *Rousseau & a educação* (Belo Horizonte: Autêntica, 2008).
26. Rousseau, *Emile ou Da Educação*, p. 573.
27. For an explicitation of this theme, see Danilo R. Streck, "The Utopian Legacy: Rousseau and Freire," in Carlos Alberto Torres and Pedro Noguera (eds.), *Social Justice Education for Teachers* (Roterdam: Sense, 2008), pp. 69–80.
28. Paulo Freire, "Concientizar para liberar (Nociones sobre la palabra conscienización)" ["*Concientizar* to liberate (Notions about the word *conscienización*)]. Originally it was a conference of Freire's in Cuernavaca (Mexico), in the Intercultural Documentation Center (Centro Intercultural de Documentación (CIDOC). Carlos Alberto Torres Novoa, *La praxis educativa de Paulo Freire* (Mexico: Ediciones Gernika, 1977), p. 112.
29. Conference at UCLA (April 14, 2002) with the title "The Structure of Messianic Time." His comprehension is inspired by the distinction between historic time and messianic time in Walter Benjamin. According to Richard Wolin, *Walter Benjamin: an Aesthetics of Redemption* (Berkeley: University of California Press, 1994), p. 51: "Benjamin counterposes now-time, 'which is shot through with chips of Messianic time,' to the homogeneous time of the historical era, which he equates with the notion of eternal repetition or *myth*. Man stands under the domination of mythical fate when his powers of remembrance fail him: that is, he is condemned to repeat. The recurrence of myth in unredeemed historical life remains an object of theoretical attack throughout Benjamin's writings" (emphasis in the original). The author continues describing how in the end of history, conceived as a mound of ruins, there is the light of the Redemption, the Paradise, that interpenetrates history and at the same time distances itself.
30. Usually translated as untested feasibility. See Ana Maria Araújo Freire, "Inédito viável," in Danilo R. Streck, Euclides Redin, and Jaime J. Zitkoski (eds.), *Dicionário Paulo Freire* (Belo Horizonte: Autêntica, 2010).
31. Paulo Freire, *Cartas a Cristina* (Rio de Janeiro: Paz e Terra, 1994), p. 192.
32. See Leonardo Boff, "Transcendência," in Streck, Redin, and Zitkoski, *Dicionário Paulo Freire*.
33. Freire, *Pedagogia da esperança*, p. 91.
34. Balduíno Andreola, "Carta-prefácio a Paulo Freire," in Paulo Freire (ed.), *Pedagogia da indignação: cartas pedagógicas e outros escritos* (São Paulo: Editora UNESP, 2000), p. 24.
35. Peter McLaren, *Che Guevara, Paulo Freire, and the Pedagogy of Revolution* (Lanham: Rowman & Littlefeld, 2000), p. 170.
36. Carlos Alberto Torres Novoa, "Grandezas y miserias de la educación latinoamericana del siglo veinte," in Carlos A. Torres (org.), *Paulo Freire e a agenda da educação latino-americana no século XXI* (Buenos Aires: CLACSO, 2001), p. 45.
37. See Jaime Zitkoski, *Horizontes da (re)fundamentação em educação popular: um diálogo entre Freire e Habermas* (Frederico Westphalen: Ed.URI,

2000); Raymon A. Morrow and Carlos Alberto Torres, *Reading Freire and Habermas: Critical Pedagogy and Transformative Social Change* (New York: Teacher College Press, 2002).

38. Paulo Freire, *Pedagogia da indignação: cartas pedagógicas e outros escritos* (São Paulo: Editora UNESP, 2000), p. 112.

39. Passetti, *Conversação libertária com Paulo Freire*, p. 67.

40. Enrique Dussel, *Ética da libertação na idade da globalização e da exclusão* (Petrópolis: Vozes, 2000), p. 441.

41. Passetti, *Conversação libertária com Paulo Freire*, p. 94.

42. See Lucía Coral Aguirrre Muñoz, "The Globalization of Capital, Critical Pedagogy, and the Aftermath of September 11: An Interview with Peter McLaren," *The School Field* vol. XII, no. 5/6 (2001), pp. 109–156.

43. Passetti, *Conversação libertária com Paulo Freire*, p. 99.

6 *Conscientização*: Genesis and Dimensions of Critical Consciousness

1. The ISEB became extinct with the military coup in 1964 and many of its members were exiled from Brazil.

2. Paulo Freire, "Conscientizing as a Way of Liberation," in LADOCII, April 1972, 29a, p. 1. In the same article Freire mentions that it was D. Hélder Câmara, archbishop of Recife, who popularized the term and gave it currency in English.

3. Paulo Freire, *Pedagogia da Autonomia* (São Paulo: Paz e Terra, 1996), p. 60.

4. Paulo Freire, *Pedagogia da indignação: cartas pedagógicas e outros escritos* (São Paulo: Editora UNESP, 2000), p. 61. In an interview for TV PUC, with Luciana Burlamaqui, a few days before he died, he expressed the same idea with an enormous plasticity. Here is the transcription of the text: "I am absolutely happy to be alive yet and to accompany this march, which like other historical marches reveals the impetus of the loving will to change the world, of this march of the so-called 'land-less.' I would die happy if I could see Brazil, full, in its historical time, of marches. Marches of those who have no schools, march of those who failed, march of those who want to love but can not. March of those who refuse a servile obedience. March of those who rebel, march of those who want to be and are prohibited to be. I think that, in the end, the marches are historic walks through the world and the land-less constitute for me today, one of the strongest expressions of the political and civic life of this nation (...) What they are doing, once more, is proving certain theoretical affirmations of political analysts, that it is really necessary to fight to obtain a minimum of transformation" (transcribed by Vítor Schütz).

5. Ibid., p. 63.

6. See Lucineide de B. Medeiros, Jaime J.Zitkoski, and Danilo R.Streck, "Movimentos sociais/movimento popular," in Danilo R. Streck, Euclides

Redin, and Jaime J. Zitkoski (orgs.), *Dicionário Paulo Freire* (Belo Horizonte: Autêntica, 2010), p. 274.

7. See Carlos Rodrigues Brandão, *De angicos a Ausentes: 40 anos de educação popular* (Porto Alegre: MOVA-RS; CORAG, 2001).

8. Francisco C. Weffort, "Educação e política: Reflexões sociológicas sobre uma pedagogia da Liberdade," in Paulo Freire (ed.), *Educação como prática da liberdade* (Rio de Janeiro: Paz e Terra, 1980), p. 24.

9. The first edition of the book *Educação como prática da liberdade*, in which is found this preface by Francisco Weffort, is from 1967.

10. Weffort, "Educação e política," p. 4.

11. For an analysis of this period, see Afolso Celso Scocuglia, *Educação Popular: do sistema Paulo Freire aos IPMs da ditadura* (João Pessoa: Editora Universitária/UFPB, 2000). According to this author, among the main movements implanted in the Northeast, between 1960 and 1964, the following deserve highlighting: o Movimento de Cultura Popular (MCP) [The Popular Culture Movement] created in May of 1960, in the Prefecture of Recife (government of Arraes); the campaign "De Pé no Chão Também se Aprende a Ler" [Barefoot one also Learns to Read], under the auspices of the Prefecture of Natal (RN), instituted in February of 1961; the Movimento de Educação de Base (MEB) [Basic Education Movement] of the CNBB [National Council of Brazilian Bishops] in partnership with the federal government, instituted in March of 1961 in various states.

12. Paulo Freire, "Entrevista," *Teoria & Debate* 17 (1992), p. 36.

13. Paulo Freire, *Pedagogia da esperança* (Rio de Janeiro: Paz e Terra, 1992), p. 37.

14. Freire, "Entrevista," p. 28.

15. See Augusto Nivaldo Silva Triviños and Balduíno Antonio Andreola, *Freire e Fiori no exílio: um projeto pedagógico-político no Chile* (Porto Alegre: Editora Ritter dos Reis, 2001).

16. See "Pablo Freire en Bolivia," *Fé y pueblo* año IV, n. 16 y 17 (1987), pp. 3–9.

17. Paulo Freire, *Pedagogy of the Oppressed* (New York: Herder and Herder, 1972), p. 27.

18. See Carlos Rodrigues Brandão and Raiane Assumpção, *Cultura rebelde: Escritos sobre Educação Popular ontem e agora* (São Paulo: Ed, L, 2009).

19. In *Pedagogia da Esperaça [Pedagogy of Hope]* (Rio de Janeiro: Paz e Terra, 1992), p. 66, there is a remarkable description of his reaction to the letters he received in the seventieth < from women denouncing the discriminatory language. "In this sense I made explicit at the beginning of these commentaries [about *Pedagogy of the Oppressed*] my debt to those women, whose letters I unfortunately also lost, for making see how much language has an ideology. (...) Then I wrote to all of them, one by one, confirming the receipt of their letters and thanking for the excellent contribution they had given."

20. See Balduíno A. Andreola and Mario Bueno Ribeiro, *Andarilho da esperança: Paulo Freire no CMI* (São Paulo: ASTE, 2005).

21. See Danilo R. Streck, *Correntes pedagógicas: uma abordagem interdisciplinar* (Petrópolis: Vozes, 2004); Matthias Preiswerk, *Educación popular y teologias de la liberación* (San José (C.R.): DEI, 1994).

22. With regard to this, see the analysis of Pedro Pontual, "Os movimentos sociais e a construção de políticas públicas nos espaços locais," in Liana Borges and Sérgio Vieira Brandão (orgs.), *Diálogos com Paulo Freire* (Tramandaí: Isis, 2005): "It is important to state that the intervention of the social movements in the perspective of the construction of public policies is a recent dimension of their actions which emerges as of the decade of the 80's, impacting the process of re-democratization of the country. It was in the decade of the 80's that the social movements developed a new comprehension about the State and about their autonomy in relation to it. A relation of necessary complementarity becomes evident between the autonomous organization in civil society and its propositional capacity with regard to public policies. The strategy of its actions begins to combine its autonomous organization with the dispute in the institutional space around public policies, both with regard to their formulation as well as with regard to their control and management" (p. 46).

23. See Giovanni Semeraro, "Libertação e hegemonia: chaves de filosofia política na educação brasileira," in Artemis Torres, Giovanni Semeraro, and Luiz Augusto Passos (orgs.), *Educação: Fronteira política* (Cuiabá: EdUFMT, 2006), pp. 19–36.

24. See Peter Mayo, "Antonio Gramsci and Paulo Freire: Some Connections and Contracts," in Carlos Alberto Torres and Pedro Noguera (eds.), *Social Justice Education for Justice: Paulo Freire and the Possible Dream* (Roterdam: Sense, 2008), pp. 51–68.

25. Lula was elected for two consecutive mandates, exercising the presidency of the Republic from 2003 to 2010.

26. About the relation between social movements, parties, and education in Freire, see Afonso Celso Scocuglia, *A história das idéias de Paulo Freire e a atual crise de paradigmas* (João Pessoa: Editora Universitária, 1997), pp. 91–96.

27. Paulo Freire, *Utopia e poder* (São Paulo: PUC, 1984), p. 6.

28. See Ana Lúcia Souza de Freitas, *Pedagogia da conscientização: um legado de Paulo Freire à formação de professores* (Porto Alegre: EDIPUCRS, 2001).

29. Brandão and Assumpção, *Cultura rebelde*, p. 75.

30. "I do not have any, any doubt that *sooner than many think, the men and the women of the world will re-invent new ways of fighting which we can not even imagine now*" [Paulo Freire, *El grito manso* (Buenos Aires: Siglo Veintiuno, 2009), p. 75].

31. Freire, *Pedagogia da indignação*, p. 44.

32. See the concise formulation, frequently quoted from *Pedagogia da Autonomia*, p. 30: "In truth, only one who thinks correctly, even though one sometimes thinks incorrectly, can teach to think correctly. And one of the necessary conditions for thinking correctly is not to be overly certain of our certainties."

33. Published in the United States as *Pedagogy of the Heart* (New York: Continuum, 2000).

34. Paulo Freire, *À sombra desta mangueira* (São Paulo: Olho d'Água, 1995), p. 17.

35. Freire, *Pedagogia da indignação*, p. 129; *Pedagogia da Autonomia*, p. 1.

36. Freire, *Pedagogia do Oprimido*, p. 27. In the English version [Pedagogy of the Oppressed] there are omitted the two first paragraphs of the Portuguese version, where Paulo Freire makes the connection of *Pedagogia do oprimido* with the previous book *Educação como prática da Liberdade*, published in Brazil in 1969 and in the United States in 1973 with the title *Education for Critical Consciousness* (New York: Seabury Press).

37. Freire, *Pedagogia da Autonomia*, p. 36.

38. Apud Euclides Redin, "Boniteza," in Streck, Redin, and Zitkoski, *Dicionário Paulo Freire*, p. 60.

39. Translator's note: In Portuguese the term *boniteza* has more of a popular connotation whereas *beleza* is more erudite, elite, and classic. The same does not occur in English. Here we could maybe contrast "beauty" with "prettiness" where beauty, though more classic, also has a much wider range of meanings than prettiness, which is more superficial.

40. Freire, *Pedagogia da Autonomia*, p. 80.

41. Thiago de Mello, "Poesia," in Streck, Redin, and Zitkoski, *Dicionário Paulo Freire*, p. 319.

42. Thiago de Mello, "Canção para os fonemas de alegria," in Freire, *Educação como prática da liberdade*, pp. 27–28.

7   Citizenship Can Be Learned: Participatory Budgeting as a Pedagogical Process

1. Peter Burke, "Democracy and Citizenship," Lyman H. Legters, John P. Burke, and Arthur diQuattro (eds.), *Critical Perspectives on Democracy* (Lanham: Rowman & Littlefield, 1994), p. 59.

2. See Hannah Arendt, "A crise da educação," *Entre o passado e o futuro* (São Paulo: Perspectiva, 1992), pp. 221–247.

3. See Richard Sennet, *The Fall of Public Man* (New York: Alfred A. Knopf, 1977).

4. "Life 'likes itself'. That is why the educators should analyze how the life of their students is a concrete life which, in its most profound vital and cognitive dynamism, has always liked itself or, at least, tried and tries again to like itself." (Hugo Assmann, *Metáforas novas para reencontrar a educação: epistemologia e didática* Piracicaba: Editora UNIMEP 1996, p. 151.)

5. For an analysis of the theoretical assumptions of participatory budgeting, see Félix Sánchez, *Orçamento Participativo: teoria e prática* (São Paulo: Cortez, 2002).

6. See the books *A participação em São Paulo*, organized by Leonardo Avritzer (São Paulo: Editora UNESP, 2004); *A inovação democrática no Brasil,* organized by Leonardo Avritzer and Zander Navarro (São Paulo: Cortez, 2003); *Democratizar a democracia: os caminhos da democracia participativa* (Rio de Janeiro: Civilização Brasileira, 2003); *Dizer a sua palavra: Educação cidadã, Pesquisa Participante e Orçamento Público* organized by Danilo R. Streck, Edla Eggert, and Emil Sobottka (Pelotas: Seiva, 2005).

7. Partido dos Trabalhadores [*Workers Party*].

8. Boaventura de Sousa Santos, "Reinventar a democracia: entre o pré-contratualismo e o pós-contratualismo," in Agnes Heller et al. (orgs.), *A crise dos paradigmas em ciências sociais e os desafios para o século XXI* (Rio de Janeiro: Contraponto, 1999), p. 69.
9. Luciano Fedozzi, *Orçamento Participativo: Reflexões sobre a experiência de Porto Alegre* (Porto Alegre: Tomo Editorial, 1999), p. 107.
10. Meeting of participatory budgeting councilors in Porto Alegre.
11. This is actually the present process of Popular Consultation in the state of Rio Grande do Sul, when on a predetermined date people may vote for given projects, either casting their vote on indicated places or through Internet. In Porto Alegre, participatory budgeting is still practiced, probably being the most lasting experience.
12. *Real* is the Brazilian currency. One real corresponds to approximately U$ 0.60.
13. This information confirms Rebecca Abers' finding that people do not mobilize only to react to difficult conditions or injustices, but also for better living conditions for them and for others (Rebecca Abers, *Inventando a democracia: distribuição de recursos públicos através da participação popular em Porto Alegre, RGS (*http://www.portoweb.com.br/ong/cidade/texto2.htm)
14. Nilton Bueno Fischer and Jacqueline Moll (Orgs.), *Por uma nova esfera pública: a experiência do orçamento participativo* Petrópolis: Vozes 2000, p.147.
15. In dialogue with the research team.
16. See Marco Raul Mejia and Miriam Awad, *Pedagogías y medologías en Educación Popular: la negociación cultura: una búsqueda* (Bogotá: CINEP s/d).
17. A typical tee from the gaucho culture in South Brazil.
18. For a more developed version of this topic, see Danilo R. Streck, "Beteiligung von Kindern und Jugendlichen im Bürgerhaushalt in brasilianisher Städte," in Thomas Ködelpeter und Ulrich Nitschke (hrsh.), *Jugendliche planen und gestalten Lebenswelten: Partizipation als Antwort auf den gesellschftlichen Wandel* (Wiesbaden: VS Verlag für Sozialwissenschaften, 2008).
19. The Participatory Budget of Fortaleza, in turn, combines territorial assemblies with assemblies according to "social segments," and youth and children and adolescents are two of these social segments. The *OP-Criança*, which has existed in Fortaleza since 2006, foresees meetings at schools and in public spaces, in an attempt to extend its own public space beyond the classroom.
20. Ângela Antunes (org.), *Orçamento Participativo Criança* (São Paulo: Instituto Paulo Freire, 2004), p. 83.
21. In Spanish, "presencia ligera" meaning to be there for and with the children and youths, but in such as way as to not obstruct their protagonism. César Muñoz, *Vivir, educar: desde la seducción, el amor y la pasión* (Barcelona: Centro de Investigaciones Pedagógicas de la Infancia, Adolescencia y la Juventud, 2003), p. 11.
22. Antunes, *Orçamento Participativo Criança*, p. 31.
23. See Arundhati Roy, *O deus das pequenas coisas* (São Paulo: Companhia das Letras, 1998).

24. Antunes, *Orçamento Participativo Criança*, p. 111.
25. Ibid., p. 122.
26. Ibid., p. 123.
27. "Participatory budgeting was not invented in a government Office or in a committee. It is the result of popular struggles ever since the FRACAB (Rio Grande do Sul Federation of Community Associations of Friends of Neighborhoods), in 1959. In 1983 the UAMPA (Union of Residents' Associations of Porto Alegre) was founded, and then low income neighborhood [*vila*] associations, welfare associations, cultural and recreational associations, which took on the commitment to fight for a better life and for a fairer society" [Sérgio Baierle, "Experiência do Orçamento participativo: um oásis no deserto neoliberal?" *De olho no orçamento* 6 (1998)].
28. Ilse Scherer-Warren, *Cidadania sem fronteiras: ações coletivas na era da globalização* (São Paulo: Hucitec, 1999), p. 63, distinguishes two types of participation in the last decades: during the military dictatorship the participatory movements tried to get as far away as possible from the state; after the democratic opening, the civil movements tried to articulate with the governments, especially at the local and municipal levels. One could add a third type of participation, this one promoted by the state and civil society, in collaboration, as in the case of participatory budgeting.
29. About the use of participatory budgeting in governments that do not belong to the PT, see Valdemir Pires, *Orçamento Participativo: o que é, para que serve, como se faz* (Piracicaba: Edição do Autor, 1999), p. 53.
30. L.S. Vygotsky, *A formação social da mente: o desenvolvimento dos processos psicológicos superiores* (São Paulo: Martins Fontes, 1991), p. 28.
31. Hugo Assmann, *Reencantar a educação: rumo à sociedade aprendente* (Petrópolis: Vozes 1998), p. 21.
32. Jean-Jacques Rousseau, *Do contrato social; Ensaio sobre a origem das línguas; Discurso sobre a origem e os fundamentos da desigualdade entre os homens; Discurso sobre as ciências e as artes. Um discurso sobre as ciências e as arte* (São Paulo: Abril Cultural, 1983), p. 118.
33. See Gabriel García Márquez, "La Proclama: por un país al alcance de los niños," in Misión de la Ciencia, Educación y Desarrollo *Colombia: al filo de la oportunidad* (Bogotá: Magisterio: 1994).

8   Pedagogy of the New Social Contract: A Few Agendas

1. Jean Jacques Rousseau, *Emilio ou Da Educação* (São Paulo: Martins Fontes, 1995), p. 9.
2. See Émile Durkheim, *Educação e sociologia* (São Paulo: Melhoramentos, 1975).
3. Rubem Alves, *Lições de Feitiçaria* (São Paulo: Loyola, 2000), p. 11.
4. See Werner Jaeger, "Introdução," *Paidéia: a formação do homem grego* (São Paulo: Martins Fontes, 2001).
5. Hans-Jürgen Fraas, *Bildung uns Menschenbild in theologischer Perspektive* (Göttingen: Vanderhoek & Rupprecht, 2000), p. 43.

6. Ibid., p. 155.
7. Carlos Rodrigues Brandão, *A Educação Popular na Escola Cidadã* (Rio de Janeiro: Vozes, 2002), p. 334.
8. Ibid., p. 335.
9. "America is triply *incommunicado*, by geopolitical frontiers, by abysses between social classes, by barriers that separate revolutionary America from the populist and neoliberal ones" [Luis Britto García, *Conciencia de América Latina: intelectuales, medios de comunicación y poder* (Caracas: Editorial Nueva Sociedad, 2002), p. 21].
10. See Cintio Vitier, *Martí en Lezama* (La Habana: CEM, 2000).
11. José Martí, *La Edad de Oro* (Ciudad de La Habana: Editorial Pueblo y Educación, 1994), p. 2.
12. Hugo Assmann, *Metáforas novas para reencontrar a educação*: epistemologia e didática Piracicaba : Editora UNIMEP 1996, p.97.
13. Ibid., p. 99.
14. Boaventura de Sousa Santos, "Seis Razões para Pensar," *Revista Lua Nova—Revista de Cultura e Política* 54 (2001), p. 17.
15. Danilo R. Streck, *Pedagogia no encontro de tempos: ensaios inspirados em Paulo Freire* (Petrópolis: Vozes, 2001), p. 122.
16. Brandão, *A Educação Popular na Escola Cidadã*, p. 359.
17. McMurtry bases this argumentation on the *Second Treaty on Government*, of 1690.
18. "He that in obedience to the command of God subdued, tilled, and sowed any part of the earth, thereby annexed to something that was his property, which another had no title to, nor could without injury take from him…He (God) gave it (the earth) to use of the industrious and rational…and labor was to be his title to it" [John Locke and John McMurtry, *Unequal Freedoms: The Global Market as an Ethical System* (Toronto: Garamond, 1998), p. 89].
19. "The defining principle of money-to-more-money circuit is that it is not bound by any national base of control or by any requirement to commit itself to any lifeserving function. It demands only to acquire maximally more money with no conversion into sustenance or service to life in between" (McMurtry, *Unequal Freedoms*, p. 301).
20. See Tarso Genro, "Estado mercado e democracia no 'olho'da crise," in Henrique Rattner (org.), *Brasil no limar do século XXI* (São Paulo: Edusp, 2000).
21. George Soros, *George Soros on Globalization* (New York: Public Affairs, 2002), p. 155.
22. *Los Angeles Times*, April 22, 2002, A 13.
23. Noam Chomsky, *Understanding Power: The Indispensable Chomsky*, Edited by Peter R. Mitchell and John Schoeffel (New York: The New York Press, 2002), p. 200.
24. Locke and McMurtry, *Unequal Freedoms*, p. 24.
25. "Actually, however, the struggle in favor of the hungry, destroyed nordestinos, victims not only of the droughts, but above all of badness, greed, the lack of sense of the powerful, is as much part of the domain of the universal ethics of human beings as the struggle for human rights, wherever it is fought (…). One of the certainties that I am certain of, today, is that, if we really

want to overcome the imbalances between North and South, between power and fragility, between strong and weak economies, we cannot do without ethics, but obviously what we need is not the ethics of the market" [Paulo Freire, *Pedagogia da indignação: Cartas pedagógicas e outros escritos* (São Paulo: Editora UNESP, 2000), pp. 129–130.

26. See Enrique Dussel, *Ética da libertação na idade da globalização e da exclusão* (Petrópolis: Vozes, 2000).
27. Pedro Demo, *Cidadania menor: algumas indicações quantitativas de nossa pobreza política* (Petrópolis: Vozes, 1991), p. 20.
28. Diego Palma, *La construccion de Prometeo: Educacion para una democracia Latinoamericana* (Lima: Tarea; CEAAL, 1993), p. 53.
29. Peter McLaren and Ramin Farahmandpur, "Freire, Marx, and the New Imperialism: Toward a Revolutionary Praxis," in Judith J. Slater, Stephen M. Fain, and Cesar A. Rossato (eds.), *The Freirean Legacy: Educating for Social Justice* (New York: Peter Lang, 2002), p. 52.
30. Chomsky, *Understanding Power*, p. 73.
31. Boaventura de Sousa Santos says the following about the dilemma of the weak state: "Since only the State can produce its own weakness, a strong State is needed to produce this weakness efficiently and support it coherently. Thus, the weakening of the State produces perverse effects which place in doubt the very tasks attributed to the weak State: the weak State cannot control its weakness" [Boaventura de Sousa Santos, *Reinventar a Democracia* (Lisboa: Gradiva Publicações, 1998), p. 27].
32. See Dussel, *Ética da libertação na idade da globalização e da exclusão*, p. 526.
33. Jung Mo Sung, *Sujeito e Sociedades Complexas. Para repensar horizontes* (Rio de Janeiro: Vozes, 2002), p. 64.
34. José Martí, *Educação em Nossa América: Textos selecionados*, edited by Danilo R. Streck (Ijuí: Ed. Unijuí, 2007), p. 83. Original article published in *La América*, New York, November 1883.
35. Mc Laren and Farahmandpur, "Freire, Marx, and the New Imperialism," p. 43.
36. See Francis Fukuyama, *Our Posthuman Future: Consequences of the Biothechnology Revolution* (New York: FSG, 2002).
37. Jürgen Habermas, *O futuro da natureza Humana* (São Paulo: Martins Fontes, 2004), p. 32.
38. Edgar Morin, *A Cabeça bem-feita. Repensar a reforma, reformar o pensamento* (Rio de Janeiro: Bertrand Brasil, 2001), p. 67.
39. See Antônio M. Magalhães and Stephen R. Stoer, *A Escola para Todos e a Excelência Acadêmica* (Proeduções, 2002).
40. See Dussel, *Ética da libertação na idade da globalização e da exclusão*.
41. Jean-Jacques Rousseau, *Júlia ou a Nova Heloísa* (São Paulo: Hucitec, 1994), p. 454.
42. Jean-Jacques Rousseau, *Os devaneios do caminhante solitário* (Brasília: Editora Universidade de Brasília, 1995), p. 41.
43. Paulo Freire "Canção óbvia," 1971, from the collection of Ana Maria Araújo Freire. In Paulo Freire, *Pedagogia da indignação: cartas pedagógicas e outros escritos* (São Paulo: Editora UNESP, 2000), p. 5.

Index

182   Index

186   Index